SECRETS OF THE STREET

MY LIFE AS IVY TILSLEY

SECRETS OF THE STREET
MY LIFE AS IVY TILSLEY

LYNNE PERRIE

WITH

CHARLES YATES AND CLARE MORRISROE

BLAKE

Published by Blake Publishing Ltd,
3 Bramber Court, 2 Bramber Road, London W14 9PB

First published in hardback 1994
Published in paperback 1995

ISBN 1 85782 117 3

British Library Cataloguing-in-Publication Data:
A catalogue record for this book is available
from the British Library.

Typeset by Pearl Graphics, Hemel Hempstead

Printed by WSOY, Finland

1 3 5 7 9 10 8 6 4 2

Text copyright © Lynne Perrie 1994
Cover photographs © Scope Features

For Stephen and Derrick for putting up with me.
They've stuck by me through thick and thin,
and have endured all my mood swings.

Contents

'Fame always brings loneliness. Success is as ice cold and lonely as the North Pole.'

Vicki Baum, *Grand Hotel*

'Fame, like a drunkard, consumes the house of the soul.'

Malcolm Lowry of the reception given to *Under the Volcano* (1947)

Foreword

Well, here it is in paperback – the book they couldn't ban. Who would have thought the story of my life could have caused such a commotion! It seems only yesterday that I walked through the awesome doors of the High Court in London, determined to fight *Coronation Street* bosses who wanted to prevent me publishing my 'warts and all' autobiography. Granada was desperate to gag me – to stop me lifting the lid on my 23 years on Britain's best-loved Street and its famous residents. So much so that they wanted my explosive book shredded before it could hit the bookshops' shelves. It was infuriating: Margaret Thatcher had no problem publishing her memoirs revealing intimate secrets about the cabinet and government. But heaven help Lynne Perrie, should she do the same about *Coronation Street*!

Granada made such a fuss that my book became more controversial than *Spycatcher*. The injunction was so ridiculous that I knew I had to fight it. But I was petrified. I had acted on stages all over the world, but I knew this was to be the most important performance of my life. I wasn't fighting this injunction just for me – it was for the whole cast, and on principle. All I wanted to do was tell the truth, but Granada wouldn't allow it. But thank

God – and to their credit – Granada in the end realised that truth must prevail, and after a few compromises abandoned their attempts to ban my book.

I wept for joy as messages of congratulations came flooding in from my friends in the cast and from the public. Others, to whom I had been less kind in my no-punches story, kept their distance. I still keep in touch with some of my good friends on the cast. After all, you can't just forget 23 years of your life. I'd spent more than two decades forging some very close friendships – and making some very bitter enemies! But as I said all along, I tell it as it is. That's why this book caused such a stir. I have no regrets. It wasn't the first time my big mouth got me into trouble – and I dare say it won't be the last.

Since leaving the Street, my acting career has taken a back seat. That was my choice. For the first time in my life, I realised that my family needed me. My only son, Stephen, has just been diagnosed with AIDS – God only knows how long he has left, but I want to spend every moment with him. For the first time in years I spent Christmas with Stephen and my long-suffering husband Derrick. We had a wonderful time doing things that other families take for granted. Time is so precious for us all right now. Stephen is staying with me in Manchester – it's so fulfilling to be able to mother him again after my acting career and boozing drove a wedge between us.

Derrick and I seem to be closer than ever. Even after spilling the beans in the book about my affairs and insatiable lust for toyboys, he is still standing by me. Any other man would have divorced me a long time ago for the way I dumped on him in the pages of this book, for the pain and upset I caused by my selfish whims and aspirations to be a star. But not Derrick. He's always been my tower of strength, always there to pick up the pieces when I've made a mess of my life. God knows how he puts up with me. But I'm glad he does. On saying that, knowing

Derrick as I do, he knows where his bread's buttered and probably thinks my book will be a bestseller which which keep him in the style he's become accustomed to.

I'm still off the booze – with the odd relapse for special occasions. As far as men go, I've had enough – for the time being at least. I don't know when I'll get back into work. I was supposed to be appearing in panto with John Inman at Christmas. However, it coincided with the publication of my book and a lot of mums kicked up a fuss about their kids coming to see me after they'd read about my antics. They were shocked to discover that Lynne Perrie could be so different from the sensible Ivy in the Street, and they weren't so keen to see me as their children's mentor. Eventually I pulled out of the show of my own accord, and not due to peer pressure, but when Stephen's condition deteriorated rapidly. My priorities changed and all I wanted to do was nurse him through his illness. I put everything else in my life on hold. I only hope that now those mums realise that first and foremost, like them, I am a devoted mother.

Since I left the Street, I have been inundated with offers of work. Chat show hosts have been fighting to get me on their programmes and fans have queued in their hundreds to get my autograph on public appearances. I have not been forgotten – and for that I am touched and eternally grateful. I will be back, after I've picked up the pieces of my life again. I've done it before. Until then I must be with my family – after a lifetime of me me me, now it's time for them.

LYNNE PERRIE
Manchester 1995

CHAPTER ONE

Near Death – and Rebirth

My eyes rolled as I dropped to the floor. I felt nothing as I hit the ground. I could have been dead. Alf Roberts, Jack Duckworth and Kevin Webster shot looks of horrified helplessness round the room as I lay there twitching and gagging for air. Jim McDonald sprang into action and rolled me into the recovery position. He put his hand in my mouth to check my tongue wasn't blocking my throat.

It could have been a dramatic scene from the top soap, but this wasn't acting. I was dying down there in the rest room at Granada's Studio One where *Coronation Street* is filmed. The helpless huddle of actors – Bryan Mosley, Bill Tarmey and Michael Le Vell – looked on in disbelief as I went through what appeared to be death throes at their feet.

I was stiff and shuddering. Michael, who plays mechanic Kevin Webster, was staring wide-eyed as I gasped for air. My pal Charlie Lawson, who plays Jim McDonald, leapt to the ground, pushed me onto my side, checked my airway was clear and loosened my clothing. People who witnessed my collapse thought I was a goner. Cool-headed Charlie played the life-saver to a tee. Somebody called the emergency services and the Granada doctor and nurse were on the scene swiftly. The speed of all their responses helped save my life.

They took me by ambulance, blue lights flashing, klaxon blaring, to Hope Hospital in Salford and straight into intensive care. When I eventually came round I was told by a doctor that I was thirty minutes away from meeting my maker – no more than that. They informed me that if I'd been left any longer and survived I would have had irreparable brain damage. I remember none of it.

The scene I've set out above is a reconstruction of what I'm told happened when I collapsed. I was out cold – completely unconscious. There was no warning before my collapse and it left me on another planet for weeks afterwards.

Three days earlier, I'd lost four pints of blood in a near fatal accident at home. This sounds silly, but I was perming my hair in the bedroom with the help of my best friend Sandra Gill when it happened. My hairdresser refused to do it, because he said you should never perm bleached hair. Now I wish I'd listened to him. But I am very stubborn and when I get an idea into my head that's it.

In this instance I went to Boots the Chemist myself and bought a suitable styling kit. I didn't use perm curlers, because I feared if I did I'd end up with awful Afro-style curls. Instead I used ordinary plastic rollers held in place with hairpins. We had almost got the job done in the master bedroom when some of the perming solution went in my eye. I immediately ran into the *en suite* bathroom to bathe it. But as I got through the door I caught my heel on a bath mat and careered head first into the tiled wall. I hit it with an awful thud and one of those hairpins punctured the temporal artery in my head.

I take about fifteen tablets a day to stay alive because of a history of heart trouble, and some of them are anti-coagulants. As a result of these drugs my blood is very thin. That night I was to see a lot of my watery blood.

The temporal artery is the one that runs in front of the ear, where its pulse can be felt, and over the scalp. It helps supply blood to the temporal lobe in your brain, which is the bit that plays an important part in the storage of memory. With hindsight this incident might account for my memory not being all it should.

The blood was pumping out of this gash at quite a rate. Sandra and I were mopping the stuff up with huge pieces of cotton wool. Almost as soon as she put a chunk of cotton wool to my head I was reaching for the next one as the blood seeped through. We had about ten sodden red pieces in the bathroom bin before Sandra decided to wrap a bath towel round my head to stem the flow.

Sandra, who regularly acts as the voice of reason, was suggesting I should go to hospital. But we were both a little tipsy and in no fit state to drive. I didn't fancy going to hospital and the next day finding some story about a Street star's home perm horror in the newspapers. When you are in a show like *Coronation Street* the media spotlight is tremendous – but you've got to accept it.

People in the public eye who get their wages as a result of their popularity have to appreciate media attention goes with the territory. I hate these MPs who hammer on about invasions of privacy when they've been caught getting an extra-marital leg-over by the press. It smacks of hypocrisy when they've been elected on the family ticket.

But on that Friday night, 4 June 1993, Sandra and I weren't having a deeply philosophical conversation about press intrusion. We were simply hoping that the bleeding would stop. I pressed the towel tight to my head for about half an hour. We both thought the flow had ceased when no blood spread to the outside of the towel. So I carefully unwrapped the turban from my head. As I peeled off the last layer of towel a gush of fresh blood shot across the bathroom and splattered against the wall. It was like a

Stephen Spielberg special effect – a cascade of bright red blood hurtling through the air. It was horrific.

That's when I knew I needed hospital treatment. Sandra ran for the phone and cracked her foot straight into the end of the bed, breaking one of her toes. She was in agony as she dialled 999. The ambulancemen arrived and I remember drifting in and out of consciousness as we headed for the accident and emergency department. I clearly recall the ambulanceman in the back saying to the driver: 'Charlie, will you put your foot down. She's bleeding like a pig.' A quaint turn of phrase, but I was in no position to complain!

When I got to hospital they stitched me up and sent me home. Three stitches in the artery stopped the blood pumping out. They didn't ask me how much blood I'd lost and I never told them. I guess they imagined I'd just come straight in. I later discovered that having lost that much blood could have contributed to the imbalance in body salts that led to my studio collapse. Sandra had treatment for her broken toe on the same night and left with two of her little piggies strapped together.

The next day was Saturday and I was off work and feeling dizzy. I thought, This thing has knocked me for six. But I went back to work. As soon as Liz Dawn saw me she said: 'You don't look well.' I told her about the knock on the head and that I didn't feel too good either. The last thing I remember on the Monday was standing at a desk with Charlie sitting in a chair. He told me the next minute I went completely rigid and fell over like a plank. He said that as I was lying there on my back I started breathing in terrible gasps and twitching. He used his first aid knowledge to make sure my tongue wasn't blocking my throat.

By the time I got to hospital I was completely zonked. Yet apparently people were visiting me in Hope Hospital and I was talking to them right as rain. I haven't a clue who came to see me. I must appear very ungrateful to those people who did come and those I never thanked afterwards for bringing flowers. But I was going through a very rough time, to put it mildly. I had five major fits and needed three brain scans.

Christine Watts, one of my friends from behind the scenes at Granada, came and later told me how I was swearing at the top of my voice on this ward with three other women. I was causing mayhem – effing and blinding like mad.

My brother Duggie came to see me. He had me in pleats afterwards when he told me what I was like. I had it in my head when he was there that I needed a golfing cap. I was lying there half dead in a hospital bed screaming at him: 'Get my fucking golf cap. I'm playing in the fucking Caribbean.' I was upsetting everybody with my bad language and irrational behaviour. In the end Sandra told Duggie to go away and get my golf cap. He did, but when he came back I'd forgotten all about it. I said, 'What have you brought me that for? I'm in hospital.' He laughed it off and said, 'It's a sun helmet in case you get a heatwave on the ward.'

I would go into these awful screaming fits whenever they wheeled me off for a brain scan. I remember nothing about these brainstorms. It was real life or death stuff.

In fact at one time I thought I had died. Now this bit I do recall. It was when they transferred me out of Hope Hospital to the private Oakwood Clinic, which is also in Salford. I was lying on this trolley being wheeled through all these hospital wards that were filled with flowers. There were bouquets everywhere I looked. News of my collapse had reached the newspapers and because it was so serious the story was all over the front pages the next day. As a result all my friends and thousands of fans who adored my screen character Ivy sent cards, get well messages and thousands upon thousands of flowers. I was on my back being wheeled past all these beautiful blooms. And I just kept thinking: 'I'm dead. They're burying me. I am at my own funeral.'

It made me think about the only person I know who did go to their own funeral – Stephen Hancock, who played Ernie Bishop in *Coronation Street*. He hid behind some bushes and watched as Ernie's coffin was filmed after his character had been blasted out of the show by two robbers in a particularly blood-thirsty murder scene. But that's about as close to it as you get, or so I thought until this day.

They were wheeling me along and I wasn't there. It was like I was watching a film. Apparently somewhere along this journey through the corridors at Hope Hospital I did go unconscious, so whether I was dreaming or not I just don't know. At the time it all felt very real – they call it an 'out of the body experience'. It was very eerie. I'd had some incredible experiences in my life, as you'll find out, but this was the most extraordinary ever.

When I got to Oakwood I was still in an awfully muddled state and just as awkward with the people round me. I started off yelling at Sandra: 'Why are you here? You should go home. I don't want you here.' She had been my best friend for years and I was treating her abysmally. Then as she was about to depart I insisted that she stay. She didn't know if she was coming or going, but she stayed by my side at all times after I'd asked her. Granada TV were picking up the bill for my treatment and they paid for Sandra to stay in a bed in my room. She was with me in that room for about a week. I couldn't bear to be without her. She is a real angel, but she told me later that she thought I was heading for the pearly gates on more than one occasion during those nightmare days.

For years I had been living a sad and lonely life. It got so much worse when I found out my only son Stephen was suffering with HIV as I'll share with you later. Ever since then I'd been walking round with a dead weight in my stomach – something inside me that was dragging me down. I spent a lot of my time getting drunk, trying to blot out the pain of thinking about Stephen. I also drank to help me cope with my loneliness – my husband Derrick spent most of his time in our bungalow in Maltby, South Yorkshire, seventy miles away from my Salford home.

But after coming so close to death I changed as a person. People who survive in situations on the brink of life and death often have a changed perspective of what it's all about and that's precisely what happened to me. The doctor's telling me to 'quit boozing or die' also helped my resolution to live a different life.

Before that near fatal collapse in the studios I'd been sliding from one tremendous boozing session to the next. Drinking myself into oblivion on brandy and Babycham or whatever else I fancied. I call my time at Granada my lost twenty-three years, because my existence revolved round drinking.

I used to have a saying that God takes the good ones first, so I'll probably still be living when I'm 187. I've been a hell of a sinner, but God must have forgiven me many times. Just like my Street character I was brought up a Catholic, although when I played pious Poison Ivy on the screen my real life could not have been further removed from hers. I was partying and screwing around like there was no tomorrow at one stage. But that's now firmly in my past.

Coming so close to meeting my maker has helped me come to terms with myself. I probably lost a bit of my ambition at the same time. Things happened to me on set after that collapse that I'd never have let anyone get away with before. Poison Ivy was losing her bite and I wasn't fighting for her. One time I'd have gone hell for leather to keep Ivy's behaviour in character. But I reached a point where I didn't care – I knew there were more important things in life, good health being one of them.

After my release from Oakwood I had gone home to convalesce. Derrick, my dear, long-suffering husband, had been by my side through the very dark days in hospital. Whenever I've needed him in my life he's been there. But we've always fought like cat and dog. Our relationship is bizarre, but we are happy with it the way it is. We've been through hell and high water together and we're still stuck with each other. So there must be a bit of love on both sides, although down the years I've had my doubts, as I'll explain.

During my hedonistic years – and there have been plenty of them – I never considered anything I was doing was wrong. I think that is why I became very cold towards Derrick and very cocky. I used to be my own boss. I was able to pay for everything I needed and I never had to think about him.

After I was ill I realized that I couldn't look back and alter the things that had happened. You can have regrets, but you're much better getting on with life and changing the things you can.

Three or four years earlier – probably even the day before I collapsed at the studios – I wouldn't have thought like this. I'd be looking back and thinking, 'Oh God' this and 'If only' that. I don't do that now. I am much more positive in my outlook.

It certainly helped me sever my links with Granada. If it had happened twelve months earlier I would have been in pieces, totally shattered by the news. But on 7 March 1994 a much stronger woman walked into the producer's office. I'll tell you that story in full later too.

Before the drama of June 1993 I'd have never dreamt of doing an autobiography. My life was something I was very confused about, but after coming so close to death things became clearer. I'll tell you the truth as I know it, and you, the reader, can make up your mind. It's been a damn good life for me. It might not measure up in other people's eyes. I know Ivy would be horrified if she knew half of what I've done! But she's gone out of my life now. So I can tell the story without shocking that old friend, at least.

When I eventually got back to work I made a major gaffe. I wanted to thank Charlie Lawson for saving my life and helping me through my darkest moments. Instead I upset him enormously with a flippant remark about his friendship with a pretty assistant stage manager. I'd heard newspapers were making inquiries about his private life and thought he'd just laugh it off. After all, he was happily married with a lovely wife and child. But he didn't see the funny side. He was furious. He blew his top at me and demanded to know who'd told me – but my mind was so shot, I didn't know.

I hadn't any idea what was happening for weeks after I came out of hospital. At first I didn't even recognize my own house or the gardeners working on my lawn. I had no idea where I was. Charlie accused me of being the one who was spreading gossip about him. I couldn't believe it. I'd been off for eight weeks – two of them in hospital and the other six in a daze at home. The only person from the studio I could remember talking to was Geoff Hinsliff, who played my husband Don. I said I guessed he must have told me about it, but Geoff denied it was him.

I told Charlie not to be such a daft bat, but he was raging. I said: 'If it wasn't Geoff I don't know who the hell it was, because I've not spoken to anyone else in the Street since I changed my telephone number.'

After that he was very distant with me. My big mouth lost me a good friend. Yet after Granada told me they weren't going to renew my contract Sandra bumped into Charlie in a newsagents. He came up to her and said: 'Tell Lynne I'm really sorry. I miss her. We've had our ups and downs. But just tell her I'm still thinking about her and

I'm sorry that things have happened the way they have.'
Now I thought that was really sweet of him. I hope if he
reads this he'll realize I'd never have said what I said if
I'd known it would upset him so.

But I'm rushing ahead. Before I tell you any more I
should start at the beginning.

CHAPTER TWO

A Contented Family

I came into the world with a bang on 7 April 1931, as baby Jean Dudley. Mind you, everything you did in my grandma's happened with a bang, because it was a tiny terraced house opposite Parkgate steelworks in Masbro, Rotherham, and the forge hammer went continually all day and all night. It was enough to drive you mad.

My earliest childhood memory was that bloody big hammer going 'boom'. Other kids might recall their first footsteps or seeing a hippopotamus at the zoo, but for me it was that banging. I must have been no more than two years old, but I clearly remember lying there and that noise waking me up. It woke me up every day we stayed at my grandma's.

My parents were staying there while they waited for a council house. I slept with them in the front room, right opposite the steelworks. I was only a little baby and that hammer used to drive me crackers. It was a swing hammer on a pendulum for flattening steel. Most of the people close by used to work at the steelworks, so locals couldn't really kick up a fuss or they would be out of a job.

Next door to the factory was Rotherham railway station and there was loads of steam and smoke all day from both of them. The grime that hung around was awful. Grandma's house was a two-up-two-down with an outside loo and a tin bath – a real *Coronation Street*-style home. It had a yard and a front door that opened on to the pavement. Between every three houses in the terrace there was an entry.

My dad Eric Dudley was contentment personified, and when he was with my mum Agnes they became contentment incorporated. They were the happiest couple you could ever imagine – never in my lifetime have I seen such happy people. All my life I remember my mum and dad kissing and cuddling. He would never go out of the house without giving her a kiss.

My grandma died when I was about two and I don't have any clear memory of that. But my grandad was still round when I was a child. He used to have a saying: '"No thank you" once got me a good hiding.' Then he'd tell the story of how his dad, my great-grandad, took him to work at a woman's house when he was aged about four. The woman gave my grandad a shilling and asked him if he wanted some stew. My great-grandad had some, but my grandad didn't. Coming across the fields afterwards my grandad said 'I'm hungry,' and my great-grandad thrashed him. He said, 'I'll teach you to say "no thank you"' and kicked him from one side of the field to the other.

From those early years I remember the spring cleaning. They used to get these huge peg rugs – which they make out of strips of old coats and bits of material knotted together – and beat them. The dust was unbelievably heavy. It was always in the air during the clean-up, and the spring cleaning seemed to last all year.

My mam used to have a black leaded stove and there was always a big pan of stew on it. It looked like a big black witch's cauldron and she just used to keep adding more stew to it.

My dad would come home from work and she'd have

his dinner ready in a matter of minutes. In my early years he worked as a bricklayer and it was very heavy manual labour. Later he got a job as a hothand doing repairs inside the brick ovens at the furnace. When he came home from work in those days he'd be wet through because the fires were still raging as he laboured. It must have been pure hell having to work in such intense heat, but my dad never grumbled.

Every night when he got home he'd stand in the garden wringing the sweat out of his towel – it was a ritual for him. He'd ask: 'Is dinner ready, Aggy?' And she'd always reply: 'In ten minutes.' Then he would go outside, where he had two planks resting on bricks in the garden. He used to lay on them and go to sleep – he'd be asleep in the blink of an eye. The work was that demanding that he came home totally worn out.

I told him he snored, but he'd always deny it. For years I tried to convince him of his snoring, so when I was older I took a tape recorder out after he'd nodded off and he heard himself for the first time. He'd start off lightly, but in no time it was a full blast snore. He even said, 'that's not me' when I taped him on the lawn, but at the end of the day he had to accept he sounded like a hog hunting out truffles.

On pay day, which was every Thursday, my dad would bring my mam her weekly treats – a quarter of Thornton's treacle toffee, a quarter of Thornton's brazil nuts, a quarter of fruit and nut and a little miniature brandy. He thought about her all the time.

When she didn't look too well he would look after her. She used to suffer with terrible stomach ache and he used to bring her bottles of liquid paraffin, which was used as a medicine in those days. He'd buy her the paraffin whenever he thought she was looking a bit pale or wan – he was so in touch with her that she didn't have to say a word. They were a very close couple –

they almost communicated by telepathy.

My father used to say to us kids, 'Don't upset your mother,' and she used to say to us, 'Don't upset your dad.' They were always trying to make life as smooth as possible for one another, it was really quaint. If we had two apples in the house mum would say one was for your dad and the other one would be divided three ways between us kids.

On Saturday nights my dad would invite his mates down to the house to play cards and chat. He was a man who loved work and he worked with a lot of his friends. He hated being off work and he loathed being poorly. Every day for his snack he took with him a great big piece of cheese, a raw Spanish onion and some of my mam's bread. We used to joke that his mates at work must love him, because he used to chomp into the onion as if it was an apple. Mam used to make him breadcakes with butter and because he ate so many onions he never suffered with colds. But if he got the flu he'd go to work with it and we'd all say, 'You'll pass it to everyone else,' but it didn't stop him. He just couldn't bear being off.

As a child there was only the one time I saw him ill, and that was when he got fluid on the knee. It must have been a condition he had picked up as a result of all the crouching down he did at work. But the ambulancemen had to drag him to the hospital. He was holding himself back with both hands on the front door frame as they pulled him outside.

I got on well with my dad, but wasn't as close to him as our Barry was. My youngest brother Barry is thirteen years younger than me, but he followed in my footsteps onto the Northern club circuit.

Barry wasn't even born when I made my first public singing appearance. When I was only three I was taken to Nottingham Fayre by my mother and Auntie Mary for a special day out – it was a very, very big event in those days. They were shouting for kids to get up and sing and my Auntie Mary pushed me up on the stage. I was only about three feet tall, but had no fear at all of the giant crowd. I simply sang my heart out. As I finished I said, 'My mother sings lovely,' and they insisted on dragging her up to do a turn. She tried to deny having a beautiful voice, but I chirped up again that she was great. What I didn't know at the time was that she was literally terrified of standing up in front of all those people. She was that frightened that her lips were shaking as she sung. As soon as she got off stage she went mad and snapped: 'Don't you ever do that to me again.' It was a real tough telling off that hit home. I would never ever do that to my mum again.

But her voice really was remarkable and she was forever singing at home. When I walked through the door after school I'd be greeted by my mum's singing. I used to join in with her and she would always change key and we'd sing along together in perfect harmony. She had a soprano voice and I have always had a very low voice, but it didn't matter – she just went straight into harmony. So I must have got my singing ability from her. She told me that my grandmother had been very musical and that she played a Jew's harp and a squeeze box. Mum used to sing to the wireless or whatever and I used to pitch in with her.

She was a happy woman despite the hard graft. She would bake her own bread and wash all the clothes by hand before wringing the washing out through a giant mangle. Kids today will probably have never seen a mangle, what with electric washing machines and spin and tumble driers. But, for the record, mangles were often on wrought iron stands with two heavy wooden rollers; to squeeze the water out of the washing you pushed the clothes between them and then turned a big handle at the side to drag the garments through. It was very heavy work and married women with children had a lot on their plates being housewives back then.

One of the worst memories of any part of my life were washday Mondays when it was raining. There would be tubs of washing everywhere and this bloody great mangle. Mother always gave the whites in the wash an extra gleam by adding a Dolly Blue, which was a little blue muslin parcel of a starch-type substance. The packaging looked a bit like the wrapper put round posh chocolates.

After the wash all the garments would be put through the mangle and the whole house would be full of steam. The washing would be hanging all round the fire and it would be really damp indoors as well as out. I knew where Bob Geldof and the Boomtown Rats were coming from when they released that song, 'I Don't like Mondays' – in those days that would have been my signature tune.

The idols of that era, and as I got older, were Dicky Valentine, Eve Boswell and Bing Crosby. Mam always used to ask for Jim Reeves records as presents for Christmas and her birthdays. They were always playing in the house, but my dad was so laid back he never took any notice of them. She had them on so much that she ran the risk of driving us all daft with his crooning.

Mum's idea of a good Saturday night was looking after my dad's mates when they came round to play cards. She used to wash her long black hair, put clips in it and part it down the middle. She used to put a clean pinny on and used to cook for them. I remember this happening from the age of about four or five.

Our mum made sure we all had a really happy childhood. We moved from my gran's to a three-bedroom semi-detached council house in East Dene, Rotherham, when I was about six. And it was there that I gave regular singing performances from the top of the stairs for my Uncle Jackie. He used to call at the house to see my mother on the way home from working on his fruit cart.

He would come to the bottom of the stairs and shout up: 'Sing "Carolina Moon" for me, Jean.' I'd come to the top of the stairs and sing for him. He was a strange-looking chap – he was a very bad asthmatic and had a hump on his back.

From an early age I was pretty extrovert and enjoyed entertaining. I used to walk round with my mother's shoes and all her clothes on, playing pretend games. Kids are forever dressing up and I was no different in that respect.

During our time in that house in East Dene I got a tiny playmate when our Keith was born. I was really thrilled to have a little brother after seven years as an only child. Because he was so precious I will never forget the day we nearly lost him. It was a sunny day and little Tommy Williams from across the road called for Keith to play out. They went off as usual to play in the back yard. Our Keith just toddled after Tommy. Shortly afterwards Tommy came running in and shouted to me mam and dad something about Keith not being very well in the water.

We all dashed outside where Keith was definitely not very well – he was upside down with his legs in the air and his head stuck beneath the water in mother's washing tub. If we hadn't gone outside straightaway he'd have drowned. He was blue when they pulled him out. He'd been deprived of air and was within a few seconds of dying. They had to take him to hospital, but he was all right at the end of the day.

We had a corner shop next door and a woman called Rosie with a club foot worked in it. I could never reach the counter in that shop. But although I have never been very big I have always had a deep voice. I probably had a deeper voice then than I have now. Anyway, this day Rosie says to my mother, 'I know what you and your Jean had for your tea. You had eggs.' Mum asked her how she knew and Rosie said: 'Well, yesterday I had these two little hands on the counter and a deep voice said: "A quarter of boiled ham for me dad's tea and me and me mother's having egg."' My dad loved ham for tea – it was one of his favourites.

A while after this, my dad got a job as a site foreman with a builder called Donald Dunk. I remember him surprising my mam by taking her along to one of the new estates he was working on and showing her a lovely plot. He'd picked this spot and said to her: 'It's nice isn't it? You'll like living here, won't you?' She never knew a thing about it – he'd just bought the plot to build a house and surprise her. Being the foreman, he could oversee the building of our new semi-detached house on Vernon Road at the Broom in Rotherham. It was a very posh new area – a bit like leafy Mobberley is to Manchester.

As kids up there we'd play a game called Fish and Chips. We'd get the dustbin and turn the lid upside down and put stones and dirt in it – the stones and dirt were the fish and chips and the dustbin was the counter. Mam used to make bits of newspaper into cones for us and I used to be chippy assistant and say to the other kids: 'What would you like, sir?' They replied: 'I'll have one fish and four penn'orth of chips.' So I'd dole them out and whoever was given the paper cone would go and empty it round the corner and come back for some more. In those days when we couldn't afford toilet paper we used to tie newspapers on a bit of string on the back of the toilet door, so there was always paper about to make the cones.

We also played a game called Buttons. You had to lick your fingers and get buttons to stick to your hands. We used to go all over looking for odd-shaped buttons that wouldn't stick to your thumb. It was a kids' game and looking back it doesn't make a lot of sense. But at the time we thought it was brilliant – it kept us out of mischief.

It wasn't always so easy to stay out of bother, because kids have a knack for doing what they shouldn't.

I remember only ever getting a good hiding the once as a child from my dad. That was for raffling off his most prized possession – a model battleship. This beautiful aluminium ship had taken hundreds of hours to put together, with all the guns and sailors on board brightly painted. Our Keith won the warship at a raffle on the Co-op field with a lucky number seven ticket. One day in the school holidays I wanted some money and decided to raffle this boat off to raise the cash. I got some draw tickets and flogged them all round the street. My dad went ballistic when he found out what I had done and my mother wanted to go and pay all the money back. I got a shilling and nine pence from the raffle and Mrs Kingston at the bottom of the road won the boat. Well, my dad belted me for the first time – it wasn't a bad beating, but the shock of him raising his hand really upset me.

After it happened I ran away from home. More accurately, I ran away to the back of the solid wooden Victorian wardrobe in my mam and dad's room. I left a note on the table for when they came in saying, 'You've hit me and I can't go on.' I even went to the tap and dropped some water all over the paper, so the ink would run and it would look as if I had been crying. I was crafty and dramatic even in those days. I used a chair to climb onto the wardrobe and then dropped down the back. I had no idea how long I would be stopping, but I took a bottle of lemonade, a twist of salt, some tomatoes, bread and butter, a lump of cheese and a blanket. My intention was to stay hidden there for a long time and give my dad a fright. They scoured the streets for about three hours and went to all my aunties and uncles without any luck. My dad said, 'She'll turn up,' and they both went to bed. Just before they put the light out my mother said: 'Eric, have a look at the back of that wardrobe.' He pulled up the chair and there I was fast asleep. He said: 'Well, damn me. I have been walking miles and she's been here all along.' He was going to wake me up, but my mum said: 'Oh, leave her there.' Dad, the big softie, said: 'She's all curled up, she'll get cramp.' But mam wouldn't be budged and said: 'It'll do her good. Let her have bloody cramp. Don't you touch her. She stops there until morning.' Mam was equally angry with me because she loved the warship, which took pride of place in the front room.

That room was a magical place for us, because we never went in there except on Christmas Day. We didn't step across the threshold for 364 days – it was a brand new room every year. And that made Christmas Day a really extra special occasion. For me getting into that front room, with its clean carpet and spotless furniture, was a bigger treat than Christmas chicken. We had chicken in those days because turkey was a lot more scarce.

I was never a kid who believed in Father Christmas, because I caught my dad delivering the presents one December 24th. But I loved it when we got in that front room to sit round the fire. Television was a new invention. John Logie Baird demonstrated a TV image for the first time in 1926, but all we had in my childhood was radio. We'd carry the wireless from the dining room into the front room for the Christmas broadcasts.

My gran also had a posh front room that nobody ever entered. It was a traditional thing to do. Instead we lived in the back room, which had a little concrete hill in the floor under the carpet. All the really rubbish furniture was in the living room and we'd spend all year in there. My parents' front room was so special that I moved the three-piece suite from it and put it into my first flat in Manchester in 1980. The sofa and chairs were still virtually new.

When I was young I went through a phase of never wanting any dinners. I'd ask for the pudding first. But I always liked my mum's bread – she baked it fresh every day herself. Us kids would scramble to get the crusts off it when it was still warm after coming out of the oven.

One Christmas we had a ham that mother had cooked herself, a pork pie she had made herself – in fact everything on the table had been made by mother or grown in the garden by my dad. He had a full vegetable garden and a greenhouse and years later when I watched *The Good Life* on telly it reminded me of those happy days. Everything was home made and my mum and dad used to go crackers when all our Keith would eat was bread and jam. This Christmas there was a table full of stuff, but because of the phase he was going through he just stuck to bread and jam. I also went through a spell of not eating anything when I came home from school, but all of a sudden I would go past and see my dad's plate and pinch some chips.

Normally at Christmas we'd all be waiting for the chicken to arrive at the table with great expectation – it was like waiting for the King, a very important event. We would chant: 'The chicken's coming, chicken's coming, chicken's coming.' It sounds strange, but it was hard to contain the excitement. Mum and dad used to pay a shilling a week at the club to pay for the goodies at Christmas and it was always a good day.

After losing my belief in Santa Claus, I'd go crackers in the run up to Christmas, searching everywhere for presents. I never have been able to mind my own business – a character trait I shared with my Street alter ego Ivy. I'd say: 'Why don't you go to shop, mam?' She'd say: 'Because I don't want nowt.' But I'd insist we needed some milk. She knew what I was up to. And I would have to find some other reason to get her out of the house, so I could go rooting round. Eventually I'd find all the presents and tell Keith: 'I know what you're having for Christmas.' Mother would go mad. She started keeping them at Auntie Edie's next door. But I went in there when I was about nine and spotted a bicycle in her hall. I asked her who was coming to stay and she said her niece, but when she never came I thought, That's mine. I told mum I was getting a bike for Christmas and she said: 'You always spoil everything, you.'

At Vernon Road my parents had a bit more money and started going out together to the Stag, our local pub. Dad liked his beer, but he never got really drunk. But mother was able to gauge how tipsy he was by asking him to say 'decision'. That was his code word. If he could go to the pub and still say decision he knew he was safe. When he returned and said 'dec, dec, decishhion,' mum knew he was drunk. He'd try and butter her up by offering to splash out on a fish and chip supper. But it made no difference, he'd still be in trouble. He only ever went out a couple of nights a week. He couldn't afford to go out every night and anyway he worked so hard as a hot-hand that he was often too tired to go out. To save time at work they often went into the furnace when the embers were still glowing and the bricks were all red hot. His job was cementing up any cracks. After working in the intense heat, he deserved a pint.

I honestly can't say I've met anybody as contented with life, but he was ever so funny without knowing it. When he got something into his head you could not chase it out. There was a fellow who bought a semi-detached across the road and knocked it into one. He had a fruit and vegetable business, with two big lorries that he moved his goods in. For some bizarre reason, dad got it into his head he was a pit inspector because there was always lots of coal outside his house. Colliery inspectors received cheaper fuel in those days. Dad decided because this chap always had two heaps of coal, instead of the normal one, that he must have been a big noise down the mine. He wouldn't accept anything else, regardless of the fact that every morning this man would jump into his cab and drive off with a lorry load of fruit and veg. Dad would say: 'I'm telling you, nobody gets two heaps of coal a month unless they are an inspector down the pit.' To his dying day, he wouldn't change his mind.

Coal was dropped off in the street and stood outside for days. Nobody would dream of pinching any. In those days crime didn't seem to exist and everybody left their back doors open. It was a lovely time and I'm glad that I lived through it. Things have changed beyond recognition. The level of crime today is horrific. Yet back then mum and dad had no qualms about leaving me to look after my brothers when they went down the Stag on a Saturday or Friday night. Our Barry was only a baby then, and I loved caring for him.

If mam had got her way, Barry would never have been born. She did everything she could to get shut of him. She sat in hot baths and drank bottles of gin regularly, but thankfully it didn't work. That was probably why my dad had a soft spot for him. He knew mum did her best to get rid of him, because he was a mistake. Dad wanted another baby, but mum was relishing her new-found freedom. Keith was growing up fast. She had two children and didn't want another. I'd overhear them talking about it. Dad would say: 'I am not very happy about this, Agnes.' She'd change the subject by saying: 'Don't call me Agnes.' Then they'd argue. She'd prefer dad to call her Ann, because she hated the name Agnes. He probably called her Agnes or Aggy as a joke to wind her up.

He was a natural comedian, which is probably where our Barry got his sense of humour. After Barry was born, mum was glad she hadn't got rid of him. So are millions of comedy fans who've enjoyed his gags over the years. He got his big TV break in *The Comedians* and is now known to millions as the comic Duggie Brown – probably most famous for his parrot gag, but that's another story.

CHAPTER THREE

Wartime Memories and Schoolday Fun

I will never forget being huddled round the wireless on 3 September 1939, the day World War Two broke out. I can still clearly remember hearing the voice of the then Prime Minister Neville Chamberlain declaring war. I was just eight and a half and didn't realize the enormity of the announcement.

But I knew it was bad. My parents started crying, and I had never seen my dad cry before. To this day I cannot forget Chamberlain's words: 'This country is now at war with Germany. We are ready.' My mum and dad were heartbroken, because they feared he would have to join the army. But it turned out that he was spared as his job as a hothand was a reserved occupation.

He still did his bit, though, and joined the ARP. During his time as an air raid warden he almost got his head blown off by a giant lump of flying shrapnel. To hear him talk afterwards you would have thought he had seen off the Hun single-handed. But me and our Duggie helped keep his feet on the ground. We were forever reminding him he hadn't stepped outside Rotherham during the war years.

Like everybody else in our street we had an air raid shelter in the back garden. The factories helping the war effort in Sheffield and Rotherham were German targets, so they didn't have to be far off the mark to make a mess of Vernon Road. There was a large steelworks nearby, so the area did suffer a lot of bomb damage.

I wasn't too keen on our shelter, which was a big one above the ground, but next door my Auntie Edie's was underground. I loved climbing down the steps into the half-light, as the musty stench filled my nostrils. There were bunk beds in case we had to stay overnight – it was a real adventure. She had a paraffin heater and we'd play cards for hours down there. It was like a little house.

Her shelter also had the added attraction of Doug – Auntie Edie's eldest son. He was about eight years older than me and I fancied him like mad. He spurned all my advances and got very fed up with me making eyes at him. I never got the chance to get really close to him, because there were always too many people around. My dad spent the air raids marching round the garden with his tin hat on keeping a watch.

One night he came down looking a little shaken and making quite a fuss. He was very agitated and said, 'Something has just come past me with such a whizz – I don't know what it was but it whistled past my ear.' There was a blackout on, so you couldn't see anything if it was a cloudy night. The next morning we got up and discovered what had missed my dad's head by inches – a two-foot piece of shrapnel. He was a bit more careful about walking round air raids after that.

When war broke out I was a pupil at St Bede's RC school. Hitler's bombs never really interfered with my studying. Not long after the family moved to the Broom I started secondary school. But the change in schools wasn't straightforward – my dad insisted I switch after catching the priest at our house asking my mum for cash. Every Thursday, the priest walked fifteen miles to get all the spare money off my mother. She was frightened to death of this chap in his sombre black coat. He expected her brass because Catholics were always expected to give to the church. One day, after changing shifts my dad was at home when the clergyman arrived. Dad was a bit taken aback seeing him and asked what he was doing up at our house miles from the parish church. The priest said he'd come to collect the weekly donation from my mother. When she gave him the money, dad told him in no uncertain terms not to come back for anymore. The priest pointed out that I still went to his school, but dad looked him in the eye and said: 'She won't be going back no more.' And so at the age of ten I started at Herringthorpe Secondary school.

It was there, wearing white ankle socks and sandals beneath a blue robe, that I took to the stage for my first role ... as the Virgin Mary. With hindsight the casting for the school's nativity play was vergin' on the ridiculous as even at that tender age I was lusting after my leading man.

The Joseph in question was my first great love. He was a lovely lad called Denzil Pearce – oh, even now I sigh when I recall his name. He had a shock of ginger hair and freckles and was all of four foot nowt, but to me he was Paul Newman.

In those days I was sweet and innocent, so it must have been a long time ago. Playing the Virgin Mary was right up my street as I'd been brought up a churchgoer. Looking at me then as leading lady in the nativity play, nobody could have guessed what I'd get up to later in life.

I've got some stories to tell, but this is when love first struck. I was ten years old and dear Denzil was my victim. It was so cute – a real schoolgirl crush. I was even shorter than my present 4 ft 11½ inches, but despite my diminutive stature Denzil was still terrified of me. I, on the other hand, was madly in love with him and wild horses would not drag me away from his side. I used to follow him everywhere. I was his shadow – I even tracked him to the boys' toilets and would wait outside. He'd snarl: 'Will you stop following me.' But I took no notice. Even in those days I was a real pushy devil.

On Saturday afternoons he would go to football matches and I'd be there. Try as he might, Denzil couldn't put me off. It didn't matter what I did or what he did to ignore me. I wasn't the type of girl who would get embarrassed. I was pretty thick-skinned even then – an attribute that was to help in later life when the odd critic had a go at my performances.

I was so desperate to date Denzil that I used to wait outside his school locker. When he arrived I'd just stand there gawping as he packed his books and the rest of his gear. Then I'd walk with him to the school bus stop. When the double decker rolled up I'd try and squeeze onto the same seat as him. I'd wait in the queue behind him to see if he was going upstairs or downstairs, then I'd follow with a girlish glint in my eye.

When he was cast as Joseph in the school play and I was made the Virgin Mary, I thought fate was on my side. But you've never seen a Mary and Joseph standing further apart. I'd be up at the front with the baby Jesus and Denzil would be cowering at the back of the stage trying to give me as wide a berth as possible. He couldn't bring himself to look at the baby during the performance, let alone at the rehearsals, in case our eyes met. He'd go right back and look over my shoulder and the teacher would tell him to come to the front. He'd shout: 'I'm all right here, miss.' He wouldn't come near me at all. It was as if I'd got leprosy. He really hated the sight of me. I don't blame him really because I'd been driving him potty all year.

Denzil was the first leading man I fell for, but he was by no means the last. Later on I actually got to kiss a few and it went even further with some others.

I chatted to Denzil but he never talked back – it was a bizarre relationship. His lack of communication didn't rebuff me at all because I was just a kid in love with him. We didn't know about sex or anything like that then. Nobody taught us how to put condoms on cucumbers, like they do in some schools these days. I just fancied him and had made my mind up I was going to marry him. It was very black and white in my mind, with no grey areas. If only real life could be like that.

I only ever tried to kiss him once, but I missed and never tried again. I told Denzil about my wedding plans and he reacted much as I expected ... he ran like hell down the football field shouting: 'She's mad.'

At the age of eleven I passed my school's certificate with top grades in maths and the sciences. I don't know how I did it with my Denzil obsession still fresh in my mind. But collecting the certificate at the town hall led to some red faces.

The girls who passed in my class were asked to give their full names to the teacher. Nearly everyone in the class had about three first names—but I was plain Jean Dudley. So the girls began reeling off their names: Mary so and so, Jane such-a-body and so on. When they got to the girl beside me, Margaret Josephine Rosemary King, I decided I could do with a couple of posh names too, so I piped up: 'Jean Audrey Diana Dudley'.

That was all forgotten about until a few weeks later when we were all in a giant auditorium at the town hall in Rotherham for the formal ceremony. The town crier was there in full costume ringing his bell and announcing the names. It was a very big event and quite nerve-wracking for some of the parents. The bell rang, and the town crier announces the name 'Jean Audrey Diana Dudley', and – you've guessed it – nobody got up. Everyone just sat there looking round, including my mother. Then all of a sudden from the embarrassing silence my mother chirped up: 'Excuse me, what was that last name?'

When he said Dudley, she asked: 'What were the other names?' He said Jean Audrey Diana. My mother looked daggers at me and demanded to know where the other names had come from. She told me she'd kill me – at the time she didn't see the funny side.

At the end of the ceremony lots of people went up because their daughters had forgotten to put a name in. But my mother was forced to go up and ask them to knock all my fancy new names out. The town crier asked her: 'What name would you like to add?' She said: 'It's Jean Dudley, plain Jean Dudley, that will do thank you.'

He looked up at her and said: 'She's just Jean – so where did this Audrey Diana come from?' My red-faced mum lied: 'Well, her Auntie Mary has always called her Audrey, because she wanted me to call her Audrey. But I insisted on Jean and she never called her anything else, so she thinks her name is Audrey. And her other Auntie Bessie calls her Diana, so she thinks her name is Jean Audrey Diana.'

The town crier looked confused: 'Well, I've never heard anything like that before'. Nobody had ever added names on. I don't think I've altered much since then. It was my first atempt at trying to be a flash sod.

Later in life I didn't have to try to be flashy – it just came naturally. When I could afford to wear mink coats I'd often upset animal rights activists who protested about fur fashions. They'd say: 'Do you know how many dead animals are needed to make that coat?' And I'd retort: 'I don't care. Do you know how many animals I've had to put up with to be able to afford this coat?' I was never shy about flaunting the trappings of success – there is no point.

After I passed the school's certificate, my dad splashed out on a piano which stood silent for more than a year because nobody in the house could play a note. Then mum decided I should go along to a piano teacher called Lottie Mainwearing. She was on the committee of the Gloops club – the children's section of the local *Sheffield Star* newspaper. She spent a lot of time raising money to send poor kids to the seaside.

Miss Mainwearing wore big hats and scarfs and was quite eccentric. She charged five shillings for the lesson and five shillings for the book and five shillings for a piano bag. Without even hearing me sing, she said: 'Oh you've got a lovely voice, so I'm going to teach you to sing and it'll be five shillings for that.'

She then told me she was a member of the Gloops club and that they had raffles for charity. She asked me to buy something to help the cause, then charged me another five shillings to become a Glooper and join the club. After selling me a purse and a piano theory book, she packed me off home, instructing me to return the following week with something for the raffle.

My mother had given me a pound, but I ended up owing Lottie Mainwearing money. I was in the front room after my first lesson, hammering away at the keys and singing 'ah ... ah ... ah ...' when my dad got home and asked: 'What's wrong with our Jean?' My mum said proudly: 'She's learning to sing.' But dad said: 'Don't be so bloody daft. She knows how to sing.'

My mother eyed my new piano bag suspiciously and said: 'You don't need one of them yet.' But I told her Miss Mainwearing had sold it to me, and a purse as well. Mum asked for the change and I explained that as well as the piano lessons I had paid for singing lessons. Mother hit the roof when I told her she actually owed Miss Mainwearing nineteen and six.

Grabbing hold of the bag, she said: 'Give me that bloody thing, I'm going to get my money back.' She stormed round to her old Victorian house a few hundred yards away on Beechwood Road. But she hadn't bargained on Lottie being such a good saleswoman. And believe it or not, she persuaded my mum to sign up for piano lessons too.

She didn't teach her pupils scales to start with – just how to play with one finger of each hand. Mum went back for about five lessons. But my mother never really grasped the piano, and the hassle over the lessons landed her with shingles which laid her up in hospital. To this day I can't play the piano to save my life, either.

But I did do my bit for the war effort with Miss Hills' class from Rotherham High School for Girls. It was one autumn towards the end of the war and we were sent off to Lincolnshire to pick spuds. Our nation needed us and our class, always immaculately turned out in our brown and pale gold uniform, was willing to help out.

The local lads needed us as well and we were just as willing to oblige them. Miss Hills did her best to stop us fraternizing with the 'enemy'. Anyone in trousers was considered a foe by our gym mistress, with her short black hair and prim schoolmarm dresses.

We outflanked her with meetings after lights out by the latrines, which were housed in a hut a short distance away from the barrack-style dormitory. Before our secret rendezvous we were forced to change into our pyjamas, something all the girls hated. If we had known we would get the opportunity to meet boys on our potato picking expedition we might have taken some floaty negligees – instead I was stuck with striped and floral cotton pyjamas. We had to traipse down a long path overgrown with grass to get to our latrine lovenest. It was not the most romantic of locations, but when you're in your teens you tend not to be too fussy.

After our first week away we had just arrived at the stage where we were canoodling with the local lads when 'Hills the Hun' spoilt our fun. She burst in on one of our midnight trysts and carpeted me and the whole chain gang. We were confined to barracks for the second week, but we still had fun singing about Hills the Hun.

During the day she wore her own school uniform and supervised as we grubbed about through furrows of mud searching for spuds. We'd wake at 7.30 am and after our breakfast we'd be out in the fields by 9 am for a back-breaking day. We used to be paid for our harvesting, but we'd give the money to school funds. As the days went on, we picked less and less potatoes as the kneeling and digging in the soil took its toll.

My next shove for the war effort involved pushing my mother's arm up her back to persuade her to take a soldier into our house. The sun was cracking the cobbles round Rotherham when I first heard the sound of stamping feet pounding through the streets. It was the army arriving in town, hundreds of smart young soldiers marching on one of the hottest days I can ever remember. The officers were knocking on doors seeking billets for the boys. By the time they reached our house at the top of the Broom there was just a handful of troops left. Two went to Auntie Edie's next door, and that left one lad to knock on ours. Mum said she didn't want him, but this poor ginger-haired lad was sweating cobs with his serge uniform on and a full pack on his back. I felt really sorry for him and persuaded her to take him in. 'Just look at those big boots, Mam. You can't make him walk any further,' I pleaded.

Her heart melted and Tommy moved into our single bedroom. He was a big cuddly uncle to me and stayed with us for sixteen months. He'd take me to the pictures for a treat and tell me about his home town of Wolver-hampton. I was heartbroken when he had to leave us for manoeuvres overseas.

Rationing caused everyone problems during the war. But I remember flouting the regulations when I sneaked into the school pantry. I stocked up with all the ingre-dients I needed for some lovely biscuits and whisked them up in my cookery class. I was particularly proud of them and when I got home mum said I'd done a beautiful job. But the smile soon vanished when she took a bite – this silly bugger had pinched salt instead of sugar.

I was regularly getting in trouble at school, but the worst hot water I landed in earned me a two-week suspension. And as you can guess it had something to do with boys. I was flicking through the pages of a dirty book – well, a Mills & Boon-style romance, which at the time was considered very risqué. It was even more risky if you were reading it in the middle of a history lesson.

Miss Hills asked me a question, but I was so engrossed in this book that I didn't hear her. So she caught me red-handed. I was hauled up to the front of the class, still clutching the book. She was furious when she saw what I was reading and sent me up to Miss Denser, our dragon of a headmistress. There was no messing about with her and after hitting the roof she suspended me there and then. I had some explaining to do when I got home. Everybody saw red over so-called blue books in those days.

I'm now in my 60s and have started shrinking. At one stage I was 5 feet and ¼ inch tall. I was proud of being over 5 feet tall – I always used to mention that quarter of an inch. People who are just about 5 feet tall are always extra careful to include the added fraction in their height. I used to say it's better to be looked over than overlooked.

I might not have the biggest frame in the business, but I've always said that on the inside there is a seven-foot woman trying to get out. And the woman inside me was released for the first time when I was thirteen. At least, that's when I lost my virginity.

It happened on Herringthorpe playing fields after an evening at the pictures, an experience I will never forget, but can't really remember much about – if that makes a bit of sense. I was much too young and it only happened because I was in the hands of an older, more experienced boy. In fact, at twenty-three, Walter was already a man.

He did the deed very skilfully, so deftly that I didn't notice what had happened. On this particular night we were walking home hand in hand after kissing in the cinema – which was about as far as kids got in those days – when Walter said, 'Let's sit down here.' It was a summer's evening and we were out in the open air on the local playing fields. Walter started messing about and I just lay back and let it happen.

Before that I don't remember anybody ever speaking to me about sex, and come to think about it, nobody ever did afterwards. It was a taboo subject in the 1930s and 1940s when I was a child. The nearest we got to sex education was giggling together as schoolgirls in the playground over romantic novels.

I honestly don't remember anything about losing my virginity – the mechanics of it anyway. Mum rumbled me the next day and said I'd been up to something. I didn't know anything about what had gone on. If I had I would have thrown my knickers away. Mum was not best pleased. She said, 'You've been messing about. There's blood in your knickers and I know why.' I was that naive that I asked her, 'Tell me!' She just came out with it: 'You are not a virgin any more.' I was shocked, because I hadn't wanted it to happen and hadn't realized it had. I still had my dolls and was playing out – just a child.

Walter lived on a posh estate in Rotherham and we lived nearby. Needless to say, I never went out with him again after that. He asked me to the pictures with him a couple of nights later, but I refused. His family moved away soon after, so it never happened again.

I never told my mum who I'd lost my virginity to, but she found a note in my diary which read: 'Walter took me in the top field and took my knickers down.' She didn't need a great deal of imagination to work out who had deflowered me after that.

I gave up going out with boys after Walter. I wasn't sure if I liked what had happened, but decided that I didn't want to do that again. I was simply too young for a sexual experience. I went through a phase of going out old-time dancing with my mother. I suppose she saw it as a way of keeping me out of mischief.

After a couple of visits this lad called Ralph started getting friendly. He was a strapping lad and he eventually asked me for a dance. But after one waltz I turned my nose up at him ... he stank of cod and chips. I danced with him again, but the smell was overpowering. It turned out his mum and dad ran a fish and chippy and my mother thought he was a good catch. I was given every encouragement to date him, but simply couldn't stomach the smell.

I stopped going old-time dancing after that. Instead I started going to dance halls with my schoolpal and best friend Doreen Bell. We went every Saturday night to the Maramba dance hall in Rotherham. We used to dance with the lads, but nothing more. After my mum's reaction to what had gone on with Walter I wasn't in a hurry to incur her wrath again.

One Saturday night at the Maramba was going to change my life forever when Doreen persuaded me to go up on the stage and sing. She was always telling me to do it and I finally got up during a talent competition. When I came off, a drummer called Ken Copley said to me, 'My brother Ron is looking for a singer for his band. He's playing at the Co-op tonight. Why don't you go up and have a little try with him?' So I went up to the Co-op and sang. That was my first audition, and I got the job.

I was delighted, but didn't realize at the time that they were all buskers. They couldn't read a note of music. But they were a great jazz band and they used to play in whatever key I was singing. I'd get into the act when they were playing and once I got in they'd follow me.

They paid me five shillings for a Saturday night. It wasn't much, but to me it was a fortune. Bruce, the sax player, used to pick me up from Rotherham and take me to the Silver Dollar club at Maltby. After we'd done our spot he would run me home. Bruce tried it on a couple of times, but was a lot older and realized I wasn't interested in him at all.

I was a bundle of nervous energy on my first night. I was making my professional debut as a singer. When I walked on to the stage Ron announced: 'We've a new singer starting tonight called Dizzy.' I looked round, thinking they'd got somebody else, but they'd just christened me Dizzy. To this day I've never found out why they gave me that name. I don't know if they didn't call me Dizzy because I acted daft. I took real pride in my performance wearing these 'Come Dancing'-type frocks. Anyway, it was my first-ever stage name.

They'd ask: 'Dizzy, what are you going to sing?' I'd say: 'Sheikh of Araby,' and they'd go straight into it, because we'd already arranged the keys. I'd also do stuff like 'Don't bring Lulu' and a lot of jazz numbers. 'Ain't Misbehavin' and 'A Long Way from St Louie' were a couple of favourites of the band, but they did all those old songs. I had a sort of jazzy voice which helped a lot.

So by the tender age of fourteen I was working on the stage. But if you'd told me then that showbiz was to become my life, I'd have thought you were the dizzy bugger, not me.

CHAPTER FOUR

Shotgun Wedding

I suppose from being young I knew what I wanted, and I made damned sure that I got it. I was tough as a rhino – and much more stubborn.

By the time I reached my teens, most of my friends and schoolmates were dreaming of settling down with a decent chap, having kids and buying their own house to raise a family. Not me. At sixteen I was a career girl with a glittering future ahead of me and earning as much if not more money than most of the skilled blokes round the streets of Rotherham.

During the week I worked as a trainee pharmacist on the chemist counter at Boots in the town centre for a wage of £5 10s. I was still living with my parents in Vernon Road and they never asked for a single penny keep, so all I had to spend my money on was me, me, me!

I suppose I had always been spoiled. Mine was never a rags to riches story – to be perfectly honest, I'd never had to do without anything. And I even got to fulfil my childhood dream of being a star singing with Ron Copley's dance band. For that I earned another five shillings a week.

But there was more to being a local celebrity than wealth. With it came a luxury that money just couldn't buy – a line of lads just dying to take me out. I spent all my money on fancy figure-hugging clothes for my stage act so that I would look far more sexy and sophisticated than my sixteen years. Not that I needed to make myself look more attractive. I always said you could be the ugliest woman on God's earth, but because you're up there on that stage, every man wants you. So I had no shortage of blokes at my beck and call. I simply didn't need a steady chap – I was far too independent, and having far too much fun to think about settling down.

That's why I didn't fall for any of the nonsense most men used to try to charm their hapless victims into bed. I'd realized from a very early age that the male of the species would stop at nothing to get their wicked way – even if you were too young to know what they were up to. While most girls were conned into believing the mere mention of the word 'love' meant a romantic wedding and a brood of heavenly kiddies to take care of, I realized it meant nothing more than a guaranteed legover.

And that was more my way of thinking too! So over the years it came as a shock to many a man who tried it on with me when I'd say: 'You can do what you want. Just don't tell me you love me.' That was just the kind of girl I was. There were a few one-night stands in those early days, cheeky blokes who wanted a bit of fun, as I did. But I wasn't foolish enough to fall for any of them and I certainly wasn't looking for commitment.

Then I met Derrick Barksby – and he changed all that. Not that Derrick swept me off my feet with his irresistible charms. Far from it. While the other fellas were a bit brash and keen to get to know me better, it was Derrick's lack of interest that got me going.

I first laid eyes on Derrick when I was just sixteen. He looked a vision in his gleaming dark tailored suit and pristine white shirt. His slicked-back hair framed his clean-shaven face. He seemed mesmerized as I belted out songs from the stage at the Silver Dollar. And he quickly plucked up the courage to ask me to dance during my break. It was the first and last time Derrick ever took the initiative to do anything in our relationship.

I was very taken with him at first. He was a master carpenter with a godly six-foot frame which towered over my tiny body. I could barely reach his shoulders as he waltzed me around the crowded room. He was a fantastic mover – but I couldn't keep up with him. I told him he was embarrassing me on the dance floor, so I suggested taking my high-heel shoes off and standing on his feet while he spun me round.

I was very impressed. I'd try to impress him too by flaunting my fancy new gold-plated cigarette case and lighter. I'd only used it for show before, but I decided I'd try a cigarette in front of Derrick. I wanted him to think I was far more mature than my tender teenage years.

It was a big mistake. After lighting up, I coughed and spluttered so much I almost died and vowed I'd never touch another fag again. To this day I have stuck to that. I only wish my first brandy had had the same effect.

Derrick started visiting the club every Saturday night after that, and we would have a dance during my break. But nothing more. He was eighteen, two years older than me, and lived down the road from the Silver Dollar with his Aunt Minnie. She used to make sure he was always well scrubbed and impeccably dressed with a clean, crisp white shirt every day, even under his overalls. He was the best-dressed manual worker in Maltby.

Our first proper date was tea at his Aunt Minnie's. She got the best china out and we sat in the front parlour, which meant we were sort of going steady. After that we started going to the pictures. We were just like any other courting couple, except I always footed the bill for our dates. If we went to the pub, I would slip him a few bob to buy a round. When we went to the pictures, I bought the tickets, and the sweets in the interval. Dad always insisted he didn't want me to tip up a penny digs from my wages: 'This is our house and I'm not having you thinking you run the place by contributing to its upkeep,' he would say. I had always been generous with money, something I'd probably inherited from dad. So I never thought twice about shelling out for everything when Derrick and I went out. At the time it simply didn't occur to me that he was the other way inclined – tight as the proverbial part of a duck's anatomy! And believe me, things didn't change when we got married.

We had been courting for weeks, and Derrick hadn't so much as tried to kiss me even though I'd lingered a lot longer on the doorstep when he walked me home than was thought fitting for a young lady. He never rose to the bait and always skipped off as fast as his lanky legs could carry him. Needless to say, it hadn't taken me long to realize that Derrick was clueless when it came to women.

But it wasn't as if I could tell him what to do. This was the frigid Forties and unmarried young ladies weren't supposed to be well versed in the pleasures of the flesh – let alone well practised in them. So to my dismay, when an inexperienced Derrick eventually decided to take the initiative, I had to lie back and act all shocked and innocent as he fumbled away under my frock.

The first time he tried to get his leg over, I almost died of embarrassment. Derrick walked me to a local field. Fields seemed to be my speciality in those days. It was a beautiful sunny day and as I bent over to fix another plaster on my poor blistered foot, Derrick started getting frisky. He was so tall I constantly had to wear the highest heels I could find and they ruined my feet – that's why I always carried a box of Elastoplast with me during our courtship.

Derrick had obviously decided the time had come for him to lay claim to his woman. I don't know to this day if he had been planning it for weeks, or whether it was a spur of the moment thing. What I do know is that it was a complete disaster.

He groped around so much, pulling my skirt up, then getting embarrassed and letting it drop to my knees again. He was frightened to death and it was obvious he had never been this close to a girl before. I felt like saying: 'For God's sake, this is how you do it.' But he was so shy, I just didn't have the heart. And of course he would have been very shocked had he known just how experienced I was.

After what seemed like an eternity, I picked myself up, brushed the grass off my frock and told Derrick I was going to catch the bus home. It must have been a terrible blow to his ego. I felt sorry for him because he was very eager – just a dead loss. I made my mind up there and then that I had no intentions of seeing him again. There was no point – he didn't know what he was doing and I certainly saw no room for improvement. As I sauntered off to the bus stop, I told him that was it, we were through and I didn't want him to bother me any more.

We didn't speak for months and I was getting on fine without him. Me being me, I'd had a few one night stands, nothing serious, but it was a damn sight more fun than being with Derrick Barksby. At this point I had hardly given him a second thought. Until, that was, I heard he'd been taking a pretty young girl called Norma Stewart out on regular dates.

Suddenly my whole world fell apart. How could that heartless, no-good brute do that to me? Had he no regard for my feelings at all? I'd forgotten about all the fun I was having – and you could bet your bottom dollar Derrick's toes would have curled had he known what I'd been getting up to since we split up. But I was heartbroken and, being a girl used to getting her own way, I was determined to get him back.

The first three months were hard going – especially for my poor mother, who had to put up with my incessant moaning and nightly crying fits in the front parlour. Mam used to go beserk trying to comfort me, saying: 'That Derrick Barksby – I'll kill him for all these nights of misery he has inflicted on me.' I was obsessed with Derrick and my rival. The thought of them together filled my mind constantly.

I was still singing at the Silver Dollar, where they had become a fixture, and I spied on them from the windows of the log cabin at the back of the stage. A couple of times I stood there with black mascara and eyeliner streaming down my red cheeks. I spent ages watching Derrick whisk Norma round the dance floor. I was filled with jealousy. Norma was very pretty, a few inches taller than me, with beautiful shiny black hair, dark eyes and a trim waist tucked into her fashionable figure-hugging dress. But I decided she was no match for me and I pulled myself together to get him back. I simply couldn't face the future without my darling Derrick. Sheer envy had elevated him in my eyes.

I knew it wasn't going to be easy and I had to work out my plan of attack very carefully. I started to get up an hour earlier every day just so that I could make sure I looked good and get to the bus stop in time to catch the same one as him. I dolled myself up to the nines, plastering on the make-up, coiffeuring my hair so it looked immaculate and wearing all my best clothes for work. It was a good job I wasn't going out at night because I was donning all my smart frocks for work and didn't have anything else to put on.

I wanted to look stunning, and I wanted Derrick to see what he was missing. If I spotted him coming round the corner I'd bend down to fasten my shoe and let a bus go past just so that he would get the chance to see me standing there in all my glory. Sometimes if he was working late I'd let three or four buses go by, praying he would turn up before the next arrived. And even though sometimes I would be frozen to the bone waiting for him, I'd smile sweetly as if I had only just arrived at the bus stop, trying to look ever so demure.

We started talking again, and I soon realized he was still interested. So I plucked up the courage to put his loyalty to the test. I spotted him dancing with Norma at the Silver Dollar, took a deep breath and waltzed over to them. Smiling sweetly, I barged between them and asked Derrick for the next dance. 'You don't mind, do you?' I asked my love rival. Of course she had to say no, and I whisked him off.

'I've not seen you for a long time,' I whispered in his ear as we moved around the floor.

'It was you who gave me the old heave-ho,' he replied. 'You said you didn't want to see me again.'

I asked him how serious he was with Norma, and he said he'd only taken her out to the pictures a couple of times. I told him I wanted to start seeing him again – and in true me style I got what I wanted. Once again Derrick was mine. I know now, though, that if he hadn't courted Norma Stewart, I would never have married Derrick Barksby.

That wasn't to be the last time my stubborn streak would get me into a sticky situation. It reared its ugly head again when my dad refused to let us get married three years later. Derrick was twenty-one and had been called up for national service. I was convinced the two years apart would be the end for us. I had become very fond of Derrick and I wanted to make sure he was really mine before he disappeared to play soldiers in some foreign country. But my dad put his foot down and refused to give his permission.

'You can wait two years, until he comes out of the army,' he yelled at me.

'But he might be sent away to another country. I might never see him again,' I protested in my dramatic fashion.

It didn't wash with dad. He'd got to know Derrick quite well over the years, and although he liked him he could see as plain as the nose on his face that he wasn't very keen on work, to say the least. Like any father, he wanted his little girl to be looked after. He was worried that likeable old Derrick was a layabout.

And basically, dad was right. If Derrick could get out of work, he would. If one of his workmates dropped his shovel to go to the lavatory, Derrick would drop his tool and wait for him to get back before he'd resume his labours.

But that wasn't the only thing that worried dad. The man I wanted to marry was also miserly. Dad had noticed that Derrick never stood his round in the pub. My father was a very generous man. He was always first at the bar and always insisted on paying for the last shout too. He didn't trust anyone who shirked when it came to getting the pints in.

'That man doesn't like work. He's an idle bugger,' he used to tell me, time and time again. 'Just look at yourself, lass. You're going to Nottingham University. You have got everything in front of you.'

I had already completed a year of my pharmacy training at the university but had another year to do before I became a fully fledged pharmacist. But I wouldn't hear a bad word said about Derrick. I wanted to marry him and that's what I intended to do.

In those days dreamboat Derrick was my idol, but I now know dad was dead right – he's just plain idle. My husband simply hates work – and today he'd be the first to admit it. In retrospect and in all honesty I knew that too. For three years I'd been earning more money than him and paying for everything – holidays, treats, nights out. But the thought of being the breadwinner never really bothered me.

However, I was a drama queen and I was convinced if we didn't get wed, Derrick would be posted to Hong Kong or Burma. I dreamt about him getting killed and I agonized over the fact I'd never see him again. As it was he wasn't posted any further than Catterick, a garrison town in North Yorkshire, about seventy-five miles away.

My mind was made up. I've always been a bossy little madam, and most of the time I got my own way, even with my dad. I wanted to become Mrs Derrick Barksby. If dad wouldn't have it, as always, I'd engineer it so that he'd have to. One way or the other I would win.

That's when I hatched my pregnancy plan. Derrick was as eager as I was for the baby – mostly because it meant a dirty two-week holiday in Blackpool and the opportunity for us to make love in a bed as opposed to the back of a car or in Aunt Minnie's front parlour. Marriage and a baby on the way also increased his chances of being posted nearer home when he was conscripted, so hopefully he wouldn't have to go abroad. And of course, Derrick knew that if he left me behind, I wouldn't waste much time finding another suitor – and the chances were I'd be snapped up by the time he got back. Or so I kept warning him.

We booked two single rooms in a bed and breakfast on a back street near the sea front just a five-minute walk from the famous Golden Mile. The accommodation was sparse and cheaply furnished, each room containing just a single bed, a stained washbasin and a rickety old wardrobe. The landlady was very severe looking – a black bun scraped off her wiry face and thin as a rake – and we knew we'd have to be very careful for her not to catch us up to anything. Sex outside marriage was terribly frowned upon in those days.

Every morning Derrick would tiptoe to my room, three doors away, and we'd get down to it. The bed was terribly creaky so we couldn't take chances making love on it. We had to haul all the blankets on the floor every time we wanted to get down to it.

We'd go to the dining room for breakfast with the other guests, praying that nobody knew what we were up to. Of course the landlady knew, all right – I could tell by the disdainful way she looked at me. But she never caught us so there was little she could do or say. 'Good morning,' I'd say to her with a knowing smile on my devious lips.

Each day we'd go for a walk on the front and return in the afternoon. Looking very tired, we'd say we were going up for forty winks. Then Derrick would sneak back to my room for another session. He'd do the same at night – but he always scarpered before I awoke in the morning.

I knew as soon as I opened my eyes, that fateful day, that I had conceived. My plan had worked. I went straight to Derrick's room and said, 'That's it. I'm pregnant.' He thought I was barmy, but I was right.

When we got home, my mother took one look at me and said, 'Your eyes are wan, my girl. You're having a baby.' Mum was telepathic sometimes and often guessed when neighbours were pregnant before they knew themselves. And she was spot on this time too.

I simpered, 'I hope not. I've just started earning loads of money.' But the smirk on my face told her she was right. She was furious.

When I skipped my first period I knew for sure, and being a mischievous sod the first person I wanted to tell was ... my dad. He was sitting reading his paper in the living room when I stormed straight up to him and said defiantly: 'Dad, I'm pregnant. You've got to let me get married now.' Derrick stood behind me. He was very embarrassed and didn't dare say a word. My dad was angry with him, but he knew who the real cuplrit was, who was behind the whole thing.

I had really upset him, and I saw a tear running down

his cheek as he whispered almost inaudibly: 'You little fool.' It seemed like hours before he said another word. He just stood there staring at us both. Then he roared: 'You don't know what you've done, the pair of you. You, our Jean, you've got just one more year before you qualify as a fully fledged pharmacist. I know you've just done it because I told you not to get married. You'll regret this, my girl.'

Luckily, my mother came to terms with it a lot easier than dad. She quite liked Derrick, so she managed to talk dad round, though he really didn't have much choice. I don't think he ever really got over it.

Derrick and I were married two months later, on 14 October 1950, in Rotherham Town Hall. It was what you might call a rush job. Obviously, I couldn't get hitched in white. Instead I bought a far more 'honest' ready-made pale silver grey suit, with a matching pink lace blouse and a hat with little pink roses on.

The only guests were my mother and father, Derrick's mate Jack who was best man, his Aunt Minnie, Uncle John, and my best friend Doreen Bell. It was a quiet affair – something I lived to regret later on in life. There were no fancy extras, no photos, no confetti or even a wedding cake. We didn't even have a posh car to take us to the reception. Instead after the quick register office ceremony, dad packed us all into his old Austin and drove us down the road to the Co-Op for a roast beef and Yorkshire pudding dinner. It wasn't a grand affair, but shotgun weddings seldom are.

CHAPTER FIVE

Working Mum

There I was, lying on my back in the labour ward of Rotherham General Hospital for the fourteenth time in as many days. Every night at eight o'clock the contractions would start, every night they'd wheel me down to give birth to my baby – and every night it was just another false alarm.

I was well and truly fed up. I was sick to death of sitting round doing nothing except stare down at this huge belly. Pregnancy had rapidly turned me from a seven-stone trim teenager into a barrage balloon. I was so big early on that people were visibly shocked when I told them I was just four months pregnant – I looked as if I was about to go into labour at any second. My stomach was so swollen I could balance a plate on it, and I was hardly able to walk.

Why I was so enormous I'll never know. I rarely ate anything because my morning sickness was so severe. The only thing I could stomach was spinach, something I'd never dreamed of eating before I got pregnant. Poor Derrick had to walk miles to find it when the fancy took me. It didn't matter what time of day or night, when I got the craving Derrick was sent packing to hunt it down. It wasn't easy to get hold of because deep freezers didn't

exist in working-class homes back in the Fifties and con-
venience food wasn't heard of. The spinach had to be
fresh – I wouldn't settle for anything out of a tin. I haven't
touched the stuff since and the very thought of it now
makes me want to heave.

I hated being in hospital. It drove me mad. I liked to
keep myself busy and after two weeks I began to get very
grumpy and moaned at every opportunity. My midwife
Sister Kirk was an angel. She was lovely to me and understood how impatient I was getting. But she also knew that
under my tough exterior was a nineteen-year-old kid who
was terrified. She helped me to relax and made my month-
long stay in hospital more fun.

Every morning she'd stop at my bed, shake her head
and say, 'You're too little to have a baby. Just look at the
size of you, you're tiny, still a baby yourself.'

'It's a bit late for that, sister,' I would yell back at her
as she wandered off down the ward.

Her words became part of my daily routine. Every
morning she'd look at me in disbelief and every evening
I'd be staring at the ceiling in disbelief as the calm midwife
told me to push.

But all my rehearsals couldn't have prepared me for
the birth when it finally came. After two full weeks per-
fecting my natural childbirth techniques, the doctors
discovered last-minute complications. Tests showed that
the baby's heart wasn't beating normally and that during
the false alerts his head was smashing against my pelvic
wall, causing him severe distress. I had to have a Caesarean section. In normal circumstances, going under the
surgeon's knife would have frightened me to death, but I
was that desperate to get the little bugger out that I gave
them my blessing.

So on 14 May 1951, two weeks after being admitted
and seven months to the day after our wedding, I gave
birth to a bouncing 9 lb 7 oz baby boy. We named our

little darling Stephen. He was a beautiful baby. Caesarean babies don't come into the world all red and wrinkled – Stephen was smooth as silk all over, although he did have a couple of red marks on the top of his head where he'd been colliding with my pelvis.

I only wish my stomach had escaped so easily. They left me with an ugly eight-inch scar on my belly, sewed both on the inside and the outside just to make sure it didn't come undone. It was held together by twenty-four huge silver dog clips. The doctors didn't trust stitches to hold and took every precaution to keep the wound together. A massive plaster going right round my back, up to my navel and down to my thighs kept the damn things in place. I was in agony and it was just as well I was kept in for a further two weeks because I couldn't walk, let alone take care of a new-born infant.

Just as I was recovering, a young nurse called Audrey came to change the bed and ordered me to get up. I did as I was told, but collapsed onto the floor. I wish I'd had a camera because her face was a picture! She hadn't realized I was a Caesarean because the sign above the bed was covered up by mistake. So they had to rip off the plaster, wheel me down to theatre again for more stitches and replace the dog clips – all without an anaesthetic. By the time they'd finished with me, you could have played noughts and crosses on my belly. One thing was for sure, I would never be able to wear a bikini again.

But that was the least of my worries. When I fell pregnant I had desperately wanted to have at least two kids. I didn't think it was healthy for a bairn to be brought up alone. I had seen the way Derrick had grown up as an only child, cold, isolated and devoid of emotion. Nothing seemed to choke him, nothing disturbed or upset him. He never showed his feelings or an iota of affection for those supposedly close to him. I wasn't going to have that for my children – they were going to grow up surrounded by brothers, sisters and plenty of love.

But soon after Stephen's birth we were told by the doctor that because he was such a big baby, compared to my small frame, my womb had been badly damaged. 'It will be six years before the tissue is repaired,' he told me as I wept in Derrick's arms. 'So don't even think about having another baby until then.'

I was devastated. This was something I had not expected. I'd always got my own way, but now God had intervened and for the first time in my life I felt powerless. There was nothing I could do.

I didn't realize it at the time, but this was the beginning of the end of my role as a dedicated mother. I believe to this day that if I'd had more little ones I would have been forced to spend more time at home, looking after my family. There would have been no time for dreams of stardom – my life would have taken a different direction completely. But it wasn't to be. I started motherhood enthusiastically enough, but looking back I think the fact that I couldn't have any more kids put a shadow over my abilities to give my all as a doting mum and wife.

As if that wasn't a big enough blow, I soon realized that I couldn't breastfeed Stephen. That made me feel a complete failure as a mother. I tried and tried to make him accept the milk, but he couldn't get it down, and something in it was making him ill. He lost weight and the doctors urged me to use a bottle. They bound my breasts up tightly and gave me tablets to get rid of the milk, which was solidifying inside and causing me tremendous pain.

All I could think was, 'Breast is best, breast is best.' Flashbacks of our Duggie as a four-year-old boy still being fed by mum constantly came into my mind. Here was I, holding a tiny babe in my arms unable to nourish the little mite myself. It broke my heart.

I took Stephen home after two more weeks on the

ward. Derrick and I had to cope as new parents, and we grew up fast. I knew nothing about babies. Luckily we were living with my mum and dad when I first came out of hospital. I'd tried to find us a place of our own, but it ended in disaster. My impulsive nature had got me into trouble again.

The week before we got married I'd found our first home – if you could call it that. It was a tiny 25-bob-a-week bedsit rented in the attic of a huge semi-detached house crammed with flats in Clifton Lane, about two miles away from my folks. My parents were quite well off and dad had wanted to help us out. They wanted us to move in with them until we got sorted out. I was adamant we did things our way and put my foot down. I wanted my independence and I didn't want Derrick to feel embarrassed. He wasn't earning much money at the time. We wanted to do things our own way, we were young and proud.

So I'd made sure we had somewhere to live waiting for us when we got back from our honeymoon – even though I hadn't paid any attention to what it was like. I'd simply picked up the keys, paid two weeks rent in advance, and we'd gone off to Blackpool. But when we returned a week later, cold and exhausted late on the Saturday night, I broke down in tears as I put the key in the door. How different it looked in the darkness: grim, damp and cold!

This was no place to start family life. In a hole built into the wall was a folding bed which had to be pulled out and made up every night. The furniture was old and rickety, the walls were a depressing shade of green and we had to share a bathroom with God knows how many other people.

The thought of my new life had filled me with excitement. It was something I had always secretly yearned for. I wasn't expecting such a bleak beginning. I'd dreamed of a kitchen filled with the smells of freshly baked bread, sweet cakes and home-cooked meats hanging from beamed rafters. And I'd yearned to show off my culinary skills by making Derrick a roast dinner with all the trimmings. Roast beef and Yorkshire pudding were an absolute must on a Sunday, and what you call dinner now was at one o'clock, and tea was sandwiches made from the left-over meat, cakes and a cup of char.

On Sunday morning I got up bright and early to prepare my new husband's feast. I'd already bought all the ingredients: a huge joint of beef, milk and eggs for the batter, new potatoes and a selection of fresh vegetables. But I got the shock of my life when I opened what I thought was the oven underneath the four hobs – it was a bare cupboard for storing pots and pans! I screamed at Derrick: 'Oh my God, how am I going to cook your roast?' I could have cried. I searched all round the flat to see if there was an oven somewhere else. I was that desperate, I even looked under the stairs and in the bathroom.

We didn't have a phone and, not knowing who else to turn to, I ran across the road to the call box to ring dad. 'You'll have to come and fetch me, I can't make Derrick's dinner,' I said.

'Give him some sandwiches,' he replied.

But I wasn't having anyone thinking I couldn't cook my own husband a decent dinner. So dad had to get on his motorbike and pick me up. He packed me and all my ingredients into his sidecar and drove home so I could use mum's oven. Dad sat there shaking his head and reading the papers as I raced round the kitchen in a blind panic trying to get everything just right. Fortunately mum had a jug with a lid on so the gravy didn't spill all over the place when dad sped up the cobbled streets on the way back. I sat in the sidecar with my helmet on, three tea-towels on my knee balancing a plate of Yorkshire puds, the jug of gravy and a huge joint of beef which could have fed an army.

We didn't stay in that flat very long. I went straight out on the Monday looking for another. We'd given two weeks rent up front and for the remainder of that time we'd go to mother's every night for tea. When I told her I couldn't find a flat we could afford, she insisted: 'Well, you'll have to come and stop with us then, won't you?' And that was that.

We moved back in as a temporary measure. Three years later we were still there. How we managed I'll never know. My folks had one room, our Keith and Duggie shared the room next door and me and Derrick were in the spare. And that wasn't all – there was Derrick's pride and joy, a wire-haired fox terrier called Sue.

For the first two years of our marriage, Derrick was away all week on national service in Catterick. He was never away for more than five days at a time and hitch-hiked home every weekend. To hear him talk you'd think he'd been on some secret mission working in the deepest jungles of Outer Mongolia and had won the war single-handedly.

He couldn't wait to come home every weekend – to see the dog, not me. He loved that dog more than anything. But my mother wasn't very impressed by the attention he seemed to be paying to that dog instead of his expectant wife.

Derrick was quiet, but he was also a determined lad who stopped at nothing to get what he wanted. He'd been spoiled rotten by his Auntie Minnie – she let him get away with murder. He honestly thought he could carry on like that while living with my mother. He decided he wanted to breed Sue and planned to mate her with a pedigree dog. He was never there to look after Sue, let alone a whole litter load of pups. So, understandably, mum put her foot down. She forbade him on the grounds that we simply didn't have the room. Unbeknown to us, Derrick went ahead and did it anyway. He skulked back off to Catterick and we were left looking after Sue, who was growing fatter and fatter by the day.

My mother soon realized what he'd done, and she was furious: 'You write to that husband of yours and tell him this dog is having pups – and it's got to go.'

Derrick came home as instructed and dumped the lot on Aunt Minnie, who never complained.

Derrick was so lazy he'd sit and watch the fire go out before he'd even think about putting some more wood on. It drove my mam mad. One day he went out running and left the fire to go out completely. She insisted we sat there in the freezing cold until he came home. When he did get back she sent him straight out to get some wood. He apologized, saying he simply didn't think. 'Well, you'll think on next time,' she said as she supervised him.

After that she regularly used to say to me, 'You are making a rod for your own back, lass. He'll never do owt, that one.' Even though she liked him, she thought I pampered him too much and that I was setting a pattern which I would very much regret. At the time I didn't consider it pampering. I used to just do it as a matter of course. She told me knowingly time and time again, 'You are making a rod for your own back, the way you mider after him.' But I had already set the precedent and his laziness was something which got progressively worse.

Apart from that, all was very happy in the Dudley/Barksby household. It was a little awkward at first, what with Derrick and me sleeping in the room next to mum and dad. Even though we were married we felt uncomfortable cuddling in case they heard us through the walls. And in those days it was a crying shame because Derrick was a super lover – he was a big lad and we'd had some marvellous sex.

Derrick was very athletic. He used to run with the

local harriers and he kept himself in very good shape. He was a miler, and many a time when we were courting he'd miss the last bus and run half a dozen miles home, so we could have an extra canoodle.

But even then he lacked any sort of emotion. It was as if I was just another part of his training schedule to get fit and keep his muscles in trim. Right from the start he didn't pay much attention to my needs.

As dad predicted, I had to give up my job at Boots just before I had the baby, and we had to rely on Derrick's measly army pay to keep us going. I'd never really had it tough. But now I had a family to take care of. I'd got myself into this, and it was up to me make the best of what we had. I'd seen lots of other women muddle through with nothing but the rags on their backs, and if it came to it I would just have to do the same. And here I was with my own family – a bone idle husband and a new-born babe to take care of. Thank God we were still living with mum and dad.

Stephen was still only a few months old when I decided to go back to work. Although my parents were good to us, I was sick of being careful with money and wanted to get back to earning my own living again. Derrick's contribution wasn't enough. At the time the papers were full of advertisements for work; there were pages and pages of jobs which simply weren't being filled. It wasn't long after that West Indians were brought in to do some of the work.

My mum, bless her, agreed to look after Stephen, so I got myself work as a clippie on the buses. It was hard work, mind. It was still dark when the alarm clock went off at three o'clock every morning as I hauled myself out of bed. It remained dark as I made the hour-long journey to Rotherham to catch my first shift on the special which left the grimy old depot at 4.30 am on the dot.

At the end of the shift I'd check the notice boards in

the station to see if there were any other shifts going spare. Sometimes that meant I'd go straight onto another service and before I knew it I was working a sixteen-hour day. Not that I minded – while Derrick was earning a pittance, some weeks I was taking home more than £12. It was an enormous amount – but I had to work for it.

True to form, that didn't dent Derrick's ego at all. In fact he'd come home at weekends and sit on my bus as I collected the fares from the passengers. Not that I had much time to speak to him, but he quite enjoyed the ride – though not as much as he enjoyed the brass.

Even though we could afford it, we didn't go away on holiday. That was something I had never experienced as a kid because dad wouldn't take any time off work. His idea of getting away from it all was a drive in the countryside at the dead of night to watch the frightened rabbits caught in the car headlights. Now and again we'd go to Mablethorpe or Cleethorpes for the day. It was a trip organized by the local Progressive Club and all the kids round our way used to go. They'd collect each week all year round to pay for the charabanc fare, and come summer we'd be off.

Those trips were still in vogue when I had Stephen, so it was a tradition Derrick and I adhered to. I'd inherited my dad's reluctance to take time off work when there were wages on offer, so it was day trips or nothing.

But my persistence paid off. I was earning so much that at last we could afford a mortgage on our own house. It was a two-up two-down mid-terrace on Westfield Road in Bramley, an area of Rotherham not a million miles removed from the cobbled streets of the soap opera on which I would spend more than two decades of my later life. It had a back yard and an outside loo. Every week I'd religiously sweep the yard, red cardinal stone the step and Brasso all the doorknobs. I was very houseproud.

The deceptive outside appearance did however veil

mayhem inside – a blinding array of vivid colours, ten layers of thick gloss paint plastered onto the walls, and old-fashioned fittings and shelves. I wanted the place transformed but I soon realized that if I wanted anything doing I would have to do it myself.

Derrick was a master carpenter when he left the army – but it was virtually impossible to get him to do any work on our new house. When he came home he wanted to relax and had no intention of picking up his tools if he wasn't getting paid. So every job I asked him to do, big or small, was met with the same response – an instant dismissal. 'That's impossible. It just can't be done, I'm afraid,' he'd say. But as far as I was concerned, there's no such word as 'can't'. If he 'couldn't' do it, I would.

At the time I had started a new job at the Argyle sock factory down our road. I worked full time operating a circular knitting machine from nine in the morning until six at night. Of course I had to combine that with looking after Stephen, keeping a home and waiting on Derrick.

I'd spend all Saturday morning baking bread, cakes, pies and biscuits, then I'd go out to do the shopping. Sometimes I'd come home, laden down with an over-flowing shopping basket, and Derrick would be sat there claiming to be starving. I'd have left a tray of sandwiches but he hadn't been bothered to even look. 'I didn't know what there was to eat,' he'd say, as he was surrounded by the goodies I'd spent all ruddy morning preparing. I had to take a deep breath and count to ten, otherwise I would have clocked him one.

So I was, to say the least, pretty busy in those early days. But I was determined my house would be perfect and that I would manage my time somehow. I abandoned any ideas of Derrick giving me a helping hand. I had already completely redecorated the place myself and peeled all the old paint off the walls with a blow torch when he was away with the army.

When I asked Derrick to fix a soap holder in the bathroom, I got the usual shiftless response: 'Can't do that. It would make a hole right through to the bedroom. Forget it.' I went to one of his mates, got some cement, sand and a leveller and got stuck in. I'd seen my dad knocking down walls, rebuilding them, plastering with a trowel and using every other kind of instrument. As well as being a bricklayer by trade, he was also a DIY enthusiast, and I had inherited his skills in that department. Nothing was too big a job for me.

Once I successfully fixed the soap dish, there was no stopping me. I was ready to tackle anything – but my next job was a disaster. There was an unsightly door which had been papered over after an attempt to extend one of the upstairs rooms. It looked appalling and I wanted the thing ripped out. 'There's nowt we can do,' warned Derrick. 'If I start tinkering with that the whole house will fall down.' I didn't listen, of course.

The following day I removed a hammer and chisel from his tool bag before he went off to work and took the task on board myself. Standing precariously on an old piano stool on the landing, I started hacking away with the hammer. As the plaster crumbled, my confidence grew. I forced the slim end of the chisel behind the wooden slats and prised part of the frame away. Success – until the ceiling started caving in. I tried to shield myself from the falling rubble but huge chunks of it knocked me off the stool. I looked up to see all the joists were exposed as well as a huge hole in the roof.

Grabbing my coat in one hand and Stephen in the other, I dashed to the bus stop. Dad would have to fix this mess before Derrick got home or I would be in serious trouble. Dad opened the door and stared at the flaking plaster and dust draped round my shoulders and in my hair. He shook his head in astonishment, almost. 'What on earth have you been up to now?' he asked. There was no time for any lengthy explanation, so after a brief chat we jumped into his car and set off.

Once again, with a little expertise dad saved my bacon. God knows what he did, but somehow he inserted a steel girder into the brickwork and stopped the whole house collapsing. Needless to say, the job I had wanted doing, was done – in a roundabout fashion.

Every time Derrick said 'can't' after that, I'd give him that knowing look, hoping it would instil the fear of God into him. He knew I'd attempt to do it myself.

As a moving-in present, dad bought us a 12-inch Cossor television set. We were the first family in Westfield Road to have a telly, and it made us instant hits with our new neighbours. When there was football on the box I couldn't get in the house with all the kids and men cram-med inside. I found it incredibly hard work, trying to bake for everyone and dish out cakes and butties without getting in the way of the picture.

By this time Stephen was a lovely kid, his cherubic face always smiling. He was never the least bit of trouble, never woke up in the early hours, never cried without good reason. I couldn't have wished for a more contented infant. But he started getting restless while I was working at the sock factory. He'd cry while I was away, and couldn't even be comforted by his ever-attentive Auntie Minnie.

I had to give up my job and we had to manage on Derrick's wage. It was tough trying to get any brass out of Derrick – he was used to me having my own money and didn't like handing over his. I'd ask him for money to pay the milkman and he'd say, 'When you learn to do as you're told.' That meant I had to hide every time the door-bell rang in case it was the milkman calling for his pay-ments. It was so embarrassing.

Derrick, being a typically tight-fisted Yorkshireman, thought he was teaching me a hard lesson in good finance.

But it was not a very effective one, and from very early on in our marriage I developed an unhealthy disrespect for money – the horrifying extent of which I will go into later.

My dad wanted to help out but I wouldn't let him give us anything. Instead I took in washing, and that kept the wolves at bay. Dick Garner lived next door with six strapping sons and four daughters to bring up on his own. His wife had left him. Understandably he found it very tough trying to manage the family and a full-time job down at the foundry. I offered to help with the laundry, and every week I washed and ironed all their clothes for the princely sum of ten bob.

I love housework. I always said that if I hadn't gone into showbusiness I would have been very happy as a full-time housewife. I thoroughly enjoyed cleaning, cooking, washing and ironing and never tired of it. I have a cleaner now, but I still find myself going over the house with a fine-toothed comb, making sure she hasn't overlooked anything.

Like most working-class mums, when I wasn't out grafting I had certain days allocated for my household chores. On Monday I did the washing, Friday was baking day, on Wednesday I would scrub the downstairs of our two-up, two-down. On Thursday I'd clean upstairs and do the yard and Saturday was shopping day while Derrick sometimes did a half day at work. If I had a job, I had to fit everything in around my shifts.

That wasn't the only routine in our house. Every Monday night, religiously, I used to walk out on Derrick and go back to my mother's. Monday was washday, and in those days it was a chore and a half. In the morning I'd pack a huge suitcase full of dirty washing and drag it to Derrick's Auntie Minnie's down the hill. It would be eight o'clock before I got home after sweating all day over the hot tub and mangle. Then I'd have to dry the clothes, look after Stephen and iron the lot. So when I got home the last thing I wanted to do was wait on Derrick hand and foot. Of course that's exactly what he expected. It was always a day that the slightest spark would cause a gigantic row.

Our Monday night fights became legendary. I'd pack my bags, grab Stephen and shout, 'I'm off to my mother's. Don't bother trying to talk me out of it.' He never did. I'd jump on the bus and dad would be stood at the front window waiting for my arrival.

'Agnes, here comes our Jean,' he'd say as I dragged little Stephen, who was walking so fast he was almost tripping up over his own feet, down their path.

'I've left him, dad – and this time it's for good. You can go and pick up the rest of my stuff while he's at work tomorrow.'

Dad would look at me and nod his head: 'All right, dear.' He knew very well that first thing in the morning he'd be driving one very remorseful daughter home to make up with her very unrepentant hubby.

It became such a joke, dad even threatened to buy the house next door because it would have been a lot less bother to build an adjoining door for me to burst through than to get the car out every week to drive me home.

I'd get back to Westfield Road and there was never any mention of the fight. That wasn't Derrick's way. Regurgitating the row wouldn't make any difference, he'd simply dismiss it. He knew I only walked out to show him he couldn't walk all over me, to show him who was the boss. But we both knew that I could never get the better of him. If Derrick didn't want to do anything, you could move hell and high water and he wouldn't do it.

As Stephen started to grow up, I realized he had taken on board his father's stubborn streak. He was a little devil, and more than a handful for any mother. He started to disappear when he was about three years old. I'd be cleaning or cooking, one minute he was by my side and the next minute – gone. Frantically I'd search every room in the house, but he was nowhere to be found. Then I'd check the yard, the outside loo, next door's garden. Not a sight of him to be had.

It became a tedious daily chore. I'd grab my coat and run down the street, where I'd usually be greeted by a smiling do-gooding neighbour with him firmly in one hand and his tiny tricycle in the other.

'It's all right, dear. I've got him.'

I'd whisper my thanks and grab his hand: 'I'll kill you, you little devil, showing me up like that. Heaven knows what people must think.'

Stephen would drag his feet behind me. He'd been trying to cycle to Aunt Minnie's for a bath. I wouldn't mind but she lived six miles away. All he knew was that it was down that long windy hill that was visible from our kitchen window. Thank God he was always stopped before he got to the bottom of it.

I tried all sorts to stop him wandering, not least of all tying him up out the back – to the disgust of my neighbour Mrs Baker, who threatened to call the NSPCC. I'd tie him with a clothes line to the post in the middle of the yard. It wasn't as bad as it sounds – I always gave him enough rope to be able to cycle round.

'You can't treat a child like that,' Mrs Baker would cry over the wall. 'It's barbaric! The poor little mite. Release him or I swear I'll call the authorities.'

I never did like interfering neighbours and I'd shout back, twice as loud: 'Mind your own business! What I do with my son is my affair, nowt to do with you. If you want to look after him while I change my bedsheets then that's fair enough – if not, then leave us be.'

She didn't like that and she hardly ever spoke to me again, though she used to spread gossip round the street that I used to set my main chimney alight whenever she had her washing out to purposely blacken it with soot. Silly woman – I didn't have the time, what with looking after that little sod Stephen.

Stephen was happy as Larry riding round and round on his bike – until he learned eventually how to undo my amateurish knots on the clothes line and set himself free. That's when the nightmare really began. He used to go to the butcher's on the main street and steal strings of sausages from the counter. He'd come racing home proudly brandishing his catch – with the furious butcher fast on his heels. Every time I had to apologize profusely and pay the man for his wares. Some weeks we'd have to have to eat sausages every night, he pinched that many. That butcher must have made a fortune out of me.

By this time I had played the dutiful wife and mother for more than three years. I loved my role, it certainly had its moments. But when Derrick's Uncle John, who was the concert secretary for the nearby Progressive Club, asked me to sing again, I jumped at the chance. The stage lights and the greasepaint beckoned – and the temptation was too great.

Uncle John had heard me sing at the Silver Dollar and talked me into standing in for a Sunday act who'd cancelled at the last minute. There were no agents in those days, so finding a turn was a damned sight harder than it is today. I went down to Woolworths to get some sheet music.

But my stage comeback was a complete disaster and I fell flat on my face. I was dreadful, singing at least four keys lower than the pianist Albert. I swore I would never get up and sing again, but Albert talked me into going back to his place for an afternoon rehearsal. I returned to the club that night with a bit more confidence and I brought the house down. Plus I'd earned £4.50 for that little stint – almost as much as I'd been bringing in for a whole week's work at the sock factory. I suddenly realized which way my bread was buttered and decided to investigate the possiblities of taking up this profession seriously.

A few weeks later I booked myself in for my first big audition to sing cabaret at the Rotherham Trade Centre. I knocked them dead on stage and took twenty-seven bookings straight off. I'd wracked my brains to think of a decent stage name to launch my new career. Derrick came up with Pirie, the name of his favourite athlete Gordon Pirie. The Yorkshire runner went on to win a silver medal in the 5,000 metres at the 1956 Olympics in Melbourne, Australia. Years later I was to travel to the other side of the globe to star in cabaret in Sydney – although I'd never have believed it if you'd told me then.

'Yes, that's got a ring to it,' I said, although I had no idea how to spell it, and it ended up as Perrie – Lynne Perrie. Derrick assumed the role of manager and was negotiating all my fees at that time. He was never happier than when he was discussing money.

Word spread like wildfire that Lynne Perrie, Little Miss Dynamite, was about to explode onto the scene, and I suppose you could say I never looked back.

CHAPTER SIX

Life's a Cabaret!

The women with those awful puff curls were sitting there over their glasses of stout. They were just like I'd imagine Ena Sharples would have been in her younger years: unsmiling with steely-eyed stares.

I'd been warned that these two formidable bleached blonde hags would be there ready to give whatever act walked on their stage a hard time. The club was smoke-filled and in need of a lick of paint. Drunken punters clinging to their pint pots were at almost every table. It was a typical night in a Northern club – except for the unfriendly faces of the sixteen or so people on the two main tables centre stage.

The presence of those faces filled me with dread. For this was the RAOB club in West Hartlepool on a Monday. And every entertainer on the Northern club circuit knew that Monday at the RAOB was crucifixion night. Other acts had warned me about this lot on the tables in front of the stage. They sat stern-faced through every act, killing the atmosphere and crucifying the artist. When I saw their glum faces, arms folded so they couldn't clap, I knew it was true. I said to myself: 'Oh bloody hell, I've cut a pot off a broken ankle to come here and they want to kill my act. I won't stand for it.'

At the back of the room there was a coach load who had followed me from my Saturday night show at the Lions club in Hartlepool. I'd had a good night there and was hopeful that they might lift the evening.

I wasn't first up. The initial human sacrifice was a guitarist who had a beautiful voice. He got a few claps, but then the resounding silence from the centre of the room slaughtered his show. In that kind of situation people on the periphery are afraid to signal their appreciation.

I was next up for the first of two spots. This group remained stiff-backed and grimacing. I thought, I'll show them. All I need is to get one of them going and I'll crack the lot. But I'd bargained on these people being out for entertainment – they weren't after that. Their idea of a good night out was something completely different. Seeing an artiste squirming on stage was their idea of fun.

I did the first spot and these people created a terrible atmosphere. Anyway, I thought for the second act I'd show them. I got two bars into the first song when I stopped, looked at the grim faces and said, 'Do you know you're famous?' They just looked at me. 'Your fame has travelled as far as Sunderland and up to Newcastle. I knew all about you two blondes with the beaded hair nets, the puff curls and the Marks and Spencers frocks. And you men there, I know all about you. You'll go down the pit tomorrow, won't you, and say, "we crucified another one last night." Well, I'm only 4 feet 11inches, but you haven't got a bloody cross big enough for me in this place.' I told them I was on £25 a night, but they could stuff it. I told them I'd done half a spot, but they could have the money for the old age pensioners' fund. I said straight that I wasn't singing in front of that mob of miseries. My hairdresser was with me and I called for her to bring my Jaguar up to the door so we could leave.

At this the club secretary got on the stage and asked

what I was doing. I gave him a piece of my mind as well. I told him he was responsible for allowing that lot to get away with it for years. I used some terrible language about this bunch. I said, 'They think they're so clever, but they're going to have to go down the pits without killing my act.' I stormed into the committee room and said, 'I'll give you a cheque for the pensioners' fund, because I don't want you putting that £25 into the committee's pockets.'

Then I walked out and as I went I could hear people walking up to the front tables and playing hell with them. For four years after they tried to get me back at that club, but I told them that was my first and last time. Afterwards I found out that they barred these two tables, so at least some good came of the evening.

Another nightmare evening I remember was up at a tiny place called the Stonehouse Violet Club near Motherwell in Scotland. The locals had actually paid for this club themselves after raising the cash through raffles, and I was on the opening night. When we got in the walls were all newly decorated and everything was spick and span. But they'd forgotten one important thing – a dressing room for the acts. I ended up changing in the committee room, but it was to get a lot worse as the evening wore on.

The stage was only small and after the organist and drummer set up I was left with about two square feet, but I could live with that. Motherwell had won at home and there was a large contingent of sozzled soccer fans. I had, as usual, two slots to do. The first went without any problems and I thought. What a lovely place. The people here are obviously all so very proud of it. But when I got up for the second spot I noticed they were all glassy-eyed. The Jocks don't half know how to drink and these were really first division boozers.

About halfway through the act the inevitable happened. All of a sudden a table shot into the air and smashed on the roof. I am stuck on this poky stage and suddenly the place erupts in violence. Tables, chairs, glasses and bottles are flying everywhere – it was just like a wild west saloon brawl in the movies, except the Texan drawl was replaced with broad Glaswegian and nobody was pulling any punches. There was blood everywhere and the language was blue. It was effing this and effing that, and one of these drunken lunatics even tried to attack me.

I was cowering in a corner on a leather settee when this huge lad waving a bottle came towards me. I started shouting at him, 'I'm the turn, I'm the turn, I'm the artist.' He eventually got the message, but it didn't matter in that place because the women were getting stuck in along with the men.

It all died down and I thought, Oh lovely. I'll be able to get out of here. Two seconds later it erupted again. At this point two members of the committee came over and picked me up and pushed me backside first behind the bar. They pulled the steel shutters down on me so I could watch the performance in relative safety.

In a few minutes the ambulances and police cars had arrived and the two families behind the fighting were either carted off or had legged it. As the mayhem subsided I told one of the committee men I was really disappointed – not with the scrapping, but the fact that I'd spent ten shillings on raffle tickets in the hope of winning a cuddly giant panda. I asked the chap if he'd sell me one. He said, 'After what you've been through, love, you can have one.' This bear was almost as big as me and I was delighted with it.

I escaped the evening with nothing more than a big bruise on my neck. My agent was driving me at that stage and we set off in our maroon Vauxhall Cresta for his home. I started chatting with the panda on the way back, because I found it about as communicative as Derrick and ten times more cuddly. I drove the agent mad nattering with this fluffy monster. All the way home he kept saying, 'Will you stop talking to that bloody teddy bear.' The more he said it the more I'd wind him up.

But not every cabaret job was a drag. One of my most memorable tours happened in the early 1960s when I worked as support act to the Beatles. I also supported the Rolling Stones, but the lads from Liverpool were the best for me. They sent me Christmas cards for about four years afterwards. They always referred to me as 'girlie', and after a while I got a bit fed up with this. I said to them 'I'm almost old enough to be your mother, so why are you calling me girlie?'

But I was very flattered by Paul's reply. He said, 'We're calling you girlie because you look like a little girl. And when you are on stage you move like a nine-year-old, so full of life. You've just got incredible energy.'

I'll never forget the first gig. I arrived at the venue and it was like trying to get to Wembley on Cup Final day, except the crowds were thousands and thousands of screaming girls. The noise was terrifying. I had never seen anything like it in my life. The shrieking and scream-ing would drown out any orchestra noise and I was horrified at the thought of having to go out there and entertain them.

I was in awe of the situation. In fact I was frightened, very frightened. These girls weren't there to listen to me – they wanted the Scouse mop tops. The Beatles were probably the first super-group ever. Nobody had excited that type of hysterical adulation before. My nerves were tinged with sheer terror. I thought, God, how am I going to face all that lot? Then I thought, Bugger it. I'm going to get well paid for this, so I'm going on.

The screaming girls didn't take a blind bit of notice. A dumpy housewife was about the last thing they wanted to see. All they were after was John, Paul, George and Ringo, and they had got me. They were shouting and yelling all the way through my first number. They were not at all interested in me. I was being ignored and I didn't much care for it.

So I thought, I'll show you. After the song I shouted 'Oy' then I just shut up and stood silent on the stage. Gradually they all took note and a hush descended. They were thinking to themselves, What is she doing? It went quiet – well, quiet enough for me to tell them what was going to happen. I said, 'Look, I'm old enough to be your mother. I've been paid to do an act and I'm going to do it. Now either you let me do this act or I am stopping here like this for an hour-and-a-half and you won't get to see the Beatles.'

In a situation like that in front of an audience of thousands of disinterested teenagers you either take control or take off. I wasn't about to leave behind a good wage for anybody, so I got them by the scruffs of their necks and made them listen to me. They soon got the message.

Once they started listening, the clapping followed, because my act was rock and roll not a million miles removed from the Beatles. They clapped faster and faster and I realized they were speeding up to try and get me off sooner. I could live with that – at least they were listening to my stuff. I was moving about and singing my heart out. The audience thought, Ooh it's not bad, this. I was booked for the one show, but their people liked me so much they signed me up for the other eleven. It was 1964 and all the shows were at coastal resorts on Sundays.

Just before the tour kicked off one of the lads said he liked Jelly Babies. So whenever I stepped on stage I was squashing these little fruit sweets with every step. Some of the girls even threw the jellies up in their boxes, so you had to be careful where you trod. I had a particular problem with the Jelly Babies, because for years I'd been kicking my shoes off and going barefoot, as part of the act. It doesn't half hurt if you stand on a box of sweets barefoot, as I found out pretty quickly.

Girls were hurling Jelly Babies on to the stage from the first act. All the boxes were tied up with ribbons and flowers. Some even had girls' addresses on them. But when the boxes split the Jelly Babies just spilled all over the floor. I used them in my act by picking one up and saying, 'this one's a boy – it's got that bit more.'

Another daft gag I used that fitted the tour was about the Beatles' recent trip to Paris. I'd tell the girls they left singing 'She loves you, yes, yes, yes' and came back singing 'oui, oui, oui.' They loved it – don't ask me why.

It was George Harrison who liked the Jelly Babies and it caught on so much that he had boxes of them sent to his home in Liverpool. He had so many that he used to get kids to drop them off at one of the Liverpool hospitals.

It is funny how saying something when you're famous can end up with you being sent a whole load of things that you can never use. Years later it was to happen to me when Catholics clicked on to Ivy Tilsley and sent me wheelbarrow loads of rosary beads, crucifixes and pictures of the Pope every time she had a screen problem. I've got hundreds of them under my bed at home and I've never come to any harm. In 1964 I never would have dreamt that the adulation the Beatles were getting would one day be mine as a result of work as an actress.

At that stage the lads had only had three or four number ones, but from the response they were getting you could see they were going to get even bigger. I'll never forget the girls going wild as they sang the hits 'Can't Buy Me Love' and 'She Loves You.' Those two songs really stuck out as the highlights in their act as far as I was concerned. But by this stage they had also had success with singles like 'Love Me Do', 'Please, Please Me', 'From Me to You' and 'I Want to Hold Your Hand'. That one was the Christmas number one in 1963 and was special for me, because Derrick was as undemonstrative as ever and I so wanted him to hold my hand.

I had always wanted to hold his hand, but being a Maltby lad through and through there was no way he'd let me in public. Even in private Derrick has never been one for holding hands, which is an awful shame. I often think we would have been a lot happier and our marriage might have worked better if he'd shown his feelings.

I never spent that much time with the boys because they came and went in either big limousines or helicopters. They really made an entrance, because with 10,000 fans waiting to see them you knew from the noise levels when they'd arrived at the theatre. It was pure hysteria outside. Even when they were playing I thought, People can't be listening to that, because there was the over-riding sound of screaming. I would be watching from the side of the stage and in a strange way I'd be sorry for the lads, because they were very good and the girls should have listened.

The boys used to have a laugh with me as I came off stage. They'd say in that lovely Liverpool twang, 'How did that go, girlie?' I always used to say, 'Oh, marvellous', because it must have been marvellous for them to know there was a full house literally yelling for the Beatles.

You can't get away from the fact that Paul McCartney and George Harrison were real heart-throbs. Paul was my favourite Beatle – a real sweetie. He was the chatty one in the group, and I was a big fan. Despite all the fame they were still pretty down to earth at that point. I don't know if they changed much after.

John Lennon was always a bit of an enigma. I don't know if he was on drugs or what he was on, but he never seemed to be with us a lot of the time. He was there in body, but his mind was on another planet. The drummer Ringo Starr was all right, but he was always a bit withdrawn.

When they were on the stage I used to shout from the wings, 'Paul, do "Can't Buy Me Love",' which was their spring number one. In truth I was as much a fan as those screaming girls. People not round in that era may wonder what all the fuss was about, but to have experienced it at first hand was something else. It was mass adoration, and looking at Ringo today you wonder why. He could never have fallen into the pin-up mode, but at that time scores of girls would have queued up to get him into bed given half a chance. It's a funny old thing, fame.

They used to spend a lot of their time in their dressing rooms at the theatres, just like the Rolling Stones. The lads in the group would just hole up and hide in there. When they were at the front of house they would be tinkering with their instruments, so there wasn't really that much time to chat. I remember meeting them for the first time. I walked up and said, 'Hello I'm Lynne Perrie,' and then went and stood at the side to watch them rehearse.

I was only booked for the one show, but they must have thought a comedienne and singer was the ideal act to go on before them. It seemed to work well, especially when I cracked a couple of Beatles gags. In the end I never did much comedy, because you just couldn't make those girls sit still and listen to jokes.

After the show, much as before, the crowds of screaming masses put the fear of God into me. I used to say, 'I'm not going through that door. I need a side door, so I can slip out.' Derrick was with me for the shows and he'd tell me which exit was safe for us to leave by. He'd say, 'Don't go out that door, you'll be trampled by the herd.' And when the lads went out to a limousine, if the venue didn't have a flat roof for their helicopter, they'd have their clothes ripped off them. Sometimes they couldn't even get into the car because the girls would be swarming all over them, just pawing them and trying to rip off mementoes of the moment they got their hands on a Beatle. It was quite remarkable to witness that type of hysteria.

Years later, when I was working with Sacha Distel I was almost reduced to that state myself by the sheer sexuality of the man. Millions of women round the world would be envious of my run in with Sacha. I can proudly boast that he shared my dressing room when we played together at Lewisham Civic Hall in London. To have someone like him who simply exudes sexuality in your dressing room would be any red-blooded female's dream.

You simply melt when you are in his presence. I was in awe of him from the moment I saw him. In those days he was the embodiment of a sex symbol. He came across to me and said, 'I'm Sacha Distel. Pleased to meet you.' Then he kissed my hand.

I was so stunned that I almost fainted. Those lips that sent women throughout Europe swooning had planted a kiss on the back of my hand! He was so charming and immediately started chatting with me. Sacha Distel – nattering with a lass from Rotherham like he was some long-lost friend. Pinch me, it isn't happening, I thought to myself. But there he was in the flesh telling me he hadn't been in England very long and what he was doing. He told me what he was looking forward to and everything he had mapped out along the way. I was sitting there listening and desperately trying not to tremble. I could really only manage yes and no in response as he chattered away. I was almost dumbstruck by his incredible charisma. I was a mature woman, but this remarkable man had reduced me to the level of a star-struck teenager. And it takes a lot to leave me stuck for words. His accent and his manner were just so delightful.

During his act you could see the women in the audience admiring his talent and longing for him to look at them. When he was singing nobody said a word.

There was no noise at all. But at the end of each song the clapping was non-stop.

Then in the middle of the show he called me onto the stage. He called to me in the wings and held out his hand. No woman would have refused the opportunity to hold Sacha's hand. I was out there in front of the audience and Sacha Distel was holding my hand. It was a dream, a fantasy – yet it was really happening. I just looked at the audience and sighed. They looked at me and wished they could be in my shoes. As Sacha started to serenade me. I was in heaven in Lewisham and just didn't want him to let go. As the song drew to a close I quipped, 'I'll give you seventy-two hours to let go of me.' But sadly the dream was over, and for Sacha it was on to the next song.

But he was genuinely a lovely man. Before he left the venue he came across to say goodbye to me. He said, 'It was lovely meeting you, I hope we meet again.' I said, 'I hope so. I really do hope we meet again.' By this stage I was lovestruck. I had gone gaga being in the company of such a charming man.

Of course he was used to the adoration. He must have underneath it all thought it hilarious how all these women were swooning at the sight of him.

On the same bill that night was another fabulous male vocalist, an Italian boy I'd known from the club's called Luciano. I used to call him Lucky and he had a very strong voice, probably stronger than Sacha's. I hadn't seen Lucky for ages and it was great having him on the same bill.

I always used to wind him up by saying he was good, but not as good as my old club pal Tony Christie. Lucky used to say, 'Who is this Tony Christie? I've never heard of him.' Tony was the Yorkshire singer who had world-wide chart success with the songs 'I Did What I Did for Maria', 'Las Vegas', 'Don't Go Down to Reno' and the million-seller 'Is this the Way to Amarillo'. I used to tease

Lucky terribly, but he wrote a lovely song for me. It was called 'Without You' and was an Italian serenade, a real heart-tugging Neapolitan love song.

I regularly played in Sunderland with Lucky. Once when he was singing I saw a woman in the audience have a real earth-moving orgasm at the sound of his voice. I was standing in the wings when this big-breasted lady with a white jumper started to shudder and shiver in front of the stage. There was no mistaking it. After his spot I told Lucky about it and he said very matter of factly in his smooth Italian accent, 'Good. That's what I like.'

When the clubs started to go down in the 1970s a lot of the really talented singers like Lucky disappeared. The last I heard of him he'd gone to Switzerland and opened a patisserie with his brother.

About two years ago when I was on *Coronation Street* a bearded floor manager called Ewan came up to me and said, 'Hello, love'. I knew his face, but it was awful because I didn't know from where. Ages after he said, 'You don't remember?' I told him, 'I do know the face, but I don't know the location.' He said, 'I was the organist for you down in Birmingham. Whatever happened to that Italian song you used to sing?' And he had to remind me, but it was Luciano's, and he asked me to let him have the music if I had any spare. I said, 'Yes, 'I've got two copies, one an ordinary club copy and another for a fifteen-piece orchestra I used in Australia.' I think I've still got it, because I've an awful memory for passing things on like that when I'm asked.

I did have a heavy crush on Lucky and would talk about him and his sexy voice freely in front of Derrick. But after meeting Sacha his name, not Luciano's, was on my lips for days. I got back home to Maltby and started telling Derrick about Sacha. After a couple of days of this he said, 'Will you shut up about Sacha Distel. You've not mentioned that Luciano once since you met him. You haven't talked about anything else and I'm fed up.' I don't suppose you can blame him really. To give Derrick his due he let most of my hero worship and silly crushes on the stars I worked with wash right off his back.

But he could get upset when the time was right. We split up during the mid-sixties and Derrick went to stay with his Auntie Minnie for several months. During this time I ended up having Freddie Starr in my marital bed.

We were both playing at the hypnotist Peter Casson's club. He was very strict, with a giant list of rules that the acts had to observe, such as no swearing, no smoking or drinking on stage, no tapping the microphone, no asking the audience if they were okay and no singing 'My Way' – the list was endless.

Freddie Starr took to the stage with a glass in one hand, cigarette in the other and proceeded to break every rule in the house. It was hilarious. He got to the end of them after about four minutes and tapped his microphone and said, 'Now it's time to sing "My Way".'

He had a brilliant stage act in those days and had everyone in stitches. He was just a natural comic. I remember once staying in showbiz digs and as we're eating our breakfast Freddie's outside halting the traffic with a vacuum cleaner – he's pretending to clean up the road. He is so off the wall – you never know what he's going to do next.

During our night at Peter Casson's I told him I'd split with Derrick and invited him home for a drink. As chance would have it, that night Derrick spotted Freddie's silver car outside the house and it was still there when he went by in the morning. He had the cheek to ask me what we'd been up to. He said, 'That car's been there at least seven hours, so don't go telling me you've been playing bloody tiddlywinks.' Freddie didn't hang round long in the morning, I can tell you. All I remember about the night before was him doing Hitler impersonations all round the bedroom. I laughed a lot, but I was so drunk that to this day I don't know if we had sex. But when Derrick asked I'd always say, 'Well you left me. I'm not getting it off you, so don't think I'm going without because I'm not.' I could be a cruel bugger to him.

When I first started in the clubs I used to make all my own outfits. I'd spend hours at home sewing sequins on. To this day if I want to add a bit of sparkle to a frock I'll stitch on my own sequins. But getting out and on the stage was an escape from the drudgery of married life. It was an injection of excitement in an otherwise dull life, and I loved it. Off the stage my clothes were never glamorous, more practical – the type of everyday woman's clothes that Ivy would have worn.

In the early years I went everywhere by bus. Having worked as a clippie I knew the routes and most of the drivers. I enjoyed it, to tell you the truth, rubbing shoulders with my old mates as I journeyed off on my new career. Looking back, none of them, let alone me, would have guessed where the end of the road was going to be: Britain's number one soap via cabaret throughout Europe, Africa, Canada and Australia and the silver screen.

But my days using the buses were numbered as more and more clubs further and further afield sought my services. It was in the 1960s that I took the plunge and ordered our first car, a second-hand Austin A30 from Clayburns of Doncaster. I'd seen it advertised in the *Doncaster Free Press* and got the garage people to bring it round. It cruised into our street and stopped outside our gate with the engine purring. It was sparkling silver blue – absolutely beautiful. To me it was an Aston Martin and a Rolls Royce rolled into one.

I got so excited and started jumping up and down. All the neighbours were out watching, and I signed the hire purchase agreement there and then. I almost passed out – I was that thrilled.

I can't remember if Stephen was there, but I recall Derrick being his usual deadpan self and giving nothing away. He was up to his usual trick of trying to bring me down when I was on a natural high. The car was truly gorgeous, nothing like the second-hand heap I'd half expected to arrive. I was vexed with Derrick and said, 'Well, do something.'

So he strolled down the path, jumped in the air clicking his heels together and said sarcastically, 'Is that enough for you?'

I said, 'Don't you love to drop people down? The car's immaculate and you're doing your best to put me off it.'

His lack of excitement infuriated me. He doesn't half try and dampen your spirits – it's a bad trait that he's always had. The miserable sod also pointed out that neither of us could drive – something I'd somewhat overlooked.

It was a small omission. I was eager to get a car to cut out the three bus journeys I was making to some of the clubs. We had to get the man from the showroom to drive it to our neighbour Bert's spare garage on a piece of land just up the road. I then paid for Derrick to have driving lessons. To save spending extra money, of course, he passed his test very quickly the first time he took it.

He started driving me round after that and he was always doing his best to look after me after the show. I'd already used the fact he was mean in sketches, and his tightness used to help me get a string of free drinks at the end of the night. I always said before leaving the stage, 'Derrick, open that wallet and buy me a rum and blackcurrant,' or whatever I was drinking at the time. With that a procession of chaps would go to the bar and buy me a drink.

I remember after I'd been in the business for years going to a club in Scunthorpe where a woman approached me and said, 'You know my husband.' I asked, 'Do I?'

And she replied, 'Oh, yes. He bought you a rum and blackcurrant when you played here six years ago.' This amused me, because someone brought me a rum and blackcurrant every night. This lady really imagined I'd remember her husband after the hundreds of drinks I'd been bought.

I suppose to him a rum and blackcurrant would have been a lot of money, but it wasn't something I really thought about in those days. I've never been bothered about my own money, let alone anyone else's. Derrick on the other hand was Mr Moneybags. He counted every penny and saved as much as he could. He worked as my agent and manager in those early days. And he loved the feeling of power. Some club secretaries hated having to deal with him, because if they didn't offer a fee Derrick liked he'd just shut his little black book and walk away without saying a word.

My book was always full up for about two years. Right at the beginning I'd be accepting shows at an agreed fee and in two years time I'd be topping the bill – with the bottom of the bill getting better wages. I never accounted for inflation and just took the bookings at the same price. That riled Derrick. 'We're not having this. Either they put your money up or they can't have you,' he moaned.

He got up a lot of people's noses. Concert secretaries would come up to me and say, 'I'll book you, but I won't be talking to your husband.' He had a reputation for being rude, because of the habit he had of walking off without saying a word.

I hated putting my fee up because I always believed in giving value for money. So if a club boss gave me £5 more I'd always try and find £5 worth of extra work to put in the act. It reached a point where I could put no more into the act and I'd be begging Derrick not to put my money up. I'd say, 'Don't do it, because I'll have to do that much more work.' He sensibly said, 'No, you don't. You're not getting paid for quantity, you're getting paid for quality. You're getting a fiver more because you are worth a fiver more.'

At about this stage I'd bought Derrick a desk and a typewriter to start him up as an agent because he was so good with money, but that was doomed to failure. I was so soft-hearted that I wouldn't let him ask the acts for commission. He worked for Peters and Lee and to this day Lenny Peters still owes him £23 for a week Derrick got him at the Scala club in Doncaster. I would never let him chase people for cash, so he had to give it up.

I used to do a lot of great gags about cash and Derrick's meanness in the clubs. I think he enjoyed it when I used him as a prop because he liked the chance to get noticed. But most of my humour was self-deprecating. Audiences always felt safe if you took the mickey out of yourself and not them.

One of my favourites was telling them that I kept my money in my knickers. I'd say, 'Once they've seen this face nobody will bother going down there to get the cash.'

I progressed from working men's clubs to soccer clubs and caravan clubs, which were a bit posher. Caravan sites started popping up all over in the 1960s as families started holidaying more and more at the seaside. My acts got more and more sophisticated and I'd be doing Nancy Wilson stuff and point numbers. As I travelled abroad that also broadened my horizons.

Early on, on one of our trips to the coast, Derrick persuaded me to enter a very upmarket talent contest. It was at the Spa Theatre in Scarborough – an altogether more ritzy venue than I was used to. But I knocked them out with my act and won the show hands down.

A chap called Charles Shadwell, the leader of the Northern Variety Orchestra, discovered me that night. He booked me to appear in his midday music hall and told me how he planned to groom me for stardom. I couldn't believe my luck, and it was all down to Derrick pushing me into that contest.

Charles invited me down to his house in Cambridge and his pub the Green Man. He took me to London, and I'll never forget being there one day and just having my nails, my hair and my make-up done. He ushered me along to the Noel Gay Agency – one of the top variety agents in the country. They sorted me out an appointment with a voice coach. But when I got to this woman and sang the Brenda Lee song, 'Sweet Old Fashioned Girl', she flatly refused to take me in. She told the agent, 'If I take away that natural thing she's got I'll take away her attraction. That rawness is what makes her sound so good.' It was a flattering thing to say.

These London high-flyers fixed me up with a string of shows. I'll never forget appearing in the Astor Club and everything was gilt-edged and ever so posh. So I'm doing my act in this club a million miles removed from the old RAOB in Hartlepool. I'm thinking, I've made it now, and as normal in the show I jumped on one of the tables. I went straight through it. This lovely gilt-covered table was made of nothing stronger than orange boxes. I didn't half come a cropper. After that tumble I immediately thought of the old saying that all that glitters isn't gold. I told them it was another one of those fur coat and no knickers places.

I was soon to have further problems among the bright lights of the big city. I was booked on at a place called the Embassy club which was in the West End. The hostesses in this club would sell tourists, mainly Americans, teddy bears or champagne for about £7. It was a lot of money in those days, but the club found that the punters were coming back the next night to see my act. The girls were really grateful I was pulling them in, because a lot of the time the place was pretty quiet – not surprisingly with the prices they were charging. These girls got commission on everything, and they'd sell the blokes two bottles of champagne and only give them one – it was that type of place.

By this stage my costumes were out of this world. My favourite was one with nasturtiums on it and frothy waves of lace underneath. It was strapless with a very tight bodice and covered in diamantes. It was synonymous with style – a real classy number.

One night after my show at this club a big fat Jewish fella was waiting for me in my dressing room. He was working with some of the top impresarios in Britain.

This fella started talking to me about how energetic the show was and how impressive my performance was. As he's talking this octopus is also pulling down the zipper on my dress. I was only young and not very sophisticated at all. I said, 'What are you doing?' But he just carried on doing it. Men had the idea that because I was so full of life on the stage that I must be a bundle of fun in bed. They were right, but this big fat slug wasn't about to find out.

I repeated loudly, 'What are you doing? What are you doing with me frock?'

He grasped me firmly and just replied, 'We can do things for you.'

At this Derrick came in, like the cavalry, right on cue and said, 'Not like that, you won't.' As he spoke he bashed him. He let fly with a right hook and caught him square in the face.

The fella shook his head and said, 'That's it. You're cancelled.' He scrapped all the work I had secured through hard work. I'd earlier passed an audition to appear at the ever-open Windmill club and would have been the first woman to do so if this slob had not stopped us. He told us to get our belongings and go.

Derrick and I went straight home. I wasn't upset with

him for losing me all that work. I was very proud of him for punching that chap. He was my hero. I'd never seen him in such a temper and I liked him like that, with fire in his belly. He acted on impulse on the spur of the moment – something he very rarely does. I thought, At least it shows he cares about me. But the big daft softie still wouldn't hug or hold me.

I recall my first trip down to London to play at the Royal Albert Hall. It was a show put on annually for the cycling clubs of Britain, and I went down to perform every year for a few years. The first time was very funny. My greatest fan at this stage was a little chap called George. He loved my show and was a widower who Derrick had got chatting to in the clubs. Derrick had offered to pick this old fellow up so he could go to more of my shows further afield, and George loved it. We reached a point that if I was going on my own I'd take along George anyway for company.

The day before I was going down to London I was driving a new Austin A35 van we'd got. I was approaching a crossroads down a hill at Bramley when I went to overtake a little Morris Minor in front. I was halfway past him when he put his indicator on to turn right. He drove right into the side of the van, and knocked us off the road.

The van turned over and I scrambled out in a right state. People from the nearby houses had come out to help and I was saying, 'Get me frocks, get me music. I'm going on at the Royal Albert Hall tomorrow.' One of the rescuers said, 'Never mind your bloody frocks and music – what about this little old man in the bottom of the van?' It was George – I'd clean forgotten about him. Fortunately he wasn't hurt at all.

The acoustics at the Royal Albert Hall were tremendous and I was very proud to have appeared on a bill there. In those days it took you about nine and a half hours to travel from South Yorkshire to London.

There were no motorways and you used to have to go through Newark, through Grantham and every town en route. As the years went on it took less and less time. I remember leaving home at 5 am to do a show with Bob Monkhouse down there. Travelling has got so much easier, thank God.

I met Adam Faith in the early Sixties. He was working at a theatre in Birmingham and I was doing cabaret at a place called the Barn restaurant at Hockley Heath. This night I was on at the Barn when Adam came in and caught my act. One of my trademarks in those days was yelling 'Yabba, dabba, doo' and kicking my shoes off. After the show Adam invited me over to have a drink with him. He told me, 'That's a great gimmick, getting rid of your shoes.' I haven't seen him since, but about six months later he discovered Sandie Shaw, who went straight to number one with her single, 'There's Always Something There to Remind Me'. Of course she came on stage without any shoes on at all. If I ever see him again I'll ask if he got that idea off me.

There were some real old characters round the clubs. One bloke, Les Booth, always used to book local Yorkshire talent that was sometimes better than the top of the bill. I clearly remember the time he booked me on the same bill as Lulu. It was very early on in her career – she was probably only about sixteen. In those days she was with the band The Luvvers, who later got into the top ten with the single 'Shout'. I was about the same height as Lulu and back then my natural auburn hair was exactly the same colour as hers and we both wore it in a ponytail. Her saxophonist said when he saw me, 'She'll go mad.' But she was wonderful with me.

I was in a dressing room with the chorus girls and a couple of other acts when Lulu walked in and asked if I'd got an eyebrow pencil. She wanted a pale brown one and with me being the same colour I had one. As I gave it her she looked round and said, 'You can't stop in here with all this lot. Come across with me. I've got a big dressing room and I'm lonely on me own.'

She had a lovely broad Scottish accent and we spent our time chatting about north of the border. I'd done a lot of touring up there – through Glasgow, Edinburgh, Dundee, Aberdeen and even on the oil rigs. She was homesick and I was happy I was able to cheer her up.

Working on an oil rig is probably one of the toughest jobs for a female entertainer. There you are on a tiny stage in front of these hundreds of men who haven't seen a woman for weeks. One night I was up before a bunch of these blokes making all kinds of remarks. They even let the stopper out of a blow-up doll and aimed it at the stage. In that kind of atmosphere you've got to be as raunchy as them or your act will die. As soon as I saw this blow-up doll rasping through the air towards me. I said, 'Mother, I didn't know you'd moved out here.' They loved it, and from that moment I had them in the palm of my hand.

It is great when you've got the audience where you want them. Yet in the early days they often had you where they wanted you. I once performed at the Attercliffe Non-Political club in Sheffield, which was a triangular room with a curtain across one corner for the artists to change behind. I was in the audience before getting ready when I noticed you could see the woman doing the first turn changing, because there was a window throwing light into the corner and putting her silhouette on show. I told them, 'If you want me on stage you'll have to find another changing room.' They kidded on they didn't realize you could see, but you'd have had to be blind not to have noticed.

But there were times when the act got the better of the club bosses. I remember playing at Wigan Theatre Club one Sunday, missing the next because Shirley Bassey was on, and coming back the following week. I had to do a band call before the show and I walked out from behind the curtain expecting to be a couple of feet from the orchestra pit. But I got a big shock – there was this expanse of stage. Afterwards I had to ask what had happened and the boss, shaking his head, said, 'Shirley Bassey'.

It turns out that she sent an army of people along a couple of days before her show and they demanded some major work be carried out before she'd appear. It was the first time I'd ever seen a stage grow by about sixty square feet and a club have toilets and a shower fitted overnight. Apparently the management had men working non-stop for forty-eight hours to get the theatre in shape for Shirley. I found out she had a twelve-page contract with the club – I only used to get the cash, which I kept hidden in my knickers.

Nothing compares to the buzz you get from performing in front of a live audience. Some of the most appreciative audiences I had were down in the Welsh valleys, Shirley's neck of the woods, where they really love their singing. But boy was it a long drive.

Once on my way down there I was pulled into a field by a police car for speeding. He drove through a gateway and I drove after him. As soon as I realized we were in a field I felt very vulnerable – I'd had a lot of early sexual adventures on this type of terrain. I didn't like the PC's approach at all. He was implying there was a way I could avoid getting booked. I got very angry with this upstart expecting a legover in exchange for not giving me a speeding ticket, so I told him straight: 'I've got your number and if I'm stopped between here and Newport I'll bring your colleagues back to this field and show them the two sets of tyre tracks.' It worked a treat – he went red and allowed me to leave.

I got my own back on him a short time later when I spotted him out of his uniform in a club I was working.

In those days policemen had to make themselves known when they went into clubs, and this one hadn't. The management threw him out after I told them what he'd tried to do to me. He was one rotten apple, but by and large I like policemen. These days I make regular donations to police benevolent funds.

All through my career I've been a very emotional person. Ivy's crying on *Coronation Street* earned me some tremendous plaudits from the critics. But I've been sobbing since my club days. I used to cry when I was happy after doing maybe five or six standing ovations for an audience that didn't want me to go. With hindsight I might have cried and got all emotional on stage because it was something I couldn't do with Derrick.

Busloads of fans used to follow me round Yorkshire. The coach load from Huddersfield always asked me to sing 'No Regrets' and the adrenalin would be flowing when I did that song. I'd just get lost in emotion because when the audience were behind you like that you had a marvellous night. Another number that I was forever getting requests for was 'My Mother's Eyes', and that song could also reduce me to tears.

I used to get butterflies occasionally before going on stage, but it wasn't just on big occasions. It could happen anywhere from West Houghton Brewers Club in Lancashire to Spennymore Country Club in the North East.

During those happy times working the clubs I appeared with lots of other acts that became successful – Rod Stewart and the Faces, Gerry and the Pacemakers and Gerry Dorsey, who went on to gain international fame as Engelbert Humperdinck, to name but three top class stars. I also appeared with Screaming Lord Sutch and the Savages. He's now infamous as leader of the Monster Raving Loony Party – which just about sums him up. He's never had my vote – my favourite politician was Margaret Thatcher. A great leader and a proper

Prime Minister – the best we've had in my lifetime, but enough about politics.

If it hadn't been for the clubs I'd have never got my break in the movies, which of course led to my television career. I was on stage at the Ba' Ba' club in Barnsley when film director Ken Loach and producer Tony Garnett popped in for a pint. I didn't know these chaps from Adam, but somebody told me they'd invited me over for a drink. I went over to their table and they complimented me on my act.

I asked what they were doing. They told me they'd been auditioning all day for the part of the mother of a Barnsley lad in a movie they were making. They said this woman's husband was a long-distance lorry driver and she went out to the pub nearly every night and left her son David the money to get fish and chips. I chirped, 'That's exactly what I do with our Stephen. I go out working and leave two shillings on the mantelpiece for his dad or the babysitter to get him a bottle of pop and some chips. And tell them not to let any other kids in who'll go jumping over the furniture.'

They started laughing when I told them that and right there and then asked me if I'd like the job. I said, 'Me? I'm not an actress, I'm a singer.' They said, 'Look, we've auditioned forty-seven actresses today and you're more natural than any of them.' I told them I couldn't because I was booked to do a fortnight in Wales, but they said, 'No problem. We'll get you a driver and let you finish about 4 pm.'

I used to leave the set on location in Barnsley and head off for Wales. I didn't like the studio car and ended up letting the driver take my Mark 10 Jag so I could get to sleep on the back seat. It cost me £80 in petrol for the fortnight and I only got £40 for doing the film. There was no repeats or anything. The movie was *Kes* and it was a great hit round the world. It ended up on the school syllabus for about twelve years. I'd have been a million-airess by now if I'd had the repeat fees from that film.

But *Kes* undoubtedly made me because I never had to do another audition after that. I got roles in a string of TV plays including *Crown Court*, *Slattery's Mounted Foot*, *Queenie's Castle*, *Follyfoot*, *The Intruder* and *Leeds United*, where I starred as a shop steward alongside Liz Dawn, who later landed the Street role of Vera Duckworth.

It even helped me land the part of Ivy on *Coronation Street*, but it wasn't to happen for a couple of years because the movie wasn't released until 1970, about two years after it was recorded. Meanwhile I carried on with my cabaret career, which was by this time taking me round the globe.

CHAPTER SEVEN

African Adventures

My trips to Africa were literally orgasmic. It was there at the age of thirty-nine that I actually achieved my first orgasm. While Derrick and Stephen were on the other side of the earth I was in heaven in the arms of an amazing lover.

I have visited Africa seven times, but my trip in January 1970 was the most memorable. It was then that I discovered I had never managed an orgasm during a love life that spanned twenty-six years. I got an awful shock when it occurred, because until that moment I thought my sex life was satisfactory. I never knew you could have such powerful feelings – in those days women's magazines were packed with recipes and knitting patterns, not the guides to sexual sensations you get in the glossies today. There must still be hundreds of thousands of women just like I was who have never enjoyed fulfilling sex.

Suave cabaret compere Roy Douglas is the man I have to thank for opening my eyes to mind-blowing passion. He simply knew how to treat a woman – he was a beautiful lover. It was none of this wham bam thank you mam stuff which many women have to put up with. It was unbelievable.

I even orgasmed on a bus as Roy talked to me. He

was such a fantastic lover. I was sitting there and he was telling me his plans for later that evening and I just went suddenly. I couldn't believe it. At first I thought it must be the heat – the air conditioning had gone off in the bus. But in seconds the feeling welling up inside me was unmistakable – it was an explosive stirring. But I'm dashing ahead again.

Roy's remarkable deep voice was the first thing that attracted me to him. In fact, I heard his voice before I saw him and I was immediately enchanted by the warmth and depth of tone. I had just walked into rehearsals at the splendidly modern Civic Theatre in Johannesburg when I heard this heavenly noise. It was Roy singing and it was a tremendously sexy sound. He was belting out 'Dear Heart, Wish You Were Here' and the words themselves are terribly moving. The song goes, 'Dear heart, wish you were here to warm this night. Dear heart, seems like a year since you were out of my sight ...' I had just arrived for the rehearsals and I joined the audience watching in awe. He looked like James Bond with lovely brown hair. He was very stylish and was wearing a loose-fitting pair of cream slacks and a neatly pressed white shirt. But I wasn't as taken by his looks as by his luscious voice – it really moved me.

My music was next in line for rehearsing, so I got up and did my stuff – the whole energetic routine. Afterwards he came up to me and said, 'My God, don't you move?' It was mutual admiration at first sight. The love came soon after.

The ten-week theatre tour we were booked on had two German acts at the top of the bill – the Gunther Kallman choir and a chap called Crazy Otto. The bombastic Germans never stopped bickering among themselves and caused loads of trouble everywhere they went. The choir-master made sure his girls got the best rooms with baths, and after a while I was sick of it. I was closing the first half of the show and going down better than these girls, so I insisted that I got a room with a bath and not just a shower.

I think they respected us a bit more for putting our feet down. It was no real hardship for the girls, because they all knew each other and they were able to double up. The Gunther Kallman choir was big worldwide and had been in the British charts in Christmas 1964 with the song 'Elisabeth Serenade'.

The Germans spending most of the time fighting among themselves only served to push us two Brits closer together. I had fancied Roy right away, but it took a good few days before we ended up in bed together. It wasn't just lust – he was such a lovely fella that we were able to talk together for hours. We spent a whole week rehearsing together and by the end of that I was truly smitten.

After rehearsals we had started eating together in our hotel rooms and the more I got to know him the more I fancied him. I shall never forget our first night of passion as long as I live. It was just like in the movies – he spent ages preparing me for the most wonderful sexual experience of my life. Some men get straight to it, but it was never ever like that with Roy.

This night he called at my hotel room to tell me they had set the food up in his room by mistake. I don't know if he'd planned it that way to seduce me or if it was a genuine error over the room numbers. Either way we ended up in bed together, but not before the most romantic foreplay I had ever encountered.

Roy had set the scene just right with roses in his room and a half bottle of brandy and a bottle of champagne to wash away any inhibitions. It was so different from my life at home looking after Derrick and Stephen. I didn't have to cook the tea, iron his shirts or wash his underpants, let alone handle any smelly socks. I was used to pampering my family at home – but on the other side of the world Roy was pampering me.

It was such a big change. We just spent our time away from work relaxing. It really put you in the mood for love, and maybe I fell in love with the whole situation. On this evening I don't know whether it was the effect of the drink or what, but I thought, Christ, I fancy him. I was missing Derrick, but being in South Africa was like being on another planet. The inevitable happened and on that very night I orgasmed for the first time.

Every time before we made love Roy would take me in the bathroom. He would tenderly wash me all over and caress me intimately before drying me down. It was ever so sensual as he showered me with affection. He made me feel like a whole woman and it was wonderful.

His lovemaking was phenomenal. He could hold himself back for ages and ages before bringing me to my climax ever so expertly. With Derrick it had never been this good and it made me feel anger towards him, although in fairness he knew no better and neither would I if I had not taken that fateful booking in South Africa. But life became so magical in Roy's company that it reached the stage where Derrick never even entered my head.

At first I thought Roy was trying a load of old flannel to get me into bed, but I soon realized that was just the way he was. If we were walking down the street he would hold my hand and hug me and kiss me as we strolled. He was very demonstrative, something Derrick had never been, and his desire to be by my side drove me wild.

During my early years I had been loved and cuddled constantly. My mother and father were very much in love and not afraid to show it. All three of us kids were enveloped in their love. But since my marriage to Derrick a lot of the loving touches and caresses had gone out of my life. A little thing like a hug means a lot to a woman. That probably helped me fall even more hopelessly in love with the ever-attentive Roy. He was my shadow during those blissful weeks when we became inseparable. Every day I had fresh flowers from him – something careful Derrick would never have done for me.

Roy became the man of my dreams. We made love every night and every morning, but it was never rushed. We would have made love more often, but the opportunity never arose as we spent the days travelling between the towns and cities we were performing in on a big air-conditioned bus.

We chatted all the time. Roy was about the same age as myself and very honest and open. He told me how he had been trying for a baby for ten years before his little one arrived. He was ecstatic about the eighteen-month-old youngster, but he had fallen out of love with his wife. He told me he loved me like he had never loved before. It was real undying love stuff and ever so romantic. I felt exactly the same.

We made massive headlines on the tour when a builder turned impresario called Ronnie Quibell staged a concert down the impressive Kangol caves. We had to descend down 200 steps to get to the wooden stage and I was very worried about bats. I said, 'If I see one I'll be up the steps faster than I came down.' Fortunately there wasn't a bat in sight, and a recording of the concert was released as a record over there. I made history as the first female to perform so far underground. It was very cold and shivery, but the acoustics were great. It was an incredible experience and something I am very proud of being a part of.

There was an added bonus having the cabaret compere as my lover ... because he was so much in love with me that I became bigger than Shirley Bassey when he was announcing my act. And it was here that I was first introduced to brandy and Babycham – a drink I adopted and later consumed by the bucketful back home as I drowned my many sorrows. I eventually got nicknamed brandy and Babycham Lil, because I drank that much of the concoction.

Despite the big build-ups Roy gave me before going on stage and the sensational times we spent between the sheets I wasn't prepared for the bombshell he was soon to drop. It happened on the summit of Table Top mountain overlooking Cape Town during an evening stroll. 'I want to marry you,' he announced. My immediate reaction was to say yes, because these had been the happiest days of my life. Yet my marriage to Derrick and having Stephen at school back home didn't make the answer so straightforward.

I was heartbroken. Meeting Roy had thrown my life into turmoil. It was a beautiful summer's evening and sparkling below us were the lights in the city and the lanterns on the boats in the harbour. I just thought, I don't want to go home to Maltby. I am happy here. I felt like crying and didn't know what I was going to do.

Looking back now, I probably had a lot of stardust in my eyes. I had three more weeks of the tour left before I had to make up my mind. But Roy's doting over that beautiful baby of his really clinched my refusal. Deep down I knew I couldn't split up his family.

I had been in this situation once before in Africa – a few years earlier on my first trip to Rhodesia, which these days is called Zimbabwe. On that occasion I rang Derrick up and told him to sell the bungalow and send me half the cash. I had set up home with a young Rhodesian military policeman called Andy and I had no intentions of going back. I suppose there must be something about the sun and the lifestyle out there that sends me a bit barmy.

Andy was the apple of my eye at the time, a strapping handsome suntanned hulk of a man with muscles in all the right places. I met him when I was doing a concert in an army barracks. Afterwards he came over and started chatting me up and I was very flattered by his attention. He started off by escorting me home, but things soon developed. He began staying at the flat all the time.

I was in love with Andy and I rang Derrick up and told him our marriage was over. He was at home looking after Stephen and I was having the time of my life touring Africa. I stayed over there for nine months after going out in May 1962 and spent Christmas away from my family.

I was more infatuated with the lifestyle than the bloke, and one day I woke up and came to my senses. I decided that I didn't want to spend the rest of my life in the sunshine stumbling round in a drunken daze, because boozing was a major part of the ex-pats' life over there. Every day they were drinking from dawn to dusk. The ex-pats were like fishes, they were always floating through the day in a stupor. They had a morning session about 9 am, then an afternoon session followed by an all-nighter. It got to the stage where you drank so much that you drank yourself sober. I'd heard this phrase before I went to Africa, but it was only afterwards that I knew it could actually happen.

Another expression that I discovered was correct was 'mad dogs and Englishmen', because when you meet anyone who has been out there for years they are very vague if not totally potty. I used to put it down to the sun 'scrunging' their brains, but of course the day-long boozing didn't help either.

I remember one morning coming down from breakfast and being greeted by a couple who had moved out from Yorkshire. They said, 'Lynne! Oh my God, come along and have a drink.' It was about half past eight and I had just got up for my breakfast. I said, 'I am not drinking,' and they said, 'Well, have a hot gin and orange.' I thought to myself, If that's not drinking then I'm the Virgin Mary.'

That was the day that I started looking hard at what was happening to me. It eventually dawned on me that I was living in an alcoholic haze. Before going to Africa I hadn't been a heavy drinker, because in Britain you were restricted by the licensing laws.

I began to realize that Africa was pretty boring, and it was so dull that the only things to keep you occupied were drinking and messing about. The blacks used to do all the work and we used to just sit out on the verandah all day, maybe occasionally dipping into the swimming pool to cool down. I realized I couldn't live like that all the time.

Getting over to Africa was an adventure in its own right in those days. My first trip in 1961 took thirty-five hours and entailed seven stop-offs for refuelling en route – these days the modern jets can do it in thirteen hours. Back then flying was a real novelty for me, a housewife from Yorkshire, and I was thrilled at the prospect. I was so excited because people hadn't truly started flying to Spain for their holidays, so Africa was a real expedition. I was so chuffed at having done it that I saved all the mementoes from the BOAC flight. I've still got them in a scrapbook somewhere.

On my first trip I had no idea that I was going to become an international cabaret star. I was just popping over for a month with artiste Derek Roy at a theatre at Pinelands. He was top of the bill, but the critics went wild for me as they had never seen such a dynamic act. One wrote: 'This girl jumps, she twists, she does everything – she's an amazing one woman energetic whirlwind.' I don't think Derek Roy was too happy at me stealing the show.

When I arrived at Jan Smuts airport in Johannesburg I found myself alone in the empty arrivals lounge waiting for the impresario Hugo Keletti. This giant of a man came walking towards me and he looked me up and down before saying, 'Lew and Leslie Grade usually send me beautiful girls with lovely curves and no talent. I think you are going to be different.' It was a back-handed compliment. He was basically saying, 'You're a little dumpy housewife. You must have something.' And of course my cabaret show went down a storm and he booked me back for season after season.

I remained at the one theatre for a month, but they never had a CV in advance so the agent Peter Tourien made it all up. He gave me a tremendous build-up and even wrote that I had come straight from the stage of the London Palladium.

When I hit the stage they didn't know quite what to make of me. The South Africans were very restrained and they treated their women like china dolls who just had to laze about all day. But I was a human dynamo in my act. I'd be telling gags and jumping about. I always used to take the mickey out of myself, because I knew nobody would object to that. I was five feet tall with a 34C chest, so there was no way I was ever going to be a glamour puss. I'd tell them all the old gags about wanting a bigger bust. I used to say, 'I've used corn plasters and boil plasters, but they still won't grow. All I want is bigger boobs, so I can get closer to a man without having to walk a long way.' It took them a little bit of time to get used to me, but they adored singers and the fact is I have got a very good voice. My main cabaret act was to establish myself as a singer first then try a few gags. If you don't get a laugh you can fall back on the singing.

But I'll never forget a first night at the Elizabethan Hotel in Port Elizabeth. There were these three Afrikaans on a table and one of them was giving me some right dirty looks. I thought, I'll have you, and went and sat on his knee. I told a string of gags and went right for the jugular. I pulled no punches and he was fuming. I asked if his wife was in and when he replied no, I said, 'Then what excuse have you got for being so miserable?' The audience loved it – all the more, I later discovered, because he was a newspaper editor.

A couple of days later his newspaper carried the cruellest crit about me that I have ever seen. It talked about this not so young, not so beautiful, not so talented English fishwife in a crocheted dress – and those were some of the kinder things. It was an absolutely outrageous review and it almost got me the sack. I wouldn't have minded, but the dress cost a fortune and I'd stitched all the gold sequins on by hand.

When the manager saw the newspaper he sent for me. He was a real coward, frightened to death by this critic. He said he was very sorry but he couldn't carry on using me as I didn't have a visa. To cut a long story short I went and got a visa and persuaded him to let me continue my cabaret slot.

The next night I went on stage the audience was up to the rafters, jam-packed full. I started the act by explaining what had happened and telling a few more gags about this editor. I brought the house down. I worked the fortnight to packed houses because everyone wanted to see the show that had such a stinging review. They all loved it, and on the last night the manager came up and presented me with a beautiful silver rose bowl. He told me I'd done the best business he'd had for twelve months and he was thrilled.

My next venue was a place called the Beverley Hills Hotel in Durban and as soon as I arrived the manager called me into his office. In those days news travelled very slowly in South Africa and he informed me that he'd heard my act had had a bad time. I told him he was misinformed and showed him the rose bowl and suggested he ring the manager of the Elizabethan.

That night I was introduced to the band – a bunch of Dutch men who couldn't read a note of music. They were Wilhelm 1, Wilhelm 2, Wilhelm 3 and Wilhelm 4, and they cannabalized my act. It was dreadful – they simply destroyed it. Afterwards the manager admitted they were no good and offered to pay me the three weeks wages and allow me to go. I told him I'd be happier having the money and staying for a holiday at the hotel. I had a ball. I was ever so thankful that the newspaper hadn't had a reviewer covering that night!

Talking about critics, I probably got one of the most complimentary reviews after performing at the Mayfair club in Durban. The owner there, Max Judy, never used to comment on his turns, because then if anything went wrong he would not get the blame. But after my first night he broke his golden rule and said, 'This woman is the greatest female performer I ever imported.' I was supposed to be doing a week, ended up doing six and was ever so flattered as he had imported stars such as Petula Clark before me.

My longest trip to Africa was a couple of summers after my first expedition. This time a holiday with my brother Keith and his wife Judy in Zambia turned into a marathon stay. They were living in the country's copper belt and Keith had a very well-paid job as a supervisor at a mine in a settlement called Mufulira. The American company he worked for treated him remarkably well and even paid for his children to be privately educated back in England.

It was while I was staying with them that I met an agent from Sunderland, whom I had known during his years in the clubs in the North East. He told me to send off for my music, my props and my cabaret costumes and he would fix me up with a load of dates. He said I could rake in a fortune, but I told him I was on holiday. It was no good, though. He persuaded me to stay with a string of dates at prestigious venues. He also charmed me into bed and I rather enjoyed his efforts. In those days Bretts club in Salisbury was the top nightspot in Rhodesia and they kept booking me back. I did a string of shows in Rhodesia, where I set up home with Andy.

The sun certainly boosted my sex drive and during my time there I also had a brief fling with a garage boss called

Ted, who was about ten years older than me. His wife had died and he took me to his mansion home after one of my shows. He must have been a millionaire, and his house was fantastic with fabulous swimming pools outside. We ended up making love, but it probably only happened because I was so overawed by his tremendous wealth. He had a servant called Fred who did all the chores and I was really very flattered by all the attention.

Soon after my arrival on the dark continent someone gave me the nickname Auntie Radish and it stuck. I used to tell the story of how I got the name in my stage act. I'd say, 'Auntie Radish me, daft as a brush – when I got here I ran straight down three flights of stairs and lay down in the sun. I said, "Burn me, burn me," and I waited a bit. The sun didn't half burn me for being so stupid and I finished up in hospital for three days with third degree burns.' I even went on stage with the yellow hospital dressing on the burns, and I think the audiences quite admired that.

During my mega break I stayed with Keith's father-in-law Fred and his wife Dosh for a fortnight. He was a very eccentric chap in his sixties who had moved out there from Macclesfield in Cheshire. He had a habit of always saying 'Shame' after everything and even more bizarrely referred to everyone on the telly as Yul Brynner. We would be watching a show and he would constantly be saying, 'Look, it's Yul Brynner.' I'd say, 'No, it's not, it's Deborah Carr.' But he'd insist: 'It's Yul Brynner with a wig on.' I'd just sit there and laugh nervously and look bemused at Dosh. His barmy behaviour further strengthened my belief that the sun 'scrunged' people's brains over there.

His most unusual habit happened regular as clockwork at 10.30 every night. He would suddenly pull himself from his chair and say, 'Right, I am going to take them for a walk.' At first I was shocked and asked, 'Who?'

Top left: My dad Eric.
Top right: Mother Agnes – contentment incorporated,
they never rowed.
Above right: Me as a baby.
Above left: As a four-year-old toddler with a pal in the local park
near my home in Rotherham.

Above left: Little Miss Dynamite – they didn't know what hit them when I exploded onto the cabaret scene.
Top right: One of my first publicity shots. I soon had a reputation as a wild thing – both on and off the stage.
Above right: Me at the Beverley Hills Hotel, Durban, South Africa. Not a thought for my family waiting for me at home.

Top: Topping the bill in Rhodesia with a few friends I picked up in a bar – life was one long party.

Left: Pat Phoenix, one of my best pals on the Street, left strict instructions for me to have her dressing room when she left the show.

PATRICIA PHOENIX
AT
THE LODGE
WINTERHAVEN

THIS PLACE is
BEQUETHED TO LYNNE
PERRIE. FOREVERMORE

Pat Phoenix
VERY

Right: My invite to the 'World Premiere' of Kes. It was my first ever film role and I was so excited – until I found out it was being held at the local cinema in Barnsley!

The Directors of
United Artists Corporation Ltd
and Associated British Cinemas Ltd
cordially invite you to attend the
OPENING OF BARNSLEY'S OWN FILM
The Kestrel Films Production

"KES"

at the ABC CINEMA, PEEL STREET, BARNSLEY
SUNDAY, MARCH 29th, 1970

Full programme commences 6.00 p.m.
" Kes " presented 7.30 p.m.

Admit
Dress inform

Top: Coronation Street's 33rd birthday party – before that famous cosmetic surgery got me into trouble. It was to be my last celebration with the cast.

Above: Switching on Blackpool Illuminations. There were no arguments about who did the honours – Doris Speed was always the boss.

Right: The first time I met Liz Dawn. We led the pickets in the BBC's Leeds United back in 1973.

My great friend, and drinking buddy, Charlie Lawson. He saved my life when I collapsed on set – and he saved my skin a few times too!

Top: The 30th Anniversary of the Street. Me with Bill Roache and Betty Driver. I borrowed a stage outfit from a drag queen pal – and stole the show!

Above: The Tilsleys arrive at number five. Me with my Street family, Peter Dudley, Chris Quentin and Helen Worth.

Top: Me and hubby Derrick. Can't live with him – can't live without him.
Above: My baby brother, comedian and actor Duggie Brown at the races. We both loved a flutter on the gee gees.

Top: My favourite tipple earned me the nickname Champagne Perrie. But behind the scenes the booze almost killed me.
Above: The first night of Peter Stringfellow's Hippodrome 'Gay Evening' in London. I always had a loyal gay following – and the lesbians loved me too!

He replied, 'Sam and Tom, the —ogs', and I said, 'But you don't have any dogs.' He said, 'Not dogs – frogs!' I couldn't believe it, but outside his back door stood these two giant bullfrogs who hopped along behind him as he walked round his garden. That was it. I thought, I couldn't live here. It would drive me daft.

Fred wanted me to go and live over there and bring Derrick and his greyhounds. Derrick had twelve dogs at that time and Fred offered to build a racetrack for them in his front garden. He was determined we were going to live there. The cheeky old bugger even wrote to Derrick and said, 'You have got to get over here. It is a wonderful life and you will make a fortune with those greyhounds.' I said greyhounds would never survive in this heat, but he wouldn't have it. Added to that I didn't want Derrick cramping my style.

Something I noticed during my trips in the Sixties was the strange pets that people kept out there. I stayed with a girl called Penny who kept giant spiders in every room in her mansion house in Greenlands, Rhodesia. She was a member of the Dutch Reform Church and they had some law about women alone at home not being able to throw parties, so she invited me to stay while she hosted a big thrash. Her husband was a multi-millionaire who had fitted the first pools out there and he had gone away on business to Bulawayo.

On the night I arrived Penny threw a magnificent bash. Before the party I tried on wigs in her bedroom and she told me I could wear anything from her wardrobe, which was crammed with thousands of designer dresses. But there was a bit of a hitch ... she was six feet tall and I was a foot shorter. It didn't stop us spending three hours going through them looking for one that fitted.

Her boy David had been hauling buckets of coal up and down the garden for three days to heat up the pool, and by the time the party came it looked like a Turkish bath with steam rising off it. The booze was flowing like a river and everyone was sloshed. In the middle of the do I went to the toilet and as I sat there I looked up and there was a spider with a body as big as the palm of my hand. The legs made it look even bigger and it was on the mirror. I thought it was some kind of ornament because my mother used to have plastic butterflies with suction pads on her bathroom mirror. I thought, What a horrible thing to put on your mirror.

I thought nothing more about it until I went to pull my knickers up and this thing moved as if to pounce. I screamed and ran out of the loo right into the middle of the party with the disc jockey and all the guests looking at me. I had lost my voice with fright and in the sheer panic I had forgotten to pull up my pants. I squeaked: 'Penny, there is a big ... a big ...' but I couldn't bring myself to say spider.

Some kind gent pointed out that I needed to pull my knickers up from round my ankles and then Penny realized what had terrified me. She laughed and said, 'Oh, you mean Fred.' I said, 'Christ! You're breeding them.' Penny then revealed they had one in every room.

She showed me my bedroom and in the corner of the wardrobe was an enormous spider she called Oscar. I was scared stiff, but she assured me there was nothing to worry about. The next morning I woke up and my finger had swollen up to twice its size. She said, 'It must have been Oscar because you have been so nervous and you have jumped as he walked across you in your sleep, so he has bitten you.' I went looking through the cupboards and said, 'Where is the little bastard?' I went bloody mad and told her I was going to kill him. She told me I couldn't because he wouldn't hurt me and his job was to keep the mosquitoes down. I was livid and told her I could make do with a mosquito net. There were nights I couldn't get to sleep for thinking about these bloody huge spiders.

Earlier Penny had said to me, 'Anything you want you can have – I will buy it for you.' At the party there was this handsome Portugese chap and I thought, I want him. He had a beautiful body and every time he walked past I kept saying, 'Penny, that's him. Buy him for me – that's what I want'. This man thought I was mad and kept swimming round the pool with his bulging biceps driving me wild. The next morning Penny woke up with bruises over her arm where I had been grabbing hold of her. The only trouble is I can't remember if I had him or not, because it was such a boozy bash.

As well as giant spiders they had snakes in Africa, and I was also terrified of them. I remember once staying in this five-star hotel complex with luxury mud-hut-style lodges in the grounds. After a show I was drinking in the open air and the subject of snakes had been discussed. I was told not to worry about the reptiles because they only came out when it rained.

As usual I was one of the last to leave the bar at about 4 am, and just as I did so it began to drizzle. I started heading back to my lodge when I realized I had to go under a series of bowers. I immediately imagined these tropical plants infested with boa constrictors, anacondas and pythons. I panicked and ran to the nearest room of one of my fellow entertainers. It was the tremendously funny deadpan Scottish comic Chick Murray's room.

He escorted me the fifty yards or so to my room. I said, 'Thanks very much, Chick,' but he then hit me with the most unforgettable line. He said, 'When you woke me you stirred the biggest snake in Africa.' I persuaded him that his trouser snake was safer going back to sleep. It took a fraction further persuasion before he made his excuses and left. And I breathed a sigh of relief – on top of all that drink the last thing I'd needed was an energetic sex session.

Drinking, as I mentioned earlier, played a major part

in the ex-pats' lifestyle over there. When I spent my first Christmas there I couldn't believe the benders they would go on. A couple of people would meet for a drink and then visit a friend's house for more booze. Then it was on to another house for a party, and all the time the group is growing as people leave their houses to join in the knees-up. It would end up with forty or fifty people out of their skulls at the last house. Everyone would be well away and people would be throwing each other in the pools – switching on hoses and causing total chaos. The moral code in Africa seemed a hell of a lot different from the one back home – anything goes in that atmosphere.

It was over there that I had my first real experiences of the casting couch – club bosses who believed a legover was part of the deal before you set foot on their stages. The nearest I came to being frightened was during one of these awful experiences at a club in Cape Town. The owner was a tall, good-looking chap who took it for granted that sex was part of the booking. He put me in a swish apartment hewn into the cliff face underneath his home and told me on my first night, 'I'll be down shortly.' I knew what was on his mind. It happened as a matter of course, but it was awful sex. I was just another notch on his bedpost. I lay back in the luxury surroundings and just thought of England. There was nothing more I could do as I was a million miles away from home and he'd already told me it was an unwritten clause in my contract. I later found out that he bedded all the cabaret acts that came through.

It was in Cape Town that I met a handsome man who was a high-flyer with the Kinekor cinema chain who turned into another one night-stand. But he was hopeless in bed, so I gave him the elbow. He was one of these blokes with loads of money, who expected you to be honoured at being held in his arms. But just like all the other South Africans I met, he was a disappointment in the bedroom. In all my time out there I never met one that was any good in that department.

My act became more and more sophisticated as the years drifted on. With each new season I also earned more and more cash and my costumes got classier and classier as well. I was so sick of the casting couch scenario that I wrote it into one of my songs with the lines, 'Drop your draws, the contract's yours.' This got a great laugh from the audiences, but only the artistes knew the truth of it all.

Another gag that went down well over there was my quickest joke, 'Speedy Gonzalez took a girl into a wood. He said, "Can I?" She said, "Will it hurt?" He said, "Did it?"' That just about summed my life up at the time.

One thing I never could come to terms with in South Africa or Rhodesia was the apartheid system and the way the blacks were treated. It was appalling. In South Africa apartheid was far worse than Rhodesia and the blacks there were treated like pigs.

On one occasion in Rhodesia I ended up in police cells for helping a black joiner get down from the fourteenth floor of the David Livingstone building in Salisbury. This young lad was struggling with a giant bag of tools, because the natives' lift was out of order. I told him to get in the lift with me. He was frightened and said, 'No, madam.' But I insisted and this poor eighteen-year-old could not refuse because he had been brought up to obey white people. After he'd got in I realized he was terrified and I chatted with him to calm him down.

But as soon as we stepped out of the lift we were stopped by a commissionaire. He said, 'You are not allowed to mix with black people. Where are you from?' I told him England. He then asked what I was doing there and I told him I was working in cabaret at the Chicken Grill in Greendale. The police arrived and asked for my passport. Unfortunately, that was at the nightclub which was closed. They took me straight down to the station and locked me up in a bare cell. I was absolutely horrified at what was happening to me for helping out another human being. I was very frightened. It was very strange being banged up in a cell in a foreign land. All kinds of horrible thoughts raced through my mind.

Before they carted me off the man showed me the blacks' lift in the hotel. The tiles and radio speakers were pulled out of the roof, the carpet was wet through and it absolutely stank of pee. He said, 'Now you wonder why we don't have them in our lift.' I was very angry and said, 'Oh yes, and you wonder why they act like that. Well, they act like that because you treat them like that. It is absolutely immoral to let someone struggle with a huge bag of tools just because a lift is broken when another one in the same building works.' They didn't like me letting off steam and kept me locked up for four hours until the club owner returned to show them my passport. The young chap Amma was whisked off as soon as he stepped out of the lift and I never found out what happened to him. They probably locked me up to teach me a lesson, because they believed very strongly in that superior race nonsense.

I once asked a boy who was a servant at a friend's house if he'd kill the family should revolution break out. 'No, no, madam, I couldn't do that,' he said loyally. 'I kill the family next door and their boy kills everyone here.' That illustrated to me just how potty apartheid was.

I got on great with the natives. The blacks were very funny about having their photos taken. They believed that if you took a snap you would take their spirit away. The lack of technology out there in the Sixties was often very frustrating and the lack of television a real pain, but what could you expect when the majority of the natives were scared of cameras.

On 21 July 1969 I was particularly furious with the lack of TV because that was the day Neil Armstrong became the first man to walk on the moon. It was one of the biggest happenings in my lifetime, and I missed it because they had no telly. I really wanted to see it and took the ridiculous step of standing on a balcony with my binoculars pointed at the moon. I was convinced I was going to see something as I had the binoculars set on their maximum. But of course I never saw a thing and afterwards I was really mad. I saw the pictures in the newspaper the next day, but it just wasn't the same.

I got up to another crackpot caper less than a year later on tour with Roy Douglas. The pair of us visited an ostrich farm at Oosthuizen, where I was told that if I sat on a particular egg it would hatch beneath me. I sat on this egg for ages, but it was just a wicked wind-up. I've got a picture of me sitting on that egg to this day. I still laugh looking back at the mirth I caused by plonking myself on it.

One day trip that thrilled me in more ways than one was to a diamond mine in Kimberley, South Africa. For services rendered to a supervisor on the visit I was given an enormous uncut diamond. It was wonderful receiving such a beautiful gift in return for a night of passion.

During a month-long break years later Derrick and I stayed at the Serena Park Hotel at Nairobi in Kenya before moving onto Keith's daughter Jenny's place in Zambia. Our luggage didn't join us until two days later, because lost baggage isn't a new phenomenon. The cases were laden down with goods from Britain for Jenny and her husband Gary and I'd only taken a quarter of the clothes I would normally travel with. In Zambia in those days you couldn't get a lot of the stuff we took for granted back home. She had asked me to stock up with packet sauces, mints and tins of salmon and I even took a couple of Harrods' Christmas puds. Another case was loaded with three model aeroplanes for Gary and a whole pile of Janet Reger underwear for Jenny.

We were very surprised to hear that the baggage was coming back to us from Johannesburg. The chocolates had melted, but miraculously the bags had not been rifled, so the gifts were intact. We had to fill in about 178 papers in triplicate to get the cases back, but it was worth it because they loved the presents.

By this stage Keith had gained fame in his own right as a cabaret compere. The cheeky swine used to come to Britain, steal gags off me and Duggie then go back and use them on the club circuit over there. He was in great demand to host cabaret nights at all the mine and golf clubs in Zambia. The jokes were always new out there, and that gave our Keith star status.

Up until then we had always described Keith as the normal brother who worked for a living. He's back from Zambia these days and running a lovely pub called the Bull Hotel in Fairford, Gloucestershire. I've called in a couple of times, and now my *Coronation Street* days are over I plan to pop down for a stay. It's a damn sight easier getting to see him there than travelling to the other side of the globe – although I wouldn't exchange those memories for the world. There was a lot of pleasure, mainly thanks to Roy Douglas, but now I'll tell you about the awful pain that came along too.

CHAPTER EIGHT

It Ain't Worth Living

The rain was sheeting down, the sky was grey and frost lay on the ground. This was Maltby in March. I'd just returned from paradise and the gentle caresses of my lover Roy Douglas to the grim reality of life at home with Derrick. He wasn't one for hugs and kisses at the best of times, but right now I needed tender loving care more than any time in my life ... I was pregnant to Roy.

It might have been a dream beginning, but I knew inside it was a nightmare ending. I had to get rid of the baby. Telling Derrick I was pregnant to another man would have taken more guts than I'd got. It would have torn him apart at that point, and the anguish over it all was already ripping me to bits.

As far as Derrick was concerned nothing had changed. He had little interest in what I'd been up to. It was straight back into the old routine. Make the tea, do the washing and work the clubs he'd booked me into for the rest of the year. Everything at home was frighteningly normal. Much, much too normal for me.

I had come home for the world premiere of my first movie, *Kes*, on Sunday 29 March 1970, and it should have been one of the happiest times of my professional life. Instead I was travelling headlong down a tunnel of despair. I was engulfed in doom and gloom. Holding the first showing of *Kes* at the ABC in Barnsley, South Yorks, was not my idea of the glitzy location for a movie premiere. I had hoped for a trip down Sunset Strip and an opening night on Rodeo Drive, though I'd have probably settled for a glamorous London venue. But I was flying half way round the globe to go to the ABC at Barnsley.

I thought at first they were kidding me. I never got invited by card – it was a telephone call and I thought someone was pulling my leg. I even told them not to be so silly, you couldn't stage a world premiere in Yorkshire. It didn't make a lot of sense travelling for over a day to get to Barnsley.

I put on a posh frock, but my heart wasn't in it. I was living life without the lights on. I was shrouded by darkness. I can't really remember what the first night was like. It must have been good, because *Kes* went on to become a worldwide smash hit. I carried on as best I could, going on the stage doing my stuff, but the spark had gone. I had all this trouble and worry on my mind and I was trying to make people laugh. Behind my stage smile I was heartbroken. I reached a point where I thought it makes no sense carrying on like this. Derrick was his usual insensitive self and could not see I was being torn to shreds. I could have just returned from Mars for all he cared. I tried to contact Roy to talk through the situation with him, because he knew nothing about the pregnancy. But our agent Claud Hunter, suspecting an affair, refused to put me in touch. He told me I should be ashamed of myself and that Roy was back home with his wife and family. For all I know Roy might have been getting the same story at his end. Claud had even threatened to stop Roy and me from working.

My deepest dread of us setting up home in a tiny bedsit without two pennies to rub together was praying on my mind. I did get very materialistic at this point because the lack of cash would have spoiled the whole romance. I thought, Keep your wits about you, girl. It was like a honeymoon in South Africa – we could never be so happy back home. I didn't want any of that love-in-a-garret stuff. It would have been too hard to survive after having enjoyed the high-life from my showbiz success. I was riddled with doubts and in an awful muddle. I could see no clear solution.

Then it came to me through the blur of self-pity: brandy and aspirins would provide the answer to my prayers. I was so mixed up that suicide seemed the only way out. I planned it in as much as Derrick was working shifts and when he was out I'd swallow the overdose. I tried it one night, but after getting them down the damn things kept coming up. I was sick as a dog, but the next night the self-destruct button was switched on again. I was determined to get it right.

I sat there with the brandy bottle and a mountain of sleeping pills. It was just like Ken Barlow's Christmas suicide scene on *Coronation Street* – buckets of tears. There I was, wallowing in a sea of self-induced grief, thinking of nobody but myself. My mind wasn't on the trauma and upset I'd leave behind. The horror if young Stephen had found me or even Derrick – that was the last thing I would have been thinking about. It was simply focused on getting out of the awful mess I'd gotten into.

I swallowed the pills by the handful, washing them down with brandy straight from the bottle. The more I took, the more hazy it got, until finally I fell asleep. I felt funny and then I passed out. As I drifted away I thought that all my problems would soon be gone.

When you are so awfully depressed you reach a point where your brain just stops functioning. I'd arrived at that stage of the journey. I couldn't take any more and I had to get out.

Not being able to talk to Roy for weeks made the need to resolve something more urgent. If it dragged on much longer the baby would have started to show. I'm only small and even Derrick would have spotted a big lump in my belly. I was having a nervous breakdown, and my way out through suicide meant it was soon going to be over.

I was very, very wrong. I woke with a plastic pipe down my throat and an awful pain in my stomach. The life-savers at the district hospital were doing their job and bringing me back from the dead. It was not the most pleasant experience, as you can imagine. I thought, Well, I've failed in that. It was Derrick who saved my life by coming home from work early and finding me lying there almost lifeless.

I can thank him for it now. At the time it only made me want to kill him, because my mind was in such a shocking state. I was still pregnant and decided that if I couldn't kill myself then I'd have to have an abortion. I still couldn't bring myself to tell Derrick what had gone on and why I'd become so desperate.

I carried out the abortion myself using a plastic tube and soapy water. It was a common way of doing it in those days, but very dangerous. Women could do themselves untold damage if they got it wrong. I took the risk because I thought, my life won't be worth living if I don't get shut of this. I won't go into any more gory details, because I don't want to make it sound like an article in the *Lancet*. I never thought of it as a baby, just a big headache I had to get rid of.

Looking back now I don't really think that I wanted to kill myself. I simply wanted to get out of the agonizing situation I was in. As I was taking the pills I remember thinking, 'I might die, I mightn't die, I might die, I mightn't die.' My mind was in a sorry state.

For weeks before it happened I had turned myself into a recluse. Wearing nothing but a dressing gown over my nightie, I'd lock myself in a room and start downing bottles of brandy and any other booze I could get my hands on to blot out the pain.

I was hurting like hell inside and poor Derrick became a target for my hatred. I made his life a misery for months and months. I'd smash glasses, the windows, the glass doors, the telly and anything else that I got hold of. During this dreadful period of my life Derrick tells me I chucked sixteen tellys through the kitchen window in rages. I couldn't tell you if it's true or not, because my mind was in splinters as well. After the glazier had been out four times, I changed to another firm for a while. I didn't want them to think I was mad.

When I went on a wrecking spree Derrick would call for the doctor. Dr Gregg was a lovely chap who understood drunks. He'd step over the shards of glass scattered along the hallway and try to calm me down. I wasn't always up to reasoning, but Derrick must have needed somebody there. I was lucky that Derrick didn't do away with me. I wouldn't have blamed him, I was so horrendous.

One day my friend Dorothy Frazer came round and walked straight in because I hadn't locked the door. She took one look at the brandy and booze spattered wallpaper round the lounge and simply said, 'Oh, how contemporary.' She was never one for subtlety. She'd also worked for years as a singer in the clubs with her organist husband Phil Freeman.

On a lighter note, I'd tried to get Dorothy and Phil into *Kes* with me when it was filmed. Ken Loach had asked the cast to bring along friends for the crowd scenes. The pay was quite good at £2 a day and all the booze they could drink. The only stipulation was that the extras should dress in neutral colours because he wanted to portray working-class austerity.

I'd invited the agent Dennis Lightowler along as well.

But I couldn't believe the gear Dorothy had got on after I told her to dress down. She was dressed louder than a Cup Final crowd. Her red hair had been bleached carrot colour and was covered with a net with coloured beads on it. Her frock was African violet and her coat was apple green. I just said, 'So this is neutral, Dorothy,' but she didn't bat an eyelid. She was the type of woman you could call for at 6.30 am and she'd still be fully made up, with her nails and hair done.

When we arrived at this pub in Barnsley where they were filming, the crew were taking all the bright curtains down and painting the walls mushroom colour and hanging brown drapes up. Ken Loach was in the middle of a conversation when he caught a glimpse of Dorothy in her get-up. His eyebrows automatically raised and he looked askance. I went up to him and said, 'Give me a brush and I'll paint her.' He said, 'She's a bit bright.' She got a big shock to find out she'd been completely cut out of the movie.

The film-makers had made a bloomer by offering all these Yorkshire extras free drink. Everybody got pissed and nobody could follow the instructions. I remember Dennis going up for a tray of ten whiskies and the barmaid asking him who they were for. He told her they were for a table in the corner, but he sank the lot himself.

It was a low-budget production and the cost of drink on that day must have been more than they paid for the hire of the central character's council house.

Meeting the camera crews and experiencing their techniques was to stand me in good stead for my future career on the small screen, although I found it hard playing the part without having an audience there. Before going on stage in the club I used to sign autographs, chat and have a drink with the fans. In the movies that just doesn't happen and it was something I missed.

Friends like Dorothy and my old pal Doreen Bell

helped pull me through my mega-depression. About five weeks after I carried out the abortion, I thought, Sod it – I've got to get on with my life. I got back on the circuit after going out for a night with friends and being collared by a concert secretary who said he'd take me to court if I cancelled his club. He'd had the booking for ages and it had been sold out for over two months. I did the show, and getting back in front of the audience breathed more life into me. I realized what I was missing and it helped me to overcome the personal trauma.

Before I could get on with my life properly, though, I had to lay the ghost of Roy Douglas to rest. I knew I had to see him again, and when I heard on the grapevine he was playing in a club in Worksop a few months later, I went along with my old schoolfriend Doreen. I saw him in the grimy setting of a working men's club and knew straight off that the magic had gone. Despite being besotted with his baby he had, true to his word, left his wife and had now started dating a croupier.

I thought about our talk of marriage – and we had both been keen on it over in South Africa – but coming back home and seeing him in a smoky social club took all the glamour away. He came and chatted to us. He told us he had left his wife, but assured me that I wasn't the reason. He simply said he got home and couldn't face being married to a woman he didn't love. He couldn't face carrying on with her.

I never told him about our baby – or the abortion – and at the end of the night we both went our separate ways. I couldn't have coped getting involved with him again, because I was just beginning to get my life back on the level.

In South Africa I was seriously considering divorcing Derrick, but seeing Roy back in England made me realize that not doing that had been a sensible decision. But I maintain to this day that I have never been so madly in love with anyone in my life, nor experienced the intensity of passion that I shared with Roy.

From that day to this I have not seen Roy. It's like that Michael Jackson song, 'He's Out of My Life'. I don't regret our time together and I've thought about him a lot since. He really was a tremendous lover. I firmly believe that everything I've done through my life has taught me something. Roy, God bless him, taught me a lot. And I am sure he'll have a wife somewhere whom he's made very, very happy.

His warmth and love undoubtedly pushed me further away from Derrick, because in our rows years later I told him he was lousy at making love. That must have made him even colder towards me. I even told him in vivid detail that I'd never had an orgasm until I'd met Roy Douglas. I really put him down, but he probably suspected I'd had a fling with Roy because I mentioned him a fair bit in my letters from South Africa.

It must be said that Derrick never did have much of a sex drive to start with. I remember when Stephen was about two years old. I was doing my decorating and I fell off a stool. Derrick's Uncle John was there and he said, 'I know what's wrong with you. You're pregnant.' I told him straight, 'I haven't had what it takes to get pregnant for six months,' and he was astounded. He thought I was kidding, but I told him Derrick just wasn't sexually minded.

I often wondered if it was something to do with me being the provider. Working in the clubs, being the main breadwinner, might have in some way intimidated him. He later told me that I'd told him I didn't fancy sex with him and he asked me how I thought that made him feel. He said, 'What's the point of bothering?'

Sex with Derrick had lost that special feel, not that it was ever really there in the first place. He would just put the telly off at 9 pm and say, 'Let's go to bed'. And I'd think, 'Oh sex. I don't want bloody sex, I want to finish watching this film.' I was probably being selfish, because if I wanted sex at 3 o'clock in the morning I wanted it then. But I would never wake Derrick up. I'd just let the feeling go and that would build up a lot of resentment inside me.

After the Roy Douglas episode I actually became frigid. I had to keep a jar of Vaseline under the bed and use that when we were making love. One night I had a cough and had been using Vick. Well Derrick came up and I put my hand under the bed and slapped some lubrication in place. Derrick said, 'I wish you'd stop using so much Vick,' and then all of a sudden he screamed. He got off me, and he was very red in a rather rude place. Poor sod could hardly walk for three days afterwards.

Sex for Derrick was like giving someone a bar of chocolate – and it was that emotional. It was taken for granted we were going to have sex when he felt like it. He used to look at women with big boobs and go, 'Cor!' and I'd say, 'You don't know what to do with these,' pointing to my own chest, 'so don't even bother thinking about them. They'd be much too much for you.' Someone told me once that the more a man handles your bust the bigger it gets, so I told Derrick, 'No wonder mine are so diddy – you never bloody touch them.'

One night I'd had enough of him and when he went to bed I decided to play a song with a message. I got this record with lyrics that said, 'Neither of us wants to say goodbye.' It was a tune about neither of you daring to leave, because you haven't got the guts to say goodbye. I must have played the single forty times before he came downstairs. He said, 'Are you coming to bed?' When I said no and asked him to listen to the words on the record, he said, 'It's driving me crackers,' and raced over to the record player, picked up the disc and chucked it on the fire. He snarled, 'Now are you coming to bed?' Again I refused. I said,' 'The fire's warm, I'm staying here.' So he took all the fuses out of the main electricity box to kill the lights and the music. I was furious and went out in the garden and started chopping wood for the fire. He came down, lobbed a bucket of water over the fire and smashed all my records. It was a case of, You will come and have sex or I'll burn all your records. It was barmy.

But when we had rows I really would go into a rage. I remember in one silly argument smashing him over the head with a shovel. I bent the shovel when I hit him as he got into the bath. Years later we still hadn't managed to get the dent out of that shovel. On another occasion I cut up all his suits and during a row when he worked in a sock factory I slashed his seventy pairs of Argyle socks.

But for all that I still loved Derrick – I must have done to have stuck by him through those years. Discovering he had cheated on me with a woman called Rose when I was cheating on him with my Rhodesian policeman Andy actually made him more attractive to me. I was furious with him. In my muddled moral code it was okay for me to carry on, but not Derrick, and the thought of another woman having him made me immensely jealous.

It turned out he had only taken this woman called Rose out three times to local pubs, but at first I didn't know that and Derrick was driving me dotty by refusing to talk about her. He wouldn't even tell me where they had gone. He was mad at me for leaving him and Stephen in the lurch. For three months while I was shacked up with Andy I never sent them any money back. Derrick must have had to sign on the social to live. He used that against me in rows for years to come, and I can't blame him for being bitter.

I had told him I wanted a divorce in the August of that year, but it wasn't until the December that he started dancing with this Rose from Rawmarsh, near Rotherham. My mother saved me from a nervous breakdown by telling me what Derrick's game was. He was refusing to tell me about Rose to wind me up, and it was working.

I was so furious with him that I'd attacked his car when he was out. I thought, Using the car I'd bought you to carry on with other women! I'll show you, Derrick Barksby. I put 4 lb of sugar in the engine and cut all the wires under the bonnet. I slashed all the seats and one of his tyres.

My mum said he'd never had so much attention in his life and he was revelling in his new role as man of mystery. I remember her telling me to ask him about where he took Rose and then peep through a crack in the door to see his reaction. Well, he sat in his chair and said, 'I can't remember' before smiling contentedly to himself. I thought, I know your game.

I traipsed up to the club one day to meet this girl, and I asked around after the Rose who had been dancing with a big tall fellow. Someone pointed her out and I went and sat near her. She was very motherly, she was lovely with a big bust. She knew I was Lynne Perrie, but obviously didn't connect me with Derrick. I swung the conversation round to her dancing partners and she mentioned Derrick's name.

She got the shock of her life when I told her he was my husband. She didn't know what to think, but I told her I only wanted to know how many times they'd been out and where they'd gone. I said my husband had been driving me insane by playing cat and mouse and not telling me anything about her. I said I didn't blame him, because I'd been in South Africa and had told him our marriage was over. She said they'd been out three times and told me the names of the pubs. It transpired that Derrick had dropped her like a hot potato when he discovered she already had three kids. Looking after someone else's offspring would have sounded too much like hard work to old lazy bones.

From the way she reacted I guessed they'd had sex, but I didn't want those details. I just used the pub names to put him down. He was a bit deflated when I told him I'd been to Rawmarsh and met Rose and rolled off the names of the boozers. I said, 'Your memory must be bad if you can't remember those three names.' He wasn't a happy chappy that day, I can tell you.

During the 1960s a lot of my temper tantrums might have been caused by the use of drugs. I'm not saying I was into hard drugs, but I regularly took tablets prescribed by the GP. In those days women were given all kinds of pills that are today deemed addictive. Derrick never knew what to make of me at all. But I realized with hindsight that a lot of my barmy mood swings were drug induced. One moment I'd be right as rain, the next I'd be yelling at him and banging his head.

I know I was hooked on some of these tablets. The doctors dished them out like sweets, and nobody ever dreamed they could have had adverse effects. I used slimming pills for about nine years. They were like black torpedoes and it turned out they were amphetamines. They gave me so much energy that I could stay awake for forty-eight hours and would be painting the walls or washing clothes at 4 am in the morning. No wonder they used to call me Little Miss Dynamite.

These days kids fork out a fortune on the stuff because it apparently keeps them dancing in clubs all night long. Of course, they're illegal now and people are much better informed these days. Then I had no idea why I was so hyperactive. But I had to counter the effects of being up all night by asking the doctor for sleeping pills. Once again they were freely prescribed.

One night Derrick asked if I was coming to bed and I said, 'I'll just have a sleeping pill.' It started to work and then I washed it down with brandy, and that sent me crazy. I stormed up to Derrick lying in bed, picked up the alarm clock and threw it at his head. It was totally irrational. I had been given a combination of uppers and downers and they were sending me round the twist. I later found out that the brandy reacted with the sleeping pills to send me potty.

But my worst trip happened when I was working away in Wales and the slimming pills that gave me energy had run out. I didn't know that these Duraphets were amphetamines back then. I just knew they got me buzzing and able to do lots more when I was feeling tired. So this particular day in a Welsh guest house I asked the landlady's sixteen-year-old son if he knew where I could get some of these Black Bomber pills like the doctor gave me. I was working two shows every day because it was the holiday season and felt I needed something to pick me up. The lad said, 'Don't worry. I'll get you sorted out. I'll see what's on the market.' I asked him what he meant by that, thinking to myself, They've got some bloody funny markets round here. He just smiled.

After a while the lad came back with a tiny little black pill, the size of a pinhead. I asked if that was it and he said, 'Yep. Don't worry, that's fifteen shillings worth.' I thought, Such a lot of money for such a little pill, but I handed over the cash. I put it in my purse and did the working men's club in the Valleys that evening. I had left my hair dryer in the boarding house and returned for it before going off for a turn at a nightclub. I called in and thought, I'll have that pill to keep me going, and I swallowed it.

I didn't know I was taking LSD, or lysergic acid diethylamide to use its full name, but very quickly the hallucogenic drug took hold. It hit me like a sledgehammer. It is a terrible thing. It is very hard to explain. But at first I started to go under and then as you come out of this heavy black state the nightmares begin.

One of the lads from a band staying in the house saw

me and said, 'If I didn't know you better. Lynne. I'd say you'd taken LSD.' I told him 'You're not getting me on drugs,' and told him what I'd taken. He then informed me I was already on acid, as it was also known. I asked for some salt water to make myself sick and get rid of it.

He said it was no good as the drug was already in my system. He told me to go with it, but I thought, Not bloody likely, and started fighting it. I fought it all the way, and every time I felt myself going under I was screaming. I don't know who was there in that house when I went beserk. But I fought and fought. I saw my soul. I saw my fingers swell up. I saw all kinds of nightmares when I was in the grip of that terrifying drug. It was like being in a fairground's House of Mirrors – everything was distorted and shrouded in clouds. My brain was spinning with it. Everything was happening very fast, but everyone was talking very slowly. It was like everybody I saw was asking me to have a cup of coffee in slow motion.

They took me and put me on a bed upstairs, and that trip lasted for two days. Every time I thought I was coming out I yelled 'Send for my husband.' The woman at the guest house realized what her son had done and wouldn't send for the doctor. During this horrendous ordeal I also remember screaming, 'I don't want to die in Wales. Please don't let me die in Wales.' The lads said I'd had the worse trip they had ever seen. I said, 'I never wanted to go on a trip. Only trip I wanted was back up to Wakefield and home.'

After that I would never go near another drug again – not even cannabis or any of the so-called soft drugs – because once you are gripped by them you don't know what can happen. Those experiences left me with a sheer terror of drugs. When Stephen started smoking I said, 'I'll buy you cigarettes as long as you promise never to accept a cigarette off anyone else.' I believe my warnings against drugs worked on him. To the best of my knowledge he has never used any. If he had, Derrick would no doubt have blamed me for getting him involved in them, because of the way I used all those slimming pills during the Sixties.

Our rows are legendary in the family. One of the most infuriating habits Derrick has is walking out in the middle of an argument. I will be blazing away and Derrick will just go and take his dog for a walk. It built up an awful resentment in me, never being able to finish a row with him. I have never been able to conquer Derrick. He would never face anything head on – he'd just go out for a walk until it had subsided.

In telephone rows he has the same approach. He hangs up before we clear the air and sort anything out. With Roy Douglas I had a taste of what life was like with a man who would listen to you. Maybe if Derrick reads my story he will understand what some of the unfinished arguments have meant to me.

For years, as Derrick knows, I worked without touching anybody, because I was so much in love with my act. But after achieving those orgasms with Roy I started looking for that special kind of magic in every man I fancied. I'll have to tell you about my happy times with toyboys, but first I must tell you about life on *Coronation Street*.

CHAPTER NINE

On the Street

Kes, I have always maintained, landed me the role in *Coronation Street*. I never had to audition. The casting director Paul Barnard had seen my performance in the hit movie on a Saturday night. On the Monday I was down at Granada's Manchester studios and he was telling me he wanted me to play an ageing dolly bird. The character Ivy would be working at the warehouse that was later to become Mike Baldwin's factory. I was told to return for filming the following week.

The part I was playing was a tarty older woman who would be scrapping with the younger girls in the packing warehouse. An actress called Mavis Rogerson was to play my screen pal Edna Gee. Mavis was a big girl and I think the director had it in his mind's eye to use us as some sort of double act, although it was only when they teamed Ivy up with Vera Duckworth that the comic situation, with the short and the tall workmates, achieved its potential.

I already had Ivy's stubborness inside me. When told I'd have to wear white boots and hotpants, I refused. There was no way anyone was going to get me into hotpants. I am glad I did. If I had worn them the character might not have survived more than those initial three weeks. They had five pairs of hotpants for me to wear when I returned the next week, but I maintained there was no way I'd put them on. I warned that wearing skimpy hotpants would turn both Ivy and Edna into caricatures. I compromised by slipping on a miniskirt, and unbeknown to me Ivy was about to totter into soap history in those high-heeled white boots.

I was quite stroppy then and also insisted on having my hair up in curls in a sort of beehive. I didn't want the beaded hair net they'd suggested – that would have made Ivy look like a harpy. By this stage I had done a film and other TV work, so I was quite confident. I told them the secret of the job for me was, basically, playing myself. It's held true throughout my *Coronation Street* career – what you see is what you get.

In those early days acting didn't really come into it. I hadn't gone into all the crying and the real acting I did later, some of which was to earn me rave reviews from the critics. I had been told during the filming of *Kes* just to be myself, and when you do that you are playing an easy part. I told the casting people at Granada that I wanted to be a normal person and not too over the top. They listened to me in the end and with a bit of compromise I got my way.

The funny thing was that during those first three weeks I had three different husbands, or should I say I would have had if I'd followed the scripts. The first week I mentioned my husband called Eric, the following week they had him down as Wilf and he was something else in the third week. I thought the scriptwriter was obviously a loony and I stuck with the first name through all three weeks.

I must have had something, because after that they kept inviting me back. The part evolved and the character got stronger and stronger. A 'past her sell-by date' glamour puss in hotpants wouldn't have had that staying power.

Although I was doing quite a bit on the Street I was still always available to take on other TV work as well. During the early 1970s I worked on *Queenie's Castle*, a Yorkshire TV comedy series starring Diana Dors. Keith Waterhouse wrote the show revolving round Queenie Shepherd's home at Buckingham Flats. I played her arch-enemy Mrs Petty. Diana was great to work with and she was a big star. I even stayed at her magnificent mansion in the Home Counties.

Her husband Alan Lake was a lovely brown-haired lad. I'll never forget that he had a part in a show he wanted to do, but he had to go to court just before rehearsals started. He believed he would go free if he pleaded guilty but he was jailed there and then for eighteen months for wounding a pub landlord. Diana was distraught – they'd only been married a couple of years earlier, in 1968. I'd have to say her home was one of the most magnificent I'd been in. I was upset by her death in May 1984.

Another star I worked with during those early days on TV was Michael Elphick, who found fame as Boon in the 1980s. Not many people know this but Michael also had a part in *Coronation Street* as Douglas Wormold, the landlord's son who tried to buy the Kabin. When I worked with him in the 1970s on the show *It Was a Good Story, Don't Knock It*, I thoroughly enjoyed it. We were playing alongside the accomplished actor Kenneth Haigh, who starred in *Room at The Top*. Michael and I hit it off right away – he was a big drinker just like me. I'd had a lot of heartache and my time in Africa had given me a real taste for the booze. Also spending so many nights away from home on location leaves you with a lot of spare time and not a lot to do. But Michael and I kept ourselves busy ... boozing. It was delightful being able to drink with somebody who didn't look down on you. Other people sometimes looked down their noses at the state I'd get into during a drinking bout. Not that I had to drink that much. Being so tiny I ended up sozzled after only a couple, but I had the staying power to see a session through to its end.

The show was filmed on location in Llandudno, North Wales, and every day after work we'd sample the delights of the hotel bar or any other bar that took our fancy. We spent two weeks there, but I don't remember much about it. Michael and I turned it into a serious seaside bender. He was the same type of drinker as me and would be with me in the bar until five or six o'clock the following morning. The director was a big Scottish fellow called Gordon Burns whom I'd often meet at the lift in the mornings. He'd say 'good morning' in his deep voice as he passed me on his way for breakfast and I'd be hoping he wouldn't realize I was just going to bed.

My arrival at the Granada studios in a brand new Mark 10 Jaguar didn't escape the notice of some of the regular members of the cast. I recall overhearing a bemused Betty Driver whisper, 'They must be paying the talking extras well.' But I'd carried on doing my cabaret work and could earn more from that in one night than from any of my appearances on *Coronation Street*.

On my first day at the studios I made a bit of a bloomer by going and sitting myself down in Violet Carson's seat. Now she played Ena Sharples who along with Minnie Caldwell, played by Margot Bryant, and Annie Walker, played by Doris Speed, were the real Weatherfield old guard. They all had their own seats and there was an unwritten rule that you didn't sit in them. There was a lot more respect for age and experience in the 1970s.

The Street studios were housed in a bonded warehouse. Twenty years ago all the cast had their own cubicles. It was nothing like the dressing rooms they have today in the Street's posh new purpose-built Studio One complex. The cubicles meant everybody could hear the conversations going on round them. There was no room for any whispering or sniping. And to be fair nobody wanted to be bigger than anybody else. It was very much the *Coronation Street* team. It changed later, because the world of television has changed and become much more competitive. People join the Street these days and want to get on and make their mark. They strive to become the star of the show. In those days it was accepted that the show was the star and we worked as a team to continue the programme's success.

The first member of the cast I met was Margot Bryant, but nothing could have prepared me for what she was really like. On screen she played Minnie Caldwell, this lovely, mild-mannered, frail old lady with smiling eyes. But off camera she was a real raver who used some terribly abusive language. The first thing she told me about were the show's countless male admirers – and you have to remember at this point she was a woman of about 70. She said, 'They are ever so sexy, very virile and many of them are very athletically built – they are forever touching your bottom and groping you.' I gaped at her. I couldn't believe what I was hearing. Here was this little old lady lusting after young men. She used to tell autograph hunters to bugger off – it was funny. A lot of her outrageous behaviour, I was to discover later, was done simply to shock. Sadly she died in 1987 after spending her final years in a nursing home.

Back then the Street wasn't a show where there was a lot of jealousy, although I do remember getting upset one night after one of the traditional actresses in the show grumbled about 'cabaret artistes coming along and taking real actors' roles.' I rang my brother Duggie that evening, hurt by what I'd heard. But he told me, 'When you go on stage, even when you're not well, you put on a smile. You do your act without anyone to cue you. You live or die by your own efforts. There is nobody helping you with the gags or the words of a song from the moment you go on that stage to coming off. You are an actress – don't let anyone tell you otherwise.' I drew a lot of strength from what he said and must admit he was dead right.

Julie Goodyear was always the one to greet newcomers in the green room and we were to become good friends later. But from the start Pat Phoenix was my biggest pal on the programme. She took me under her wing and looked after me. It was Pat – the legendary Elsie Tanner – who warned me about Bill Roache being a real ladykiller. He was a right stud in the early years, and Pat told me to watch out for him. Bill, who plays Ken Barlow, was the Weatherfield heart throb in those days. When I arrived he spent a lot of his time playing bridge in the green room with Doris Speed, Graham Haberfield, who played Jerry Booth, and Bryan Mosley. I've never really mixed with him. And in more recent years he kept himself to himself in his dressing room during his time at the studios. He most definitely put his days of sowing wild oats behind him.

He was a Druid, which struck me as a very odd thing for clean-shaven Bill to be. Until I met him the word 'Druid' conjured up images of grey-bearded men in white gowns, prancing round Stonehenge. He was also into astrology, and had studied the subject. I remember pestering him to look into my horoscope. He drew charts up for quite a few of the cast, and after several months of repeated requests he did one for me. He asked me my date of birth and all that. Then he went away and used logarithms in the compiling of the chart. He had a very deep understanding of the stars and planets. A couple of months afterwards he presented me with a detailed chart. I was most impressed by his astro-analysis.

One thing he touched on was my relationship with my father. He said it was never a really easy relationship. What he said was very true, because I very much respected my father. He was on a sort of pedestal, because from my early days he had only needed to look at me in a certain way to indicate his disapproval. I never had the same relationship with my dad as I had with my mum, and he highlighted this in the chart. I was fascinated by the whole thing, particularly the reference to my dad.

Only a few years before I had lost my father in the most horrible circumstances – not that death is ever pleasant. He died in Rotherham General Hospital on 5 August, 1969 at the age of 62 from a ghastly form of cancer. The disease first came to light about eighteen months earlier when a little raspberry-shaped blemish appeared inside his mouth.

He was a funny chap with fixed views, and one of them was that he never ever believed that man would walk on the moon. He used to say, 'The day they land on the moon the world will end.' It was ironic that just a couple of weeks after Neil Armstrong made that giant leap for mankind from Apollo 11 the end of the world had arrived for dad.

For years my father had sucked on a pipe. He hardly ever lit up, just sucked it. I often wonder if the nicotine from the end of the pipe had in some way caused the mark that was to lead to his death. When he first went into hospital they performed a biopsy on his growth. At no stage did he ever tell me or mum that he had cancer. In fact nobody mentioned that word then, they just told him he had a growth.

A short while later this raspberry mark started appearing on the outside of his cheek. It was a bit worrying, but not that much. Then one day he asked me to give him a lift up to the local shops, and he jumped out of the car before I stopped. The car door hit that blemish on his face and it started to bleed.

Later I was to blame myself for his cancer spreading – even though the doctors assured me that wasn't the case. I was terribly upset at hurting him, but he put on a brave face and told me not to fuss. I saw him next about a week later and he had a little plaster on his cheek.

I was never to see him alive again without a plaster on his face. The size of the plaster just grew and grew. He came along to one of my shows in Wakefield, West Yorks, and didn't want a drink. He asked for a cup of tea and when he sipped it, it was too hot for him. But I noticed something really odd: as he slurped his brew it was seeping out from under the plaster. At that point I never dreamt he had a hole in his face – I was only to find that out as he lay on his deathbed.

He became progressively worse. My mother later blamed the furnaces for causing his cancer, because she recalled the hundreds of times he came home with burn marks on his face. It reached a point where dad would go nowhere without a can of air freshener. He came to my house and insisted on sitting by the back door and squirting his air freshener. I asked him why he was doing it and he replied, 'I have to do this, because my sore smells.' I was later told that cancers do give off a pungent odour, and he must have been getting the stench of it from inside his mouth.

One day they took him into hospital, because he had lost so much weight. He was only about 5 ft 4 in tall, but was a broad man and very dapper. He was always very proud of his appearance and liked to keep himself smart. But in the hospital they put him on a drip and we saw him fading away in front of us on a side ward. It was very distressing.

I'll never forget visiting him after about three or four weeks. I had a sense of foreboding, and when we got towards his room I saw his drip outside the door. I told mum to wait while I went in first, but I couldn't stop her following me through the door.

The horror hit me first. Nobody had told us he was dead. But there lying on the bed, lifeless, was dad. And they'd taken away the plaster that had been on his face for well over a year. He'd protected both me and my mum from the horrendous sight that plaster hid – a hole clean through his cheek. It was an awful sight. The hole was up round the edges, and the crust encircling it made it look like one of those moon craters. You could see straight into his mouth – his tongue and teeth, everything. We both screamed. I wished I could have saved my mother from that sight. It was what he would have wanted.

It was only then that the hospital staff told us he had died, which was pretty obvious. I started ranting and raving and playing merry hell. I told them my dad had hidden that hole in his face from us for eighteen months, but that they had completely robbed him of his dignity by removing his plaster. Before we arrived we had been told to expect bad news, but nobody had told us just how bad.

They tried to say they had seen it all before, which is very true but no consolation to someone who's just seen their loved one laid out on a bed. They were trying to bundle me out of the hospital because I was making such a commotion.

In my grief I was bashing the nurses. I was so vexed with them and so shocked and horrified by what I had seen. My mother died in spirit on that day, although it was over a decade later that her body went to the grave and peace at last. This family tragedy made me very reflective over Bill's astrological chart.

At about the same time as I was pondering my future in the stars, I suspected it was curtains for my Street character. The warehouse where Ivy worked erupted in a ball of flames after three delinquents dropped a cigarette during a break-in. Mavis had been a bit off with me all week and I didn't know why. She asked me if I'd read the scripts and I told her of course I had. But the fact that her character Edna was being killed off hadn't registered. The script said: 'Edna walks through factory door and then we see the fire.' I told her I knew she got caught in a fire, but she told me, 'I am dying.' She was obviously a bit upset about it, and then the situation dawned on me. It wasn't just a room going up in smoke, but the whole warehouse. I immediately thought, That's the end for Ivy too. It very nearly was, because after the fire in October 1975 I was written out for a spell.

Mavis's death scene was spectacular. I hope she'll forgive me, but it was a marvellous thing to watch. I had never seen such a dramatic special effect in my life. The episode ended with her walking through the warehouse door and the next minute a ball of fire blasted through it onto the street. I'm not giving away any big secrets when I explain that after she walked through the first door she went through a second door and after she'd gone through that to safety the pyrotechnics boys created their explosion.

Being a pyrotechnician in television must be one of the most fun jobs in the world. They are called on to create huge fires or explosions as special effects – it's like being well paid to enjoy Bonfire Night every week. A couple of years ago they did another great fire and explosion on the Street when Des Barnes poured petrol over a motor boat.

After Mavis went up in smoke, so to speak, they introduced her husband Fred Gee. He was played by an old sailor called Fred Feast who had already appeared on an occasional basis, but was set to become a regular like myself. They also brought in a husband for me, a chap called Bert Gaunt, who used to play the piano for me when I worked at the Dragonara at Leeds. Years later when I landed a full-time contract with Peter Dudley as my husband Bert Tilsley this chap sent me a hilarious letter saying: 'Dear Ivy, I am very surprised to find out that while you are still married to me you have another husband and a son I know nothing about. I don't ever recall the black negligee or having the pleasure of you in it. The lad has turned out nice, but he doesn't look anything like me.' The letter went on in a similar light-hearted vein and ended 'Yours fondly', which was very sweet of him.

On the day of the fire Eileen Derbyshire, who plays Emily Bishop, went down with a fit of the giggles, and it infected a few of us. Now Eileen is very much a lady who keeps herself to herself. I probably know no more about her today than when I went into the show twenty-three years ago. She is a very private person indeed. But she does have a very dry sense of humour. On this particular day one of the extras touched a nerve with her as we shot the evacuation scenes following the tragic blaze. The flames were supposed to be approaching liquid gas tanks and the whole of the Street was in jeopardy.

The extra in question was an ageing chap who had one line to speak: 'Is this where the tea and sandwiches are?' This old man kept repeating his line and every time he did it his voice got deeper and he got louder and louder.

Eileen thought it was hilarious. She was serving the tea and she couldn't hold the tray still, she was laughing that much. I was supposed to be crying my eyes out after discovering Mavis had perished in the blaze as Julie Good-year and Betty Driver brought me in, but both Julie and I were wetting ourselves.

This extra just kept increasing the volume and we could hear Eileen shaking with laughter as the teacups clattered together. She was having a really hard time controlling her chortles and I had to put plasticine between the cups to cut out the rattling.

Then all of a sudden someone noticed this fellow wasn't wearing the hearing aid he'd arrived with. He was deaf and didn't realize how loud he was talking, poor old sod. He'd taken it out because he didn't think people wanted to see deaf aids on TV. He was instructed to put it back in and somehow we finished the shot without giggling – although I had to keep my face down during the filming in case someone set me off.

Eileen was just like Jean Alexander, who played Hilda

Ogden – when something set her off that was it. Jean was a smashing character. There was no edge with her at all. She was so different from her nosey screen persona, but she had given Hilda her own mannerisms. She was greatly missed by many of us when she left the show in December 1987 after twenty-three years.

She and her screen husband Stan, played magnificently by Bernard Youens, were for me the greatest comedy double act of all time in British soap. Bernard was a smashing chap, who was a very accomplished bridge and Scrabble player. He had awful arthritis in his knees and never walked round much after filming. I'd get him a sandwich from the canteen during our lunch breaks and a couple of small bottles of Bell's whisky.

His portrayal of Stan the working-class slob made him a national institution. They even set up a Stan Ogden Appreciation Society down in Newton Abbot and members referred to him as 'the greatest living Englishman'. Bernard was sixty-nine when he died in April 1984.

After the inferno scenes I was written out of the show for over a year, but was still as busy as ever on the cabaret circuit. I was to return to the Street in 1977 after Mike Baldwin opened up his jeans factory. It was great to be back. It was just like rejoining a load of long-lost pals. Pat Phoenix summed up the spirit of the cast in those days when she said, 'If you kick one of us, we all bleed.'

I immediately hit it off with actor Johnny Briggs, who played my nasty screen boss Mike Baldwin. Ivy always spoke her mind on *Coronation Street* – something I had in common with the character. It was the producer Bill Podmore who wanted Ivy back to play the part of the factory's sharp-tongued shop steward. I used to love working with Johnny and we had a lot of great scenes together. I was in my element as the vigilant union rep, and the part of the penny-pinching boss was made for Johnny.

Ivy was always trying to get the better of Mike, but he always came out on top. It was to work out that way off screen as well when we argued. Johnny is very like Mike in as much as he's very good at getting his own way. We used to clash regularly for the cameras, and I always looked far worse on the screen. Johnny was filmed by a camera above him as he sat down and I was always filmed from below as I stood up. The type of filming they used on me was known in the business as 'nostril shots' and they were awfully cruel, highlighting and exaggerating every line on the actress's face. It took me months to work out why I looked extra worn on the box. Those shots gave Ivy her granite face and made her look such a hard cookie during union negotiations.

A few actors and actresses in the show know how to hog the camera. My first run in with this kind of behaviour happened during scenes in the Rovers Return with Doris Speed who played pub landlady Annie Walker. Doris always positioned herself right in front of the camera; she'd check she looked all right in the monitor then launch into her lines. If you were standing beside her she wouldn't give you so much as a glance as she spoke to you. It was very disconcerting. I had always been brought up to look at someone when you talk to them. She had this style down to a fine art – she was absolutely wonderful at addressing all her words to camera. There were occasions when I felt like tapping her on the shoulder and saying, 'Doris, I'm over here.' But you daren't, because you always had a lot of respect for the stalwarts in the show.

Others in the cast were far easier to work with. My favourite will always be Pat Phoenix, who played my screen supervisor Elsie Tanner. We had some hilarious times together over the years.

One funny, yet very painful, incident sticks in my mind. In the script Ivy was involved in a blazing row with Elsie. I was sitting at a sewing machine and Pat was standing beside me when I suddenly felt a pressure on my index finger. I guessed that the needle foot that holds the cloth in place while you sew had jammed onto my hand. The next minute Pat, God bless her, looked down at the machine, went grey and keeled over.

I had been trying to carry on with my lines until this point when I tried to stand up to look at Pat over the top of the machine. I couldn't get up at all, because the needle had gone right through my fingernail and through the finger. I was pinned to the table, with the needle bent like a fish hook underneath so I couldn't pull it out. There was blood everywhere, and the sight of that had made Pat pass out.

Johnny Briggs had come across by this stage to have a nosey and the first thing he said in his usual chirpy style was, 'you'll have to pay for those jeans.' I wasn't in the mood for laughing. I was whisked off to hospital to have the needle removed, but returned to the studios afterwards to finish filming.

Coronation Street has always been full of fantastic characters, but I was overjoyed one day in the canteen to meet a very old friend of mine. I had just walked in on a break to pick up a sandwich when I saw top cabaret artiste Jill Summers having a cuppa.

I had met Jill years earlier in Liverpool when I was doing the clubs and she had been very good to me. I walked over to say hello and ask her what she was doing. I was delighted when she told me she'd landed a part on *Coronation Street* working as a cleaner alongside Hilda Ogden at the newly opened Capricorn nightclub.

Jill is one of those characters who are larger than life. She once had her own TV series called *Summer's Here* and was a very big attraction on the clubs. She has a blue rinse hairdo on the screen as Phyllis Pearce, but off camera she has the bluest tongue imaginable. Women after they've passed a certain age can get away with all kinds of bad language without anyone saying anything to them. Jill is now in her eighties and falls safely into that category.

When I first met her she was in her fifties and it was in the dressing room of a beautiful club called Allinson's at Litherland, Liverpool. The only problem with this place was that it didn't have any toilets in the dressing room. There wasn't even a sink, because in other clubs when you were really desperate you could always use that if needs be.

Many singers and artists are the same, they find that they need the loo just before they go on stage. If you don't go you simply have to shut it out of your mind for an hour or so and then two seconds after you finish you need the toilets straight away.

This particular day I had on a very flamboyant turquoise outfit in a beautiful silk material, with diamantes down the sides and ostrich feathers round the arms and neck. It had been made for me by a friend, Barry Anthony, who worked on the clubs himself as a female impersonator. It had cost £450, which was a lot of money then, and I didn't want the audience to see it until I made my entrance. But I was desperate for a wee and the only toilets were out at the front of the house.

Jill realized my predicament and said, 'Hang on. I've got just what you want.' She got a chair and reached into her case on top of the wardrobe and lifted down what appeared to be a hat box full of wrapping paper. She undid the wrap to reveal a very ornate glass with glitter and custard yellow stuff round the rim, like the ones you sometimes get on special offer from petrol stations.

This glass smelt very strongly of Dettol. It was horrible. I asked her what I had to do. She looked at me with raised eyebrows and said, 'You hitch your skirt up and put it down there and piss in it.' I said, 'I'd never done it before,' and she said, It's either that or go out front.' I put the glass under my skirt and started weeing.

All of a sudden I felt my hands get very warm and wet

and a big patch appeared on my dress. 'You dirty sod,' said Jill. 'Why didn't you cut yourself off?' I looked at her a bit puzzled and hurriedly handed her this glass full of pee. She matter-of-factly threw the contents through the window before rinsing the glass with disinfectant and carefully packing it away. Meanwhile, I went and stood beside the radiator to dry off the damp patch like a naughty schoolgirl. For years afterwards she was telling everyone this story about me wetting myself.

I'll never forget the first time I saw Jill use the glass, which was later that same Sunday afternoon. Just after she got it out there was a knock on the dressing room door and a chap wanting a word with her. Jill by this stage had the glass under her skirt, but said to let the chap in. He started discussing dates with her and she had her diary out. I thought she must be holding it in. She told the fellow she'd meet him in the boardroom to discuss cash and waved him off. As soon as he'd gone she slipped out this glass full to below the brim. I was amazed – she'd been peeing as they talked. I was so impressed that I had to ask her how she knew when to stop and she explained it was just something you learn.

She asked me where I was staying and I gave her the name of some showbiz digs in Liverpool. She told me to cancel the accommodation, because I was going to Southport with her. She booked me a lovely double bedroom at the hotel, but I wasn't prepared for what was going to happen the next morning at breakfast.

We were in the main dining room and there was a coach load of about seventy pensioners filling up the rest of the seats. Jill followed me into the breakfast area and asked in that gravel-voiced bellow of hers, 'Do you use talc on your crotch?'

I was flabbergasted. My face went beetroot red as I tried to hide my embarrassment. I blurted out quietly,

'How do you know?'

She said loud as ever, 'Because it's all over the fucking

toilet seats.' In front of everybody. I could hear the sound of pensioners choking on their cornflakes all round the room.

I loved her from that day. She was so open and honest. Jill was my kind of woman.

I later got invited to a really wild party at her lovely semi-detached house in Wakefield, West Yorks. You'd not think, looking at Phyllis Pearce on the telly, that she could host such a way-out bash, but believe me she did. It was bizarre in as much as there were beautiful women mingling with very straight men, and booze was flowing like water. They would get this weird mix of people together then sit back and watch the reactions during the conversations, as it dawned on each the lifestyle of the other. The girls would just be invited along as friends.

Jill made friends with everyone wherever she went – she was such a wonderful character. Years later after she'd become established on *Coronation Street* she still hadn't changed. She would be swearing like a trooper and nobody would bat an eyelid. I remember once being in company with her and the manager of Manchester's posh Midland Hotel and every other word was a rude one. But he just accepted it as part of her conversation.

I do vividly recall the day she shocked the Street's producer in the late 1980s, Mervyn Watson. He was a very quiet, grammar-school type, who has now moved on to a high-flying position with the Beeb. This afternoon Jill had been to the ladies and for a bit of mischief had hitched the back of her skirt into her bloomers. She came back into the studio and walked across the floor in front of him. His eyes started to pop at the spectacle he saw before him. Stunned Mervyn started nudging those round him and we were all pretending to take no notice. He said, 'Have you seen Jill?' And we said, 'Yes. What's the matter?' He wasn't the type to come out and say, 'She's got her dress caught in her knickers.' We just let him stew. It was ever so funny – Jill played the part of an absent-minded old dear to perfection on that day.

Days like that, filled with fun, make me very glad I took the contract with Granada when it was offered to me in 1978. Priscilla Johns, who ran the casting side of things, had been trying to get hold of me lots of times for appearances on the Street, but I could rarely make it as my cabaret work took me all round the country. She eventually got so fed up of chasing after me that she told the then producer Bill Podmore that if he wanted me he'd better give me a contract.

I have to say that whether to take the job on the Street at all was a close-run thing, because at the same time I was offered a good part in the John Schlesinger movie *Yanks*. My co-star in that would have been Richard Gere, and the film became a box office smash.

During wartime I had my own run in with the Yanks – well, one six-foot tall magnificent specimen of manhood from the USA, at least. It happened when I went up to Bradford to help out at my Auntie Winnie's pub. The place was packed to the rafters with American GIs, and their accents were fascinating to me.

I used to go and sit on the wall outside during breaks from helping out in the bar. And it was on one of those occasions that an American airman started to chat me up. I can have been no more than fourteen, but I knew what this chap was getting at. I was so thrilled by his deep Southern accent that I let him kiss me. I was very proud of that kiss. He looked a bit like Mel Gibson, only taller. I told all my friends about it back in Maltby, because everyone thought the Yanks were irresistible. It might have even gone further as I was so enchanted by him, but Auntie Winnie intervened. She'd seen enough local girls join the pudding club, so she sent him packing before anything developed, and ordered me back inside.

Derrick always used to liken me to Auntie Winnie, because she was a talker. She nagged and nagged at my Uncle George, who was forever saying, 'Yes Winnie, no

Winnie'. Derrick always said her nagging drove poor George to his grave.

So when I went along for the audition for *Yanks* at the Leeds Variety Club I had first-hand knowledge of what they were like. Schlesinger's right-hand man, Noel Davies, told me to go on stage and ad-lib. Afterwards I was told I should go along and meet John Schlesinger. But before the meeting I was warned he disliked actresses, I was told he preferred proper women he could mould into the part. I thought, Charming!

I met Schlesinger, who was a major name since the success of *Midnight Cowboy*, in a posh hotel suite. I immediately knocked him off balance by telling him that he looked just like Ronnie Dukes, except Ronnie didn't have a beard. He said, 'Do I really?' I said 'Yes'. Then he said, 'Who the hell is Ronnie Dukes?' I explained he was a tap dancer on the clubs, who did his act with a piano player and his wife who had a beautiful voice. So he said, 'I remind you of him?' And I said, 'Yes, except he doesn't have a beard.' Schlesinger didn't know what to make of it and simply said, 'Oh'.

Then he told me he wanted me to pretend I was in a telephone box and an American GI had tapped on the door to try and use the phone. So I just let fly: 'We've been in this war for four years, so don't be coming along at the finish thinking you've won it. And you can leave my daughter alone, because she's got enough nylon stockings to last her a lifetime.' I carried on in similar fashion. It all just flowed off the top of my head. When I came outside Noel Davies told me that Schlesinger loved it and there was a part for me as Mrs Sheldon, the corner shopkeeper. He told me that the five day's worth of script could be spread over five weeks, because Schlesinger liked me.

This left me with a dilemma when the Street offer came in. But my agent Barbara Priestland helped me make up my mind to take the *Coronation Street* job. She told me that for five weeks' work on the movie I could end up with just three minutes on the screen, but if I did eight scenes with *Coronation Street* I was virtually guaranteed that six would be shown.

I continued with my cabaret work safe in the knowledge that I'd soon be getting offered a contract by Granada TV, but I never dreamt that I'd also get to play a part in *Yanks*.

I was up in Scotland working at a nightclub created on the site of the old airport at Aberdeen. In those days I used to drive home no matter where I was appearing, so after motoring through the night I arrived back in Maltby at 5.30 am. Derrick told me that Stan Josephs from the City Varieties wanted me to be at Keighley, West Yorks, at 7.30 am. I said there was no way and he could 'tittle off'. Until Derrick mentioned the magic word: it was for *Yanks*. As soon as I heard that I thought, I'm not going to bed. I was so excited I couldn't wait to get going.

When I arrived to discover the part was just six words I thought, I am not doing this. I rang my agent Barbara, furious, and said, 'the character hasn't even got a name – it's just "woman in railway station" – and there's no way I am doing it.' Barbara told me straight: 'Shut your face. You are getting a week's wages for those six words.' It worked out about £70 a word.

To top it all, my only line stole the show. It was used in all the reviews. Barry Norman showed it and in the States the line apparently drove them crazy. The line came in a scene where a pregnant girl is being walked along the railway station and this chap says, 'Make way for my girlfriend. She's pregnant.' My character then says, 'So is half the bloody town.'

After I gave up the part in the film Priscilla Johns' pressure for me to be given a contract paid off and I was signed up by *Coronation Street* for three years. In the space of twelve months I was to get a new family on the screen, but away from the cameras the death of my mum was to cause heartache.

CHAPTER TEN

Tilseys Arrive at Number 5

Pat Phoenix saw me just before the press conference and shook her head. 'You need to look a million dollars if you're announcing your arrival full time on *Coronation Street*,' she said. ''Ere you are chuck. Throw this over your shoulders,' she said as she passed me her magnificent mink coat. 'If you're going to do anything, my dear, do it with panache.'

That was Pat's by word – 'panache'. She had dashing style in abundance and no one could match her. I was often the willing recipient of her fashion advice. As she stopped cars and trucks during the rush hour with a wave of her almost regal hand, I was the dumpy housewife chasing behind her yelling, 'Pat! Don't go too fast. They can see you, but I'll get killed.'

The new family on *Coronation Street*, the Tilsleys, met the press and told them they were buying Deirdre Langton's terraced house at number five for £7,000. Everything went swimmingly as we posed for pictures skipping arm in arm along the famous Weatherfield cobbles. I played the part of the elegant actress as best I could. I'd had media attention before, but never this much.

All of a sudden I noticed the PP embroidered into the

mink. I desperately tried to hide Pat's initials. I didn't want the gentlemen of the press thinking it was a case of knickers, but no fur coat. Pat, on the other hand, was a case of fur coat and no knickers' – she never wore any pants.

The first scene we shot as a family was at Christmas 1978 when I was stood on the cobbles and said, 'What do you think then, our Brian?' He replied, 'It looks all right to me, mam.' I told him, 'Well, I think we are going to buy it.' And that was it. The Tilsleys had arrived.

My Street family – husband Bert, played by Peter Dudley, and son Brian, actor Chris Quentin – were to provide me with much happiness. They gave me the warmth and love I was missing at home. Derrick remained as aloof as ever. He liked the dough from Granada, but wouldn't dream of moving across the Pennines to be with me. On screen the Tilsleys were going to be dealt as much trauma as I was to get in real life. It's sometimes hard coping when your whole life seems to be filled with grief and aggravation.

At first I enjoyed a honeymoon period on the show. I was the barbed union boss and later the meddling mother-in-law when Brian married Gail. Poison Ivy was making her mark on the Street. When I started out, Bill Podmore told me he saw me as a second Ena Sharples. I never wanted that. I was determined to become the first Ivy Tilsley. I've never been content to settle for second best.

Chris Quentin was like a son to me. He always sent me a card and flowers on Mother's Day. He was ever so sweet, and like a mother I was proud of how well he was doing. He was a good-looking young lad and the women went mad for him. He'd just have to walk along the street and girls and fully grown women would swoon. He always used to send me these massive bouquets and I'll never forget what was written on the first. I saved the card, which said, 'If I had not got a mum and had to have another one I would love it to be you.'

He was a real gymnast and must have been very athletic in bed, although I never found out at first hand. We didn't have that type of relationship. We would talk about the separate nights of passion we'd had when we got together in the studios. And I'd go on stage during my cabaret slots and say. 'Have you seen that son of mine, Brian? He does sixteen backflips for a girl even when he's trying to say no.' Oh God, he was energetic.

But the trouble with him was he'd extended the top half of his body a good bit more than his legs with all the workouts in the gym. In my eyes he was always a little out of proportion. But his popularity as a heart throb was greater than any of the good-looking young actors we've seen since in the Street. He lost a lot of money when the restaurant he opened went bump, but Chris worked really hard to pay off his debts. Afterwards he became more careful with his cash and vowed not to let it happen again.

In those early years on the Street I carried on doing cabaret and made personal appearances as I revelled in my heightened fame. Peter Dudley or Johnny Briggs often accompanied me on my PAs. Johnny was always happy to have me signing autographs at the front of the car show-rooms or wherever we were while he spent time hob-nobbing with the directors, trying to do a deal. He was always out for a quick buck or a decent discount.

Then when his business was done he'd come out to the front and throw a few dozen autographed photos to the fans. I have always joked with Johnny that he's not aged since he played the part of an RAF man in a Sixties show. I reckon Johnny has a picture in the attic that's getting wrinkled and worn just like Dorian Grey had in the Oscar Wilde book.

Johnny has always been a cheeky swine. He'd come away from every PA with carrier bags crammed with goodies. When I asked what he had he'd say they were freebies he'd been given. I'd go mad with him: 'You sod – no wonder you allow me to do all those autographs.'

Peter, on the other hand, hated me spending ages signing photos after an appearance. He'd moan: 'You're spending too much time with the peasants.' I didn't agree, because without the fans the show would be nothing. I was happy to give them my time. After all them switching on their boxes at home earned us our bread and butter.

Peter had enormous style. He was a champagne and top hotels kind of person in private. He also had a wicked sense of humour. Many a time when I was preparing to put one of Ivy's grumpy faces on, he would turn to Chris Quentin just before we went on camera and say, 'Just look at your mother's face, son: Hitler in knickers.' Then we couldn't act for laughing.

Early on I regularly did Tuesday night shows at the Blue Dolphin nightclub in Filey and Peter used to drive for me. I'll always remember the night he knocked me right off my form when he interrupted my act with an outburst from behind the stage. I'd just finished singing when this voice over the PA said. 'Can I let your mother out of the cupboard? She needs a new rubber sheet in there, because the old one's all wet.' His timing brought the house down – they knew it was Bert from the Street. I said, 'I'll kill you when I get my hands on you, Bert.' The punters loved it. He was never happier than during his years on *Coronation Street*.

He was a proper theatrical type and had never experienced the cabaret star's intimacy with an audience. When I'd stop to sign 600 or 700 autographs after a show he'd be fuming.

On one occasion Peter invited me to dinner at the countryside cottage he had shared until recently with his boyfriend. We dined together before going off to a show, and everything was just right. The table was set like a work of art with all the correct glasses for the drinks. He really enjoyed his cooking and would have made a good chef if he hadn't been such a great actor.

It was agreed that I'd spend the night at the house after the show. I went down a storm during the cabaret and we celebrated when we got back to his place with champagne and Curaçao, the blue-coloured liqueur that tastes of orange peel. I'd also been drinking in the club and it didn't take much in those days to make me maudlin.

My real-life marriage was a mess. There was no romance and we'd been living apart since I started on *Coronation Street*. I spent my working days in the week staying at Manchester's Midland Hotel for the first couple of years. Every night I'd be out drinking to fill in the lonely hours, spending a lot of my time simply supping with my co-stars in the Old School bar – Granada's staff drinking club.

This night at Peter's house I got more and more maudlin as the drinking continued. I wanted a cuddle. A loving embrace from my husband Derrick was nowhere to be had and Peter my screen hubby was a more caring substitute. I asked him right out: 'Peter, can I come to bed with you? I don't want to screw you, just sleep in your arms.' He was gay and started to sober up immediately. He said, 'What?' I said again, 'I want to sleep with you.' He said, 'I'll tell you now you can't change me. It's been tried and it cannot be done.' I insisted: 'I don't want to change you. I just want to be close.'

Well, he put on his best Bert voice and said, 'Not bloodly likely, lady. Come here. Let's get you up these stairs, you've had enough.' He knew me only too well.

Once upon a time I actually believed that men were only gay because they had never found the right woman. Years later my son Stephen was to put me straight on that score.

Peter dropped me on the bed, and went down for a

couple more drinks. But when he came back upstairs he started moving the furniture in his room. He pulled the chest of drawers to the door and barricaded himself in the bedroom, pretending to hammer wooden planks across the door to keep me out.

The next morning he laughed about it. He thought it was hilarious. He feared I'd wake him up in the middle of the night with that determined glint in my eye and try to to get my wicked way. He told me that after hammering about for a bit he heard me snoring in the room next door and he knew he was safe. He said, 'When I put you to bed you were neither use to man, woman or dog.'

When he told me what I was like the next morning I couldn't believe I'd been so daft. But I used to get that way in drink. I'd be so legless that I'd never know even when I'd had a leg over. My lonely life as a Street star led me into a succession of brief flings – including one with a handsome leading man from the soap. But I'll tell you about my rampant sex life during my *Coronation Street* years later.

Peter, like me, was a big friend of Pat's. She helped him get about ten parts on the show before he landed the steady role of Bert. He'd played a disc jockey, a shop salesman, a sales rep and a host of other minor characters.

Roy Barraclough was another who had about five or six small parts before joining full time as Rovers landlord Alec Gilroy.

We had some great fun on the set and some of the storylines in the early 1980s were incredibly strong. The scriptwriters were never stale. Their stuff was the best in soap in those days. Poison Ivy came into her element after Brian married Gail Potter, played by the wonderful Helen Worth.

The plot when they moved into their new house was a *Coronation Street* classic. Three or four days after they had moved in Ivy was very angry at not having been invited round. In those days when Ivy was furious, I developed a trait of polishing the three brass jugs in the living room. It was her way of burning off that famous Ivy fury.

On this day Bert went out to the Rovers and bumped into Brian, who told him to bring me round for Sunday lunch to stop me moaning. On the way we popped into the Rovers for a quick drink – and bumped into Gail's mum Audrey who was there with her boyfriend. She said she was going to Gail's, but Ivy tried to put her off by saying they weren't in. Bert got angry with Ivy but she insisted they couldn't accommodate everyone as they only had four chairs.

As you've guessed, Ivy and Bert go round for dinner and Audrey arrives. Half way through the scene I had to storm out, taking my handbag. But as Sue Nicholls, who plays Audrey, enters, I noticed that the handbag was gone. The next minute it was back on the settee. As I tried to flounce off set, I couldn't pick up the handbag. Bewildered, I spotted Johnny Briggs in the corner laughing like hell with his cheeky face all crumpled up with mischief. And when I opened the bag I saw why. He'd packed it with a 4 lb stage weight, a tin of dogfood and a tin of asparagus from Alf's corner shop. Everyone was in pleats – if I'd pulled too hard, I would have wrenched my arm out of its socket.

The director, Steve Butcher wasn't in on the joke and he called for quiet. 'There is an awful lot of laughter down there. What's going on?' But nobody could tell him with a straight face.

There were always lots of practical jokes behind the scenes. I remember on Sue Nicholls' first day getting set up terribly by Julie Goodyear. Earlier in the day Julie had me looking at her bum for a boil. At first I said no way, because I'd read of Julie's reputation as a lesbian in the newspapers and I told her to go to the nurse. I told her to try looking in a mirror, but she said none worked and the one in the dressing room was too public. I even suggested she ask Peter Dudley, and she made out as if she was really hurt. She said, 'Well, you soon find out who your friends are.'

She appeared genuine, so I thought it'll do no harm if I have a quick look for her. She moved onto a set of stairs by the door and started manoeuvring her backside into my face. I was lifting the edge of her black gym knickers to one side and then the other looking for this lump.

All of a sudden I noticed she was shaking. I asked, 'What's up?' She was convulsed and I looked up and there was Peter Dudley bent over face to face with her laughing his head off. There was no boil – the pair of them had just put me on the spot, so to speak. I said, 'You swines, you've set me up. I'll never speak to you again.'

Later that day I went in the green room and Sue came and sat down. Now she is an honourable – the daughter of the former Tory MP Lord Harmar Nicholls – and ever so posh, but lovely with it, a real lady. As she sat down there was a ripping sound. And she said, 'Ooh Lynne, I think I've split my trousers. Will you have a look?' I said, 'Don't you start with me.' I really thought Julie had put her up to it. Then Julie looked across at Sue and pointed to me and said, 'Dyke, dyke,' indicating I was a lesbian – a real case of the pot calling the kettle black. So Sue got up and moved to a chair in the furthest corner. She never spoke to me all day, just kept looking at me. I said to Julie afterwards, 'You sod. You always set me up.'

Another time she had me going was when she and the fellow who played the milkman Harry Layton set me up in the Old School. I was sitting with the pair of them when this big coloured chap came and sat opposite me. He said 'hello' and I replied with the same. He then stared at me and said, 'Don't you remember me?' I asked, 'Should I?' He then mentioned the name of the Beaufront Hotel I used to stay in on the seafront up at Roker. I said, 'Oh, you're from up there.' And he said, 'I can't believe it. You still don't remember me.'

He then proceeded to describe the room I stayed in and all the equipment I packed in it. He was spot on. I never went anywhere without my sewing machine, sun lamp, slimming machine and rowing machine. By this stage I was getting to feel a bit uneasy. Julie and this other chap were sitting there straight faced taking it all in.

I wracked my brains and decided I couldn't have been that drunk that I've had this big black man and not remembered. Now in drink I did have one-night stands that were very hazy, but I was sure I'd have remembered sleeping with a black man. Then he proceeded to tell me, 'We had a lovely night.' I thought to myself, I don't want Julie to hear this. I said, 'I'm telling you, I don't remember.' This beautiful-looking young lad of about twenty-eight looked ever so hurt and said, 'I've never been forgotten before.'

Suddenly I turned round and these two beside me were killing themselves laughing. I asked them what they found so amusing and they told me they'd teed me up for it. Once again I'd fallen for a Goodyear practical joke hook, line and sinker.

Another of my Street pals in the early days was Liz Dawn, who played Ivy's battleaxe buddy Vera Duckworth. We'd first met during the filming of *Leeds United*, a play by the talented writer Colin Welland, who I'd worked alongside doing *Kes*. Coincidentally, in *Leeds United*, I played a shop steward who led the factory girls out on strike. That was the first Play of the Month to cost more than £250,000 to produce.

I hit it off with Liz, who played one of the factory workers, straight away – we got on like a house on fire. She's fun to be with, but she's scatty. I'd tell her a joke and she'd look at me with a glazed expression. Nothing had registered and I'd have to ask her if she'd got it. And if somebody else told her a gag I'd more often than not have to explain it to her. One of her performances when we were both on *Coronation Street* almost got me jailed. That was the time when Liz stood in the witness box at court for me in real life. I had to my eternal shame been charged with my second offence of drink driving. I enjoyed my booze, but after the first ban had sensibly concluded that champagne and motorized chariots didn't mix.

A salesman friend of Johnny Briggs, who wanted to bed me, spiked my drinks and that was what led to my downfall. I spurned his advances in a Manchester watering hole, but without my knowledge he'd been sticking double vodkas into my tomato juice. I even told the court I found this chap drunk and a bit offensive.

I was only nicked after nearly killing myself in a car crash. I know I would have killed myself if the drink driving had led to the loss of another's life, as so many do. In those days I used to get a train from Manchester across the Pennines to Sheffield and pick my car up at the station for the thirty-minute drive home to Maltby.

This particular night I actually fell asleep at the wheel of the car at a roundabout over the M1 motorway. Fortunately I hit a bollard as the motor careered out of control. That lump of concrete saved my life – it stopped the car falling about thirty feet onto the carriageway below. In 1979 it wasn't law to wear a seatbelt and as a result of not having mine on I knocked myself out when I hit the steering wheel. If I'd been any taller I could have gone through the windscreen, but sometimes it's a blessing to be petite.

I started coming round and there was this handsome blond chap tending to me. I kept drifting in and out of consciousness, but as I did so I managed to get a few words out. I kept repeating, 'Don't fetch the police, I think I've had too much to drink.' The effects of the alcohol had hit me after I came into contact with the fresh air at the railway station. I knew I felt tipsy but couldn't understand why, so I stupidly decided to drive home. Eventually as I lay there with blood streaming from a cut above my eye I came round long enough to hear this young chap's reply, 'My dear, I am the police.' If I'd been able to focus earlier the uniform, blue flashing light and panda car would have given him away.

I was taken off to hospital and the police were allowed in to breathalyse me. It was only afterwards that the nurse told me I should have pretended to be concussed, because she would not have let them wake me. I said, 'Thanks a lot. Why didn't you whisper that in my ear earlier?' I escaped from the crash with nothing more than six stitches in a nasty cut on my eyebrow.

The next morning I rang my agent Jack Denman from a hospital bed to cancel my work. I was in no fit state to go on stage. Jack was furious and thought I was pulling a stroke. The cheeky devil even rang me back at the hospital to check I was telling the truth.

I was fuming and told him, 'I almost died.'

In court a few weeks later I was to wish I had died shortly after Liz took the book in her right hand and said those words: 'I promise that the evidence I shall give shall be the truth, the whole truth and nothing but the truth.' Her performance had to be seen to be believed – it was so funny. I was sat there in my fur hat, trembling at being the star of this particular pantomime. We laughed about it afterwards, but at the time I saw a prison sentence staring me in the face.

Liz took to the stand and immediately after the oath there was confusion. The lawyer said 'Sylvia Ibbotson', which was Liz's married name, and they had to clear that up, because everyone recognized her as Vera Duckworth. Then she was asked how she remembered the night in question. Liz told them that was the day the pair of us had been chasing Pat Phoenix round trying to get her to open a bottle of German wine from a case she'd been given. She added that I couldn't have had a lot, because Pat wouldn't open a bottle. As she said this I started to sink into my seat. She told the truth but was completely gormless and had that blank look on her face.

She was then asked how she remembered the date and said, 'It was the day before my grandmother's birthday and we always put a thing in the paper, because she's dead now. And I know her memorial was the next day, so I know the day in question.' Then the lawyer told her she could come out of the witness box. She looked over at me and I sank lower and lower into my chair. I thought, I've had it now. Then she asked, 'How do I get out?' 'Same way you got in,' I replied curtly.

If she'd been the only witness I believe I'd have been jailed for three years. Luckily Johnny Briggs had done a good job on my behalf and told the court how his pal had spiked my drinks.

I had to subpoena the salesman to attend court, because it turned out his ex-wife was chasing him for about eighteen months' backdated alimony. He was furious, because the case made the papers and she caught up with him. It served him right for spiking my drinks.

The magistrates, God bless them, didn't jail me. The chairman of the bench, a middle-aged woman in a bile green hat, however, banned me from driving for three years and fined me £150. Afterwards Liz was triumphant. She said: 'I must have been good. They didn't even cross-examine me.' I told her straight: 'My barrister daren't because I'd have been put in bloody prison.' She was unperturbed and revealed how one of the people who spends all day listening to court cases from the public gallery told her she was one of the most honest witnesses he had ever heard in his life.

The court case drama was in December 1979. The month was to become even more traumatic for me. My mum had been in nursing homes for quite a spell. It was hard putting her into the hands of professional carers, but we had to for safety's sake. She was going dotty – a victim of senile dementia. As I've already mentioned, she died in spirit when my dear dad departed this life.

Our Keith had taken her off to Zambia after the funeral with the best of intentions. But it was the first time she'd been abroad and with hindsight it may have been wiser leaving her in familiar surroundings. She returned and I'd done all the sorting out at home, thinking, like Keith, that what I was doing was for the best, but looking back it might have been more sensible to allow her to face her grief in that house with those possessions of my dad's that meant so much.

After returning from Zambia she became more and more confused. I'll never forget the time she came to stay at my house one weekend and she put on a terrible exhibition in front of the TV set. It was a chilly night and I suggested changing my mum for bed in front of the fire. She looked at me and said, 'You can't undress me in front of him.' Derrick was out so there was nobody else there. I asked, 'Who?' And she replied, 'Reginald Bosanquet.'

I laughed nervously, thinking to myself she must be joking. But she was adamant. She had her back to the box, but she whispered, 'He's a lovely man. He comes to my house every day and says "good evening" and I say "good evening" back. Then just before he goes he says "goodnight" and I say "goodnight". He has lovely manners.'

I couldn't believe it. Here was my mum dressing up and looking her best for a dishy newscaster on the telly in the mistaken belief he could see into her room. I had to change her in the bathroom. I did her hair and had her dolled up to the nines. She walked back into the living room right in the middle of the news and smiled at the set before saying very deliberately and in her poshest voice, 'Good evening.'

Just before this bizzare episode, the neighbours in Vernon Road had been complaining about mum leaving her phone off the hook on the street's party line, so nobody else could make or receive a call. The final straw came when Myra, her next-door neighbour, found mum wandering down the road in her slippers and nightie during a snowstorm. Then we knew we'd have to get someone in to look after her.

We started off booking private nurses to go to the house until 10 pm, but they were putting her to bed at 7.30 pm and nipping off early. Next I decided she'd have to come and stay at the bungalow in Maltby, but at this time I was getting more and more entrenched in *Coronation Street*. Derrick took umbrage and moaned that he'd not be able to look after her while I was away at work.

So I made the heartbreaking decision to put mum into a home. We found a lovely private nursing home in Sheffield, and she enjoyed it at first. But after about six months she really deteriorated and all they did for her was get her up, wash her and sit her in the corner of this tiny room.

We heard about a new council home opening in Worksop and moved her in there. It was much better, because she was able to mix with the other residents. But she started saying she wanted to go home. I'd resigned myself to giving up the Street to care for her. But before I'd taken any action mother suffered two cerebral haemorrhages while she was in there and the doctors advised us against taking her home.

Then she got a clot in her leg and gangrene set in. She was very ill. Duggie and I went to see the doctor and offered to pay to have her limb amputated in an attempt to save her life. But the doctor explained that he wouldn't do that to his own mother. It hurt like hell when they turned her over. 'Please don't move me over,' she'd plead. But they had to move her to prevent bedsores, and she'd scream in agony. It tore us all too shreds, our nerves were in tatters.

The night before she died I stopped up with her. I couldn't sleep seeing the pain she was in. The next morning was New Year's Eve and I was working at Granada. I had to go and smile for the cameras, but my heart was breaking knowing my mum was close to death.

A couple of days earlier a nurse told me they'd put her on strong morphine to help her cope with the pain. She was lovely and caring and told me that the level of morphine mum was on meant that she had four or five days left to live at most.

Suddenly I jumped out of the make-up chair. I was compelled to phone the home. I got through, only to be told mum had died two minutes earlier. I was distraught. I found out later that our Keith had called Duggie from Zambia at exactly the same time to find out how she was. Duggie then rang me, because he didn't know I knew. Despite being miles and miles apart, we remained a family. We all made the phone calls simultaneously, a kind of telepathy between siblings.

I still cry now when I think how sad the loss made me feel. It wasn't a very Happy New Year for any of us. My mum wasn't together enough to appreciate my achievement in landing a role on the Street and my dad died before I hit the TV screens. He would have been more proud of our Duggie's success than mine. Duggie was always his favourite.

My life had already been thrown into considerable turmoil by the driving ban. I had just started hunting for a flat near the Granada studios when my mum died. I gave up looking. But later in 1980 my great friend Johnny Briggs, who was as big a wheeler dealer as his character Mike Baldwin, told me there was a flat going near his in the newly developed St John's Gardens, just a stone's throw from the studios.

Johnny was one of my regular boozing buddies in the Old School and I respected him for giving sound financial advice. He encouraged me to invest in this place close by. It was the beginning of the booming Eighties, and with Margaret Thatcher leading the country investments in bricks and mortar looked bound to grow. City centre properties were all the rage, so I bought one.

At about this time the name 'yuppie' was coined for the young upwardly mobile professionals who were springing up all over. They were moving into the flats round us. I quite fancied some of these repectable young chaps in their smart suits. I have always been one for younger men, particularly toyboy types with long hair.

Shortly after I moved into my swish pad I decided on a party for all my friends. It was a little cramped as the place only had one bedroom with a minute kitchen and a lounge and I was expecting about thirty-six people. But I was determined to make it go with a bang.

I put a half a dozen bottles of Dom Perignon in the fridge to chill, which was the best bubbly in the world at that time. Pat Phoenix was there and Julie Goodyear, and considering it was such a small bash they certainly made an effort in dressing up for the occasion. Mervyn Watson, Bill Podmore and Chris Quentin suddenly disappeared, though how they managed that in my flat I'll never know.

When I heard popping sounds coming from the kitchen, I had a fair idea what they were up to. I walked in and there were the three of them knocking back the bubbly on their own. 'This is the place to be,' said Chris. I told them I was saving the champers to give everyone a glass at the end of the night. There was plenty of other booze in the fridge, but oh no, that simply wouldn't do. Luckily I hadn't invited Derrick. I knew it just wouldn't be his scene. And thank God I hadn't – he would have died to see about £500 worth of bubbly disappear in less than an hour.

Liz was at the do and she was really sloshed. She'd get in states almost as bad as I did in those days. She bounced off people as she walked across the room and slurred, 'You got any Max Bygraves?' Everyone at the party was enjoying the modern stuff I had on the stereo, so drunken Liz got fobbed off. But she was in a real rowdy mood and seemed intent on causing a scene.

It wasn't long before that happened. Liz with her raucous voice asked Bill Podmore's girlfriend Millie for a cigarette. Now Millie has a very authoritative voice and she said, 'I hope you know you are taking my last one.' At this Liz got the hump and launched into an astonishing tirade. She said, 'Who do you think you are? Just because you are living with Bill Podmore doesn't mean you can talk to me like that, because you can't.' It was a terrible outburst and so uncalled for. Millie after all was handing over her last fag.

Millie took off and I heard her say, 'William, we are going home.' I asked what had happened and Millie said, 'Never mind, Lynne. It isn't your fault, love.' Millie went downstairs and Liz chased after her and tried to prevent her getting in her car. She was still stuck in the middle of her diatribe, reaffirming, 'It is only Bill Podmore can get shut of me.'

Her husband Don was doing his best to drag Liz away. He kept repeating, 'Sylvia, Sylvia.' He always referred to her by her real name – just like Derrick has always called me Jean. But Liz wasn't listening. She said, 'I don't care. She is not going to treat me like this.' It was a very big row. And as is often the case, it was all over nothing. We were all gobsmacked when Liz came in after Millie had gone and sat down.

At 3 am, after everyone had gone home and I was clearing up, the telephone rang. Liz had got home and realized as she sobered up what she'd done. As I picked up the receiver I heard her sobs. 'I'm going to get the sack,' she sobbed. I tried to placate her, but was well oiled myself.

The next morning she bought a giant box of flowers and sent them to Millie. But the dozy bat hadn't checked the spelling of her second name. She told me she'd made a second bloomer, but I calmed her down and told her Millie would understand. She knew, like the rest of us, what Liz was like after a few scoops.

I was always very houseproud and loved having visitors round for dinner at the flat. I remember once cooking roast beef and Yorkshire pud for Duggie, his wife Jackie and Johnny Briggs. My obsessive tidying came to the fore when Duggie popped to the loo. He came back and inquired where his glass had gone. I was such a busy body that I'd picked it off the table, washed it up and put it away – all in the space of a Jimmy Riddle.

Johnny lived just along from me. Peter Dudley was also to buy one of the flats nearby. We joked that we were turning St John's Gardens into Weatherfield. When I decided to move on, Johnny was at hand to sell me his-two bedroomed top floor flat. I'd decided on moving because I was fed up hearing the noise from the flat above.

A judge and his barrister wife lived directly on top of me. She would clatter round the wooden-floored kitchen in her heavy court shoes every morning and at night he had a very irritating habit of dropping his heavy law books on the floor. At first I thought he was taking off his boots when I heard a thud and I was waiting for the second bang.

It was only after I bumped into his charming wife on the stairs that I discovered he was dropping his books. She was one of the few people in Britain who didn't watch *Coronation Street*. She didn't recognise me – it was a pleasant change. When she asked me what I did for a living I had to explain I appeared on the programme.

This pair were more noisy than my new neighbours in the flat opposite Johnny's old pad. The girls across the hallway at Porchfield Square had hundreds of boyfriemds they entertained all day and all night. I recall several occasions when a member of the mucky mac brigade scarpered when I opened the flat door just as they were building up the courage to press the doorbell.

When I had a housewarming at that place I brought in outside caterers, but the flat was still too small to have the spread laid out inside. I commandeered the landing so they could set up the buffet there. Fortunately the girls were very discreet.

Johnny gave me a good deal on the flat – knocking £6,000 off the asking price of £45,000. I rang him late one night and he agreed to let me have the flat cut-price. I thought he must have had a drink, but the next day he'd remembered the conversation and said, 'Once I've given my word the deal is done.' That is Johnny for you – a man of his word.

He knew me better than anyone else on the Street. He knew I was an electronic gadget addict. If there was something new on the market I'd have to have it, regardless of the fact that I would be bored with it in a matter of weeks. So mischievous Johnny spread the word round the set that if anyone wanted anything electrical, all they had to do was rave about it to me. I would then send out for it, get fed up and sell it to them half price when they offered to take it off my hands.

One great gadget I bought was a knitting machine. It cost hundreds and I immediately went off on a week-long course to Bath to learn how to use it. Derrick thought I'd flipped, spending so much cash on the lessons. I stayed in a top hotel down there and was one of only three women on the course. One was an ex-headmistress from Ireland and the other was a Cockney market trader.

Well, they say the Irish are thick, but by the end of this course she was the only one who had made a jumper. A lovely job it was as well, with a great big black and white bulldog's head on the front. I'd knitted a collar and a couple of welts for the cuffs.

The Irish lady kept calling the instructor away to give her personal lessons every ten minutes, so me and the other girl Margaret decided on the first day to have a long lunch in the pub. She liked a drink as much as me and we got on like a house on fire. She invited me along to her caravan in the evenings. We'd drink and play cards until all hours.

It was really relaxing, a great break. Needless to say we never got much knitting done.

Derrick couldn't believe how little I'd achieved in the week after splashing out on the lessons. He was absolutely furious with me. I told him a little white lie and said I'd been praised for my splendid first-time efforts.

I'd told Johnny Briggs I'd knit him a golf jumper, and for weeks he kept asking me where it was. After a few weeks he said, 'Lynne, just knit me a scarf.' Time went on and I'd still not got round to it. Next time he asked about it in the Old School I told him I'd do him a willy warmer instead. He joked, 'That'll take all of an ounce of wool.' Everybody in the Old School heard it. There were a few raised eyebrows, I can tell you.

That's the way he was, a real character and always up to something. But we were both very lonely during those drunken years in the Street and spent a lot of time drinking and eating out together. Like me, Johnny was away from his family and also found it difficult to fill in the time. We found comfort in each other's company.

We were both pals with a chap who was on the management side of things before Granada started making lots of redundancies just after the TV franchises were announced in October 1991. I can tell the tale with impunity now he's left the company. I have always been slightly accident prone. But after smashing a finger in a fall on set, he told me it was possible I could take action against Granada. I told him I couldn't do it, but he said they were insured for such eventualities.

I'd tripped over a coil of electrical cable that had been left lying on the floor. I was eager to get into position for a shot with Liz Dawn and Eileen Derbyshire when I tripped and smashed my hand. Two fingers were mashed together in the tumble and my knee was aching. I got about £6,000 compensation for the broken fingers. I was stunned at the size of the payment, but having said that I'll have a wonky finger for the rest of my life.

I was so keen to continue my work that I insisted coming back on set with my fingers bandaged. But the first take during this row with Emily and Vera had to be reshot when I thrust my bound hand in the air. Everyone looked at it and for the sake of continuity it could never have been broadcast, because earlier shots in the scene had no sign of the dressing on. I kept my right hand behind my back and waved my left hand during the finger-wagging row. At the time they told me I'd get arthritis in the joint, and right enough I'm starting with a bit of that in the knuckle now.

Another embarrassing incident on set which I can now look back and laugh at is the time Liz Dawn held a cat which peed over a row of girls in the factory. Her character Vera had to hold the moggie up for the storyline, but the poor beast had been in a box for ages and as soon as it came out a spray of wee just washed all over about four of us.

The best of it was nobody jumped out of the way, because we were all mesmerized by this stream of piddle that was squirting straight at us. We just stood there wondering when it would stop. It was the last scene of the day and we had cat pee on our overalls and in our handbags. They had to send us home after that – nobody could work on with the awful smell.

I thoroughly enjoyed the Street in those early days. One night Pat Phoenix and her future husband Tony Booth visited my tiny flat. Pat was always one to speak her mind, particularly after she'd had a drink, and she started to slag off my taste in art. I had a painting as a centrepiece that she considered appalling and told me so in no uncertain terms. The next day she was ever so apologetic. I suppose Tony must have told her she'd overstepped the mark. But I wasn't upset.

When Geoffrey Hughes, who played binman Eddie Yeats, heard the story he said, 'She'll be outside your flat with a 9 ft by 9 ft Van Gogh.' Bless him, he was right, well almost. Pat presented me with a fabulous oil painting in a wonderful antiquated gold frame. She was always giving me presents.

I'll always remember the time I presented her with a leopard skin handbag after one of my cabaret trips to Africa. Pat accepted the gift graciously, but explained at that stage she was into beauty without cruelty so wouldn't be carrying the bag. I've got a lion skin bag and an elephant skin bag. I can't be doing with the anti-fur lobby and explain to them if approached that minks are pests and the best place for them is in a coat.

Julie was always amazed by Pat's generosity. After the incident with the painting Julie said to me, 'I wish she'd insult me – I could do with something like that.' On the surface Julie and Pat got on, but underneath I knew Pat wasn't a fan of Julie. She saw her as a young pretender to her crown as queen of *Coronation Street*.

Even to this day I describe the Rovers as Annie Walker's pub. I used to say that if I left the show I'd like to return as a gargoyle and they could put me on Annie Walker's mantelpiece. My views about that have changed over the years as you'll discover.

I always try to be nice to people. Courtesy costs you nothing, but can be very rewarding. I was always happy to chat with the girls in make-up or wardrobe. If you are pleasant with people you'll find a reward in it. Everyone behind the scenes of *Coronation Street* would natter with me.

My favourite backroom boy was Vinny McNally, a prop man, who had been on the show for over twenty years. He was a real friend to the stars and was particularly loved by Pat Phoenix. She adored him for his friendly conversation and pleasant manner. In the morning if I'd not had breakfast I'd nip into his room and ask him to rustle up some toast. He would always oblige and say, 'Yes, love. Do you want Marmite on it?' He'd go out of his way to do you a good turn.

He was a very quiet chap who spoke in hushed tones. When he popped on the set he would always whisper to us, 'Tilsleys are the best, Tilsleys are the best.' He was tremendously loyal, or so I thought. I later discovered he also used to say, 'Duckworths are the best' when he was on the set with Liz and Bill. The crafty sod must have been buttering everyone up, but a good word never does anyone any harm. The technicians were great and always asked me to sit with them in their corner of the Old School bar.

Drinking at Granada reminded me of my days with the ex-pats in Africa, where their social life revolved round booze. I'd decided the existence out there was empty and shallow. At the time of my greatest TV fame I hadn't realized I'd fallen into the same sort of trap. I reached a point where I was too tired to commute the two hours between Maltby and Manchester and started staying in the big city away from Derrick. I got into a habit of visiting the old pubs round the town to fill in my time. It wasn't an existence, it was a non-existence, but that hadn't dawned on me then.

There I was, a major TV star, and I was stumbling round bars, bored and lonely. I was lost for years in that alcohol-filled vacuum. While I was doing it I remember feeling very happy, but there was no lasting joy inside. I was actually living in fairyland with all these big stars off the telly.

It was a transient lifestyle. All the other actors and actresses were moving through and I was trapped there like a travelling salesman filling in time away from home – except my time away from home amounted to most of the time, and unlike a roaming sales rep I spent it all in the same city. Looking back I know I've missed at least fifteen years of my life when I could have been useful in other ways.

At the time you do it because in a way it is what is expected. The star's glamorous life takes you out every night, and while you are out you are inevitably drinking. I loved it when it was happening.

As you get older you get wiser. There is no point moping about what might have been. You have to face it that you can't alter what has happened. I was enjoying the boozing and with me being so small it didn't take much to leave me reeling. I drank with pals from the Street who had problems in their home lives as well. Solace is often found in optics behind a bar, in my experience. As my soap pals suffered personal crises I gave them a shoulder to cry on and a proper drinking companion. What more could an unhappy soap star want? But drinking to excess and to the exclusion of everything else makes you become very selfish. You don't realize it is happening. You just look after yourself and don't think about anybody else. My drinking was to get much, much worse before it eventually got better. In the eighties I regularly got into shocking states after boozing binges. Yet no matter how drunk I got I had a built-in protection mechanism of not allowing whoever dropped me home into the flat.

One night I'd had a lot to drink and decided it would be a good idea to weigh men's privates on the talking scales in the ladies' loo. Julie Goodyear was drinking with me at this stage and realized I'd had too much. She kindly helped me home.

Now I must have said to her, 'You're not coming in,' because that was an instinctive reaction. It was a standing joke at Granada that I never let anyone in the flat. But the next day Julie told everyone she had been inside. I told her she couldn't have, but she said, 'How come I know you've got an ashtray in a drawer beside your bed and you don't smoke.' I denied it, but she was right. I was so blotto that to this day I don't know what happened when we got back.

It's funny how when you're drunk you have the strangest habits. Mine was always putting my knickers in the bath. I could be out cold and I'd wake up to find my

Top left: Me and musician Derek Hilton – we kept the cast entertained at Street parties. When Julie Goodyear saw me walk in in that frock she said: 'What a f..king entrance!'

Top right: My darling skinflint Derrick. He's so mean he won't even buy a newspaper and goes to the bookies every morning to read them instead!

Above: My return to the Street after my brush with death. More than 1,000 fans turned up to wish me well.

Top: Freddie Starr – he pranced around the bedroom doing impressions of Adolf Hitler! *Above left*: Actor Tim Woodward lets me sniff his aftershave!

Above right: Roy Douglas (in white shirt) – he introduced me t[o] my first orgasm at 39.

Top left: My second screen husband Don, played by Geoff Hinsliff. 'You're too old to be with Don,' he told me.

Top right: Geoff was angry when I stole his limelight at the 30th Anniversary Party.

Above: Me, Geoff and Denise Black. Geoff was always asking the scriptwriters to let his character have an affair – he wanted Poison Ivy out of his life.

HOT FLUFF
THE WEBSTERS YORKSHIRE
BITTER CESAREWITCH

BELLE VUE 1990

My three great loves (apart from toyboys!) during my lonely years on the Street – the one armed bandits, the booze and the greyhounds.

Top: On honeymoon with Derrick in Blackpool. I was 19 and pregnant with Stephen – it was a shotgun wedding, but the only way my dad would allow us to get married!
Above: Me and Derrick on holiday in Jamaica – a far cry from the days when we had to scrimp and save.

Top: Derrick looked a picture – when I could tear him out of his old scruffy overalls.
Above: Our only child Stephen. It broke my heart when I found out he was HIV positive.

The whole Coronation Street cast at the Royal Command
Performance in 1989. Johnny Briggs and I were inseparable.

Top left: I wept on Julie Goodyear's shoulder after Manchester failed to land the Olympics.

Top right: Here's me reading about my cosmetic surgery in The Sun.

Above: One of my closest friends, millionaire businessman Kevin Horkin.

pants in the bath. If that happened I knew it had been a long night.

At the time when I was drinking myself into such ludicrous states I never thought I was doing anything wrong. It is odd how things change. Nowadays if I did that I'd be dicing with death. I fully understand boozing to excess is wrong for me.

In the mid-Eighties there was a lot going on in Manchester. The Stalker affair blew up surrounding the RUC's alleged Shoot to Kill policy in Northern Ireland. And amazingly I found myself in the middle of the police investigation into John Stalker, the deputy chief constable of Greater Manchester.

I'd been to a wonderful party up at businessman Kevin Taylor's sumptuous mansion home near Bury, just on the outskirts of Manchester. He'd sent a white Rolls Royce to collect me, and it was champagne all the way. The do was for his fiftieth birthday party and there was no expense spared. I sang for the guests and John Stalker accompanied me on the piano. Kevin was a pal from Manchester's Variety club where a lot of the Street cast drank in the 1980s.

This party hit the headlines in June 1986 because Mr Stalker was pictured with a shady gangland character called Jimmy 'The Weed' Donnelly. There was a big to-do about it, because Donnelly admitted contacts with Manchester's 'Quality Street Gang', the people behind most of the city's major crimes.

I was flabbergasted. Detectives from West Yorkshire telephoned and wanted to quiz me about the bash. They were looking into Mr Stalker's behaviour. He had already been taken off his two-year inquiry into the Royal Ulster Constabulary. A lot of people said he was getting too close to the truth and he was pulled off it for the purpose of a cover-up.

I didn't like the questions these officers were asking me.

I told them John Stalker had played the piano for me and he was a charming chap. Kevin Taylor was a respectable businessman. A picture was published somewhere of me in Kevin's giant swimming pool looking naked. But I told the police I was wearing a costume. It was just that the costume did not have straps on. I'd had a good drink at the celebration and couldn't remember every detail. But I am sure there was no funny business going on. The picture in the paper was the nearest I've ever been to becoming a Page Three girl. And at the end of the day both Mr Stalker and Kevin Taylor were completely vindicated.

I've always enjoyed a good party, but my boozing has got me into bother more than once or twice. The headline read 'Intoxification Street' over one story about my drunken antics on a night out at the lovely Foo Foo Lamar's nightclub in Manchester.

It was a Yuletide thrash and I confess I'd supped too much. I took to the stage to sing 'My Way', but told the assembled audience, 'I'm sorry I'm too pissed to sing.' My straight talking was what caused the problems. One of the revellers took exception to my use of a rude word. Me and my big mouth struck again – another own goal inspired by alcohol.

Peter Adamson, who played Len Fairclough, had been a big boozer in his time – a real hellraiser. But he reformed. He went to AA and dedicated much of his time to helping others beat the bottle. He always used to say I fancied him, which wasn't true. He was written out of the show in December 1983 for repeatedly breaching his contract by talking to the press after a very unpleasant court case. He was cleared of the charges against him.

The writers killed him off in a motorway crash. As the years went by a lot of Street regulars were to die on the roads. I often joke that the roads round Weatherfield must be the most unsafe in the world. At the time of writing I'm praying that Ivy doesn't go the same way.

The year 1983 contained a real-life tragedy for me as well when my screen husband Peter Dudley died of a heart attack. Peter had suffered awful stress after being accused of cottaging and committing a homosexual act in a public toilet. I firmly believe the charges against him contributed to his death.

He maintained his innocence and told me the only way a policeman could have seen into the public toilet was if he had stood on a ladder and peered through a window. The whole court took a trip to these toilets and had to climb a ladder to look through the window just as Peter said they would. And the fellow he was supposedly caught with had yellow boils all over his face. I just couldn't believe it was true, because he wasn't into acned adolescents.

A year earlier Peter had suffered a heart attack even before the charges against him were aired in court. He was never the same after that. But I'd visit Peter after work and cook him meals every night.

Granada couldn't be faulted for the way they looked after him. They paid him all the time he was off. The company is very good like that, as I was to discover later myself. He returned to work, but after the stroke he was unable to put any emotion into his voice. He did really well to return at all. Half his brain had been damaged and he was left walking with a limp.

Bill Podmore was forced to take action. By now the press had nicknamed him the Godfather of Coronation Street after Ernie Bishop was blown away in that robbery. But it just wasn't a fair description of Bill. He was a caring human being and a great friend to me. He came to parties at my flat and I regarded him as a pal as well as the boss.

I saw the caring side in action one cold night. I heard footsteps pass my window and looked out to see Bill going to Peter's flat next door. I thought, Oh my God, it's bound to be bad news, because Bill wasn't one for making unannounced home visits.

He called at my flat after Peter's and was really cut up. He told me he had suggested that Peter should get a smaller place which wasn't so expensive. But Peter said he was happy staying near the studios. Now Bill had gone there to give him the bullet and explain to him that Granada couldn't keep paying him forever. But he couldn't bring himself to do it. He said, 'I just couldn't tell him, Lynne. He looks so ill. He was very jocular with me and I hadn't the heart to tell him.'

Those were the words of a very considerate human being, yet people insisted on calling him the Godfather with its mafia hitman connotations. If he was the Godfather then it was for the way he looked after *Coronation Street* and the cast. He told me once he hated giving people the sack and only did it for the sake of the show.

Just before Peter passed away after a heart attack in his flat in October 1983, I had been hospitalized following a severe bout of angina. I collapsed at Manchester's Piccadilly railway station and was recovering at Salford Royal Hospital when Peter was brought in.

A nurse told me that my husband had been admitted. Now Derrick was standing in the room with me, so I guessed who she meant and quipped, 'See, he really thinks he's married to me.' When I discovered he had died of a massive coronary seven minutes after arrival I immediately regretted making that wisecrack. But with hindsight that's just how Peter would have wanted it. He was always so full of fun.

My collapse had brought Derrick back to my side, and we decided to try and rekindle our love for each other with a romantic second honeymoon. Against doctor's orders I flew to Antigua in the Caribbean and to my amazement was greeted by a *Sun* reporter on the beach. This chap called Nick Ferrari, dressed ever so smartly in his suit, came across the sands to me and Derrick and introduced himself.

He'd been sent to cover the US invasion of Grenada,

but was diverted to Antigua when he found out I was on the island. I couldn't believe it. There was America on the verge of war and I was the centre of this reporter's attentions.

As the years rolled by the Street started falling more and more under the media spotlight. The soaps are probably more popular today than they have ever been, and that is in part due to the focus the media puts on the shows. I often say to fellow professionals on the Street, 'Don't knock the press. We need them as much as they need us.'

When I returned from Antigua I was amazed to see snaps of Derrick and myself all over the *Sun*. It was like having your holiday snaps published before you'd taken the film to the developers. The reaction we got from people was tremendous. As we walked through the airport everyone was staring at us. They all knew we'd just been on a second honeymoon.

I arrived back at work and had to do some really harrowing scenes: the death of Bert in hospital. It was all so close to the real thing. I genuinely broke my heart crying. Bill Podmore had insisted that the scenes be done as delicately as possible to spare Peter's loved ones any further heartache. Peter had such charisma and was so warm I suspected they would never be able to find someone to fill his shoes. Ivy was to go through a period of loneliness and I had plenty of experience to call on.

At the same time I was losing my big pal, Pat Phoenix. She wanted to do other things and was written out. In the show she met up with her old flame Bill Gregory and they went off to Portugal together.

Her final generous gesture to me was bequeathing me her dressing cubicle. In 1984 when she left we did not have dressing rooms, just cubicles in the bonded warehouse. Pat pinned a note up with her bequest. The cubicle opposite was Johnny Briggs', and when nobody was looking he sneaked over and wrote on it: 'As long as she keeps quiet.'

Some other wag then inserted on the note: 'Very quiet.'

Pat revealed she had been suffering from pleurisy before she left and had not been at all well. But less than two years, later in September 1986, she was lying on her deathbed, a victim of cancer. I had planned to visit her, but Tony Warren, the creator of *Coronation Street*, told me the doctors didn't want anyone to see her. I later found out he had seen her and Jill Summers had visited and all Pat was asking about was my whereabouts. I really wish I had made the trip. Tony later told his story to a newspaper and I was upset because she died the day after he told me to stay away. I think Tony was trying to protect Pat. He was a big friend and maybe thought she would rather not have people see her so ill.

She was given the last rites at the Alexandra Hospital in Cheadle, Cheshire, but still married her devoted lover Tony Booth. He was desolate after her death – as were millions of soap fans who still adored her for her portrayal of Elsie Tanner.

At her funeral I saw grown men weep buckets of tears. I saw Johnny Briggs cry for the first time on that day. Pat was buried in style – as I've said before, she did everything with panache. A jazz band played 'When the Saints Come Marching In' and her funeral was a proper showbiz occasion.

Julie Goodyear and I both attended without any knickers on. We did it as a tribute to a great actress and a fantastic friend.

CHAPTER ELEVEN

The Sunny Side of the Street

I had made lots of friends on the Street, and it was wonderful when we were reunited for the thirtieth anniversary. It had been billed the most glamorous, star-studded bash for years – hundreds of celebrities putting on the glitz to celebrate Coronation Street's thirtieth birthday. Anyone who was anyone would be there – many big names from the world of film and television, politicians and three decades of Street stars reunited for the first time. Cilla Black was to host the party, the Queen had sent a good luck telegram and Cliff Richard would sing Happy Birthday via satellite live from his concert at Wembley Arena. And to top this fantastic accolade, it was all to be captured on camera for network television.

There hadn't been so much activity around the studios for years. The whole place was buzzing in anticipation. But the orders to the cast from the powers that be at Granada were loud and clear: *everyone*, must be there without exception – and make sure you look the part.

Look the part? That night was the first time I had ever been called glamorous by a newspaper in my life – let alone since I joined the Street as dowdy housewife Ivy. I'd really gone to town, as everyone had, to make this an extravaganza to rival any Hollywood party. I knocked 'em dead with my gold lamé jacket and new wig. I felt a million dollars in it – but little did everyone realize that I'd borrowed it from a drag queen pal who used to wear it as part of his act.

We were all expecting a lavish buffet with caviare, smoked salmon and lashings of champagne. It was the least we could expect for such an occasion. After all we were celebrating thirty years of being Britain's top TV soap. Instead we were greeted with huge vats of the Rovers' hotpot served on paper plates with plastic forks. Of course, the TV cameras didn't catch that spectacular event on film. And it was spectacular – what with us tackling supper in all our finery and jewels. Everyone was starving by the time the speeches had ended, until they wheeled out the grub and you could hear everyone groan, 'Oh, no! Betty Turpin's bloody hotpot!' But there were hundreds of people there and to water and feed them all with the best would have cost Granada an arm and a leg.

What a shame Pat Phoenix couldn't have been there to give it that touch of panache it so desperately needed. I still believe we should have dusted off the cobbled stone image and put on a bash worthy of the occasion. Instead it smacked of penny-pinching. We were offered just one glass of champagne – except for a quick toast when Doris Speed, who played the original Rover's landlady Annie Walker, made a special appearance and got a standing ovation when she walked onto the stage.

That was a very touching moment for us all. Doris was almost ninety and not in the best of health, yet she had made the effort to come along knowing the night wouldn't have been complete without her. The tears streamed down my face and I even saw a few hardened actors shed a tear or two.

After the formalities, the cameras were switched off and the fun was supposed to start. We'd all been sat there for what seemed like an eternity while the show was filmed, and were gasping for a drink. So by the time the party began, the queues to get served were about a mile long and the chance of getting so much as a sniff of the barmaid's apron were so remote it didn't seem worth it.

Derrick was rather pleased. He hardly ever had a drink, and instead suffered in silence as I made up for the both of us. Greyhounds were his only vice. And it was always a relief for him – and his earholes – when I couldn't get my hands on a bottle.

Needless to say it was good fun being back together again, and we had a giggle. It was wonderful to see all the old faces – Michelle Holmes, who played Rover's barmaid Tina Fowler, Doris and Chris Quentin whom I'd hardly seen since he quit the show as Brian Tilsley in 1989.

I loved Chris like he was my own son. As I've said, there was always a close bond between us, though it was nothing sexual. But we used to lark about and flirt a lot anyway, it was in both our natures. It hurt me terribly when I found out via a newspaper report that he was to be axed from the show while he was away on holiday in the States. He came back and asked me if I knew what was going on. But I didn't have the heart to tell him that I'd had words with the powers that be, and that the papers were right. He was out of the show.

'Surely they wouldn't have brought me back from America just to kill me off?' he asked over and over again.

'I don't know son,' I lied, not able to look him in the eye. 'You'll have to ask the producer.'

It left for a very dramatic storyline for his departure. Brian was stabbed to death outside a nightclub after being caught in a clinch with a mystery blonde. His behaviour towards me, however, on the night of the thirtieth party was something my husband Derrick found very offensive. It almost ended up in a punch-up. Chris grabbed me round the waist, bent me over a table and started to thrust his pelvis into my backside. I knew it was just a lark –

and that Chris had obviously succeeded in finding a drink or two where I had failed.

From the corner of my eye I could see Derrick was getting a little hot under the collar. Understandably, he didn't always feel comfortable in the company of actors – luvvies who acted the goat and did anything for attention. And he didn't take it too well when Chris started making rude suggestions, saying: 'It would be like f...ing my own mother.'

'Go back to Middlesbrough and try it with her then,' I'd retorted as I tried to push him off.

But Derrick was not amused. He grabbed Chris by the scruff of the neck and clipped him round the ear, saying, 'That's enough.' Chris looked stunned and walked off sharpish. But there were no apologies from Derrick. 'Get your coat,' he snapped at me. 'We're leaving.'

So we left. The most memorable event in the show's history and for the first time I was forced to take an early, and sober, cut.

Granada had had a party every year, but nothing as fancy as the thirtieth anniversary. The birthday celebrations usually ended up with me, Liz and Bill Tarmey entertaining the rest of the cast with a song or two. Not that we ever got any thanks for it. I put a stop to that after the twenty-fourth bash after I overheard one of the cast saying, 'Oh no, not her again!' I wouldn't mind if I was getting paid for it, but it was a free show. I thought, Sod this for a game of soldiers. I wouldn't have gone to it but for Johnny Briggs pestering me to go along – he threatened to drag me along if I didn't show up. We were like a double act, Johnny and me, and we had a good laugh together. He was always looking for a partner in crime.

I had been looking really frumpy as Ivy and so I decided to make an effort with my own appearance. I have always been a method actress and I didn't like to wear wigs to make my character look dowdy. So I let my dark roots grow because not many women can afford to go the hairdresser's every week to have their hair tinted – and being realistic, neither could Ivy. I liked my character to be as realistic as possible.

But that wasn't conducive to a glamorous night on the town where all the co-stars of the show were naturally, though unwittingly, competing to steal the show. I had my roots bleached and my hair totally re-coiffured and bought the most amazing evening gown you could imagine. It was beautifully tight-fitted with pleated chiffon, a typical Rita Hayworth number in shimmering white drapes. I'd seen it so many times tempting me from its home, a tiny boutique in the city centre near to the studios. It was a size eight – but I was determined to shed a stone and have it for myself, even though it cost £750.

I dieted for weeks to get into that frock, and after a full manicure, facial, body massage and hairdo I felt like a million dollars when I walked into that do draped in my new fox fur and covered with diamonds. Unfortunately I was a little late. I could hear the speeches going on inside and tried to creep up the stairs and through the back door not wanting to make too much of a fuss. I thought they would all be standing round the podium with their backs to the door. But as I walked in I realized to my horror it was a sit down meal – and everyone was facing me. My face must have been a picture as I stood in front of all those people, but Pat's words came back, and I was after all dressed to kill: 'Panache darling, always do it with panache.' I smiled, sauntered to my seat and joined Johnny.

Julie Goodyear walked over to me, shaking her head, and said, 'You sod. What a bloody entrance! You stole the show.' I'd wanted to keep a low profile. In fact I hadn't been there long when I decided to slip out quietly. As I made my way towards the lifts, David Plowright came up and said, 'You have not sung for us yet, Lynne.'

'No, and I'm not likely to,' I replied, always with a little more courage once I'd had a few drinks. 'I could have been earning £600 tonight at the Flamingo Club in Blackpool and I turned it down to come here – and if you think I'm singing here for nowt, you've got another think coming.' Of course, me being me, I got up, did a turn and entertained the troops.

I missed the next party when Bill Podmore ordered me to stay at home because I was ill. Wrapped up warm, I stayed in my flat and watched the fireworks from the window. Until the thirtieth, when we ordered to attend, I didn't want to go to any more. I simply lost interest in it all.

The drink totally transformed my personality. I would do and say things I'd never dreamed of when I was sober. I suppose it was the same with everybody. Except that four or five years ago I realized I was hardly ever sober. Drinking was part of my life, the lifestyle of a star. But I never touched drugs, even when they were offered to me.

Once I *had* innocently inhaled pot at a party in London with Pat Phoenix. All her friends were smoking marijuana joints and I got high because the room was thick with the acrid smoke. The next thing I knew I was out of it – and asking Pat to put me to bed. She couldn't stop laughing the next day, but I could remember nothing. 'Oh darling, you were so funny,' she said. 'You kept calling me mummy and telling me how happy you were.' I couldn't remember anything and that scared me.

I decided to steer clear of so-called recreational drugs after that. When I was offered cocaine by a famous actor I told him there was no chance. I had been invited by the cast of a new Granada soap *Families* to the trendy Manchester nightclub the Hacienda to celebrate the first series. The show was an absolute flop and didn't last five minutes. But as Johnny Briggs told me later, they'd only wanted me there to raise the show's credibility and profile.

'It's only your name they're after because you're a Street star,' he told me later.

I accepted the invite and jumped into the actor's Porsche. On the way he took a detour and we stopped at the flat he was sharing while he was staying in the city. I couldn't believe my eyes when we stepped inside. He took out a piece of folded paper and carefully laid the white powdery contents on the table and arranged it into lines.

'What the devil are you doing?' I asked, being as naive as ever.

'Watch,' he said as he rolled up a ten pound note and started snorting the stuff through his nose. 'Now your go. It'll do you good,' he said handing me the note.

'Not bloody likely,' I said as I pushed it away. And he was visibly shocked. He couldn't believe that a woman with a reputation like mine, a real party-goer, hadn't tried cocaine. 'And I have got no intentions of doing so, so when you're ready, we'll go to this club.'

Needless to say, Johnny was right. They just wanted a star hanging round with them – and someone to buy the drinks. I ended up footing the bill for practically the whole evening as I paid for round after round of drinks. I hadn't noticed at the time, but my purse was a lot lighter the next morning.

After that I thought I was even more clean-living than I had already kidded myself. So when on another night out my friend and regular boozing buddy Charlie Lawson said I drank too much, I took up the gauntlet. 'I'll give it up for two months,' I slurred.

Charlie laughed as I downed another brandy and Babycham and staggered towards him. Removing a diary from his jacket pocket, he opened it on the day of his birthday, saying, 'Sign here – and if you can stay off the booze until that date, I'll give you £1,000.'

He was a fine figure of a man, a fantastic actor with a RADA background. Sometimes he'd look so striking,

I'd think I was staring at a young Lawrence Olivier.

I scrawled my signature on the blank September entry and as Charlie helped me into my taxi he laughed: 'Take her straight home, driver – no stopping off for another – and make sure she's inside the flat before you leave.'

They were always his parting words as I slumped into the back seat of a cab. It was always Charlie who made sure I got home safely. He was more like a son to me than a workmate. He even called me mother. Don't get me wrong – Charlie liked a drink himself, but he was always there to make sure I didn't wake up under the same bar I'd drank myself into oblivion at the night before. He was a good pal – though he also knew I was a prime candidate for a wind-up on set when things were quiet. Not that he would ever say things were quiet when I was around. He used to abuse me about my incessant chatter.

Once Charlie bought a box of Trill birdseed, and while I was doing a tear-jerking scene with Don I saw the letter-box of the door open in the corner of my eye. I tried to keep my concentration, but suddenly there was a thud and this box of budgie seed hit the doormat. After I finished the shot, I took the box over to Charlie who was reading the *Independent* in a corner and emptied the bloody lot over his head. It went down his trousers, shirt and everywhere. He had to go into the toilets and take everything off and shake it all out. After that he said he'd buy me Swoop – food for eagles – because I was noisier than a budgie. He ribbed me constantly about my talking, but when I'd go off on holiday for a couple of weeks he'd say, 'We ain't half missed you, missus.'

One day I had a bet with Phil Middlemiss, who played bookie Des Barnes. He reckoned I couldn't remain quiet for five minutes. I lasted three minutes before I opened my blasted mouth. No one was surprised, least of all Charlie.

He was also a bugger for practical jokes. He regularly

used to move Ivy's religious relics around the set so they would be in a completely different place. One day the crucifix would be hanging on the wall above the fireplace, the next it would be on the sideboard. He would joke, 'No Papists in here' – a throwback to his early days in Northern Ireland, no doubt.

Once he moved the whole set of No. 5 to the other side of the studio. I'd gone on set one day and it took me ages to find the Tilsleys. I was walking round saying, 'That's not my furniture. Hang on, that's not mine. Where's everything gone?'

Another time he hung a huge ladle from the kitchen on the wall where the crucifix should have been and he turned the picture of the Pope back to front. If the viewers had seen some of the things he did they'd have been shocked. I don't know how I managed to keep my face straight – though I almost cracked up when I spotted Ivy's porcelain Cocker Spaniel mounting a statue of the Madonna on the mantlepiece.

But when he saw me worse for wear, his attitude changed and Charlie stopped larking around and became very protective towards me. 'Time to go home now, Mother,' he'd insist when I had too much to drink. And no matter how much I protested, Charlie always knew when enough was enough and I was taken home.

Many a man would, and in my case often did, take advantage of a woman in that state. But not Charlie, who was always the perfect gentleman. He even declined my offers of a late nightcap of Jameson's Irish Whiskey in case I tried to take advantage of him. Of course he always made a joke of it: 'You don't think you're getting me in that flat on my own, do you?'

It was a standing joke amongst all the young lads that I was a bit of a raver, and they all used to pull my leg. They'd all be worried I was after them, and of course I played up to it. But Charlie knew what I was like. He'd seen me in action with the young lads, teasing them, getting more and more drunk and seeing them take my indecent proposals seriously. And he kept a firm eye on me. I'd told him that before he came into the Street there were many times I'd woken up next to a complete stranger, cringing with embarrassment and totally unaware of what the hell had happened the night before. But my one-night stands and lust for younger men during those murky days of drink were a common occurrence and make a chapter of their own, which I shall tell you all about later.

By this time, I had earned myself the nickname Champagne Perrie for my drinking antics. The press started to focus on the fact that I was a good-time girl. I thought it was a giggle. Sure I liked going out, I liked a good drink, who didn't?

My 'problem' surely was nothing more than the fact I hated going back to the miserable two-bedroom flat across the road from the studios where I lived alone.

I wasn't the only one. Many of my colleagues from the show would end a long day with a relaxing drink in the Old School across the road from the studios. It's just that I stayed longer than most, that's all. That's how I fooled myself in those days as I drank myself into a stupor night after night – remembering nothing the following day.

I'd spent many drunken nights in the Old School. It was private for Granada staff, which meant there was never any shortage of famous faces inside. There were always stars filming for just a few days or weeks on a drama series, meeting up with producers or simply calling in to see friends. If autograph hunters had been allowed in, they would have been in their element. But it was a strict sanctuary for televison workers only, and was probably the only place for actors to escape the public gaze. We incurred the wrath of our TV bosses if we stepped out of line on the outside.

It was a lively bar, not plush or anything flash as you might imagine for a celebrity hang-out. It was down to earth and normal – and believe me, when you can't leave your home without being heavily disguised, normality was something we all yearned for. It seemed like years since I had been able to walk along the road without hoards of people swarming round for autographs or a chat. Even a trip to the supermarket for a loaf of bread or a pair of tights could become an utter nightmare. I'd be so pre-occupied trying to keep my head down that I would get totally confused.

Once I was in Sainsbury's getting a few items in my lunch hour from Granada when two women started staring at me. They had obviously recognized me, but I was in a terrible rush and simply didn't have the time to stop. You know that if you stop for a chat you'll be there all day as more and more people recognize you. That's only fair when you spend so much time in their living rooms – the viewers think they know you and they want to talk like old friends. That's fine if you're not in a rush, but I didn't have the time that day. I kept my head down as they started whispering my name. 'It's Ivy Tilsley. Look, it's Ivy.'

As the attention died down, I thought I'd got away with it, but as I made my way to the check-out I heard this almighty roar: 'That's not Ivy Tilsley,' shouted a ferocious old lady wobbling towards me with the aid of a Zimmer frame. She edged right up to my face and called me an impostor.

I would normally be pretending it wasn't me and would have joked: 'I wish I was. I'd love to have Ivy's money.' But I found myself chasing after her, defending my namesake: 'I am Ivy Tilsley. I'm telling you, it's me.' But she wouldn't have it. I felt extremely miffed.

There was none of that in the Old School, which was a haven from the outside world. There was always a hard core of drinkers left at the end of every evening, desperate for just one more for the road, much to the dismay of the long-suffering barman. He simply couldn't get shot of us. Still propping up the bar at the end of the night there would usually be me, Charlie and a handful of technicians.

The bar wouldn't open until five o'clock in the evening, but Johnny and I would manage to finish at three or fourish in the afternoon and we'd be gasping for a drink, or early doors as we called it. We'd ring the barman and tell him to let us in through the back door. Not that we were frightened of Granada catching us boozing so early. The bosses were quite lenient with us then and we could do more or less as we pleased – as long as we kept it from the watchful eyes of the public and the media. But in those days all-day drinking was against the law and we had to make sure we weren't spotted by the local constabulary.

By the time the rest of the actors started piling in, I'd be half cut. Of course the intention was always to stay for just one or two drinks, but it never quite worked out that way. That was in the days when I used to keep chilled bottles of Dom Perignon behind the bar because they didn't keep it in stock. In those days it was *the* champagne to drink – and it cost more than £70 a bottle – but I was tired of drinking the cheap stuff.

My reputation as the Granada lush had been born. My tiny stature meant it didn't take too long for me to get inebriated, so onlookers would think the three brandy and Babychams which had gone straight to my head were really a bellyful of champagne and a bottle of best Cognac. I was also taking pills for my heart and that simply speeded up the effect. My doctor was always telling me, 'Stop trying to keep up with the lads, Ms Perrie. You'll kill yourself.' In reality I was drinking the lads under the table. I never listened. I didn't care what anybody thought about me.

It didn't really help matters that once I started drinking I couldn't stop, and that sometimes meant carrying on all night. 'I'll stay just half an hour,' I'd promise myself, convinced I didn't need a drink. 'I'll just buy a pal a pint and have a quick chat.' Of course, the more alcohol I got down me, the more excuses I'd make not to go back to the misery of living alone.

Derrick had refused to join me in Manchester, preferring to stay put in the bungalow in Maltby across the Pennines. At the time I was grateful in a way. His absence gave me the freedom to do exactly what I wanted – and at the time I thought I was doing just that. I was so wrapped up in the stardom, the jet-set lifestyle, the men who lavished attention on me and of course the wealth. I had no idea then, as I realize now, that I was lonely and extremely unhappy. The realization of that would only come later. Much later.

From being young I'd revelled in the fact that I was always the life and soul of the party, that people loved my company, that I made them laugh. I had no inhibitions and I loved to shock people with my saucy language, raucous jokes and outrageous behaviour. Now I look back and shudder.

Derrick had given up trying to get me to stop drinking. He'd seen me in full swing while he was driving for me during my early years as Ivy Tilsley. I used to pick up money for singing in clubs, opening bars and other personal appearances, and he knew then that I wouldn't leave without knocking back the line of drinks bought for me by the fans as I was signing autographs. Some nights there'd be thirteen brandy and Babychams: 'Let's go,' he'd say. 'You've had enough.'

'Don't dare tell me I've had enough,' I'd snipe back. And just to drive the point home, I never left a single one.

I just thought he was boring. If he couldn't adapt to my new life, then that was his problem, not mine. I was so selfish it never occurred to me that he actually cared. But by then I had given up any notion that Derrick cared for anyone except himself.

At the time I would sup with anyone who'd let me buy them a drink – and there were plenty of freeloaders who hung around knowing I was paying for the booze. I didn't mind as long as I had company. I would even invite the taxi drivers who picked me up from the Old School to the pub for another drink when I'd clearly had enough. They all knew me as a regular punter, they didn't mind. And they knew I gave the biggest tips in town.

It seems ridiculous really that I needed to call a cab at all. I only lived 200 yards away from Granada. When I moved to Salford I could regulary be seen in the Albert Park drinking with the cabbies. The newspapers soon got hold of the news and even installed somebody in the pub to sit and watch me get legless. Once I was caught leaving the loo and I was in such a state they saw my skirt tucked into my knickers. It was funny when it happened to Jill Summers because she had done it for a joke. I was just sad, rolling and very lonely.

Even when I invited friends around for a meal it turned into to a marathon booze session. Once I planned a quiet dinner for myself and Jill Summers back at my place. I prepared avocado pear soaked in vintage port, steak Diane cooked in brandy, and strawberries doused in kirsch. Washed down with wine we were absolutely plastered. The following day I had the most tremendous hangover. Jill told everyone it was the booziest meal she had ever had.

But most evenings I did without the food. They were spent in the Old School and it was difficult to prise me away once I had started a session. 'I won't be long,' I'd tell the taxi driver as I ordered just one more drink from the bar. Then I'd get carried away, buy another round, have a gamble on the fruit machines, another drink and completely forget he was there. One driver waited so long, his battery went flat and he had to call base to get them to send a replacement car. I eventually came out and said to the newly installed cabbie, 'You're not my driver,' and he explained the four-hour wait with the headlights on had ruined the other fella's battery.

My cab fare was always in the region of £30 once the firm had added the waiting time, then I'd tip the driver £20 for being so patient. Basically what amounted to a £1 fare in a cab – or two-minute walk across the road – cost about £50 a time. But I never walked anywhere. I always said if I could get my car up the stairs, I'd drive it to the loo. And money meant nothing to me then.

But back to my bet with Charlie – which I was deter-mined to win. For almost two months I stayed off the booze. I still went into the Old School and tried to carry on my life as normally as possible. I was pleasantly surprised that it didn't really bother me – and my name on the Street changed from Champagne Perrie to Perrier Water! Every night I'd have a glass or two of mineral water, though I would generally get home a lot earlier than if I had been out on the razzle.

The only hurdle was Johnny. He was a bugger, always putting temptation my way: 'Give this woman a brandy,' he'd say. 'I can't stand you drinking bloody water, you're boring.' But I stood my ground. It wasn't the money I wanted so desperately to win from this bet. I wanted to prove that I didn't need the booze, that I drank for pleasure and not out of necessity.

How proud I was to come to the end of that term, booze free. I'd done it. Of course that needed to be celebrated, and on 1 September, the day I thought I was released from my wager, I walked straight into the Old School and ordered my favourite tipple. As I knocked back the first few mouthfuls, I raised my glass to Charlie who was sat at the other end of the bar and hadn't noticed me walk in. 'Happy birthday, Charlie. You owe me £1,000!' I beamed.

The whole place seemed to grind to a halt and an almost deafening silence descended upon the room. 'My birthday is the 17th, Lynne. You've blown it, Mother!' he said as he took out his diary. There, staring me in the face, was the page I had signed 17 September.

All credit to Charlie, he refused to take the money at first, but I insisted – a bet is a bet and I never go back on a wager. 'You'll take it Charlie, or I'll rip the whole lot up,' I said.

Losing £1,000 meant nothing to me. I often carried huge wads of notes around – well I never knew when I might need it. My pride was more hurt than my bank balance. But to me, that's what stardom was all about, having plenty of money – and spending it.

Charlie wasn't destined to keep the cash for ever. He later had a bet with young Simon Gregson, who played Steve McDonald, that he couldn't catch a pigeon in his lunch break. Simon set up a trap consisting of a bit of bread and a box propped on a wooden stick with string tied to it. When a pigeon came and pecked the bread under the box, Simon pulled the string attached to the wood, which fell down, dropping the box over the bird. He actually caught two if memory serves me correctly. 'I hope you're going to hand the money over Charlie,' I said to him. 'Remember, a bet's a bet.' Charlie gave him the grand because he was a man of his word.

Not everyone on the Street threw their money around. While I was a total spendthrift with no regard whatsoever for money, my colleague Bill Waddington managed to play his tight-fisted character Percy Sugden without too much trouble. It was virtually impossible to squeeze any money out of Bill. If I had the reputation of being the Street lush, he was the skinflint. When anyone mentions his name to me, one particular incident always springs to mind – and it should have been scripted and put in the show.

Let me set the scene: it was a bright June afternoon in the summer of 1991. Bryan Mosley, who played Alf Roberts, had just had a heart attack and it was a big shock for all of us. The show had only recently started going three times a week and many of the cast members feared the gruelling new schedule. At the time it was just a worry, but it soon became reality for us all, as I found out later. When Bryan was in hospital the flowers arrived by the van load and the nurses could hardly attend to him, there were so many bouquets and baskets by his bedside.

As a matter of courtesy and tradition, we had a whip round on the set every time someone was in hospital. I usually volunteered to do the collections on such occasions. Well, let's face it – I was the set busybody, and the one with the biggest mouth.

I always said that if there was one character in the Street that most suited my real-life personality, it was Hilda Ogden. I'll be the first one to admit that when some rumour was bounding round, I'd bring it out in the open. That's just the way I am, probably too honest for my own good.

So because I always spoke my mind, no one got away without contributing at least a fiver – or I'd make sure everyone else found out about it. It wasn't always that easy with old Bill, however. Whenever there was a sniff of a collection he'd disappear. I usually caught him slipping out of a side door as fast as his legs could carry him. 'Oh, I've not brought a lot out with me today,' he'd mumble when I tackled him. 'I only have enough for a spot of lunch in the canteen.'

From any other pensioner, this would have been acceptable, but Bill Waddington wasn't short of a few bob. He'd regularly say, 'I didn't become a millionaire by handing my cash out willy nilly.' I don't know if he really is a millionaire, but he owned racehorses and that was enough for me.

I'd heard his excuses time and time again during my collections, and this time I wasn't going to stand for it. With anybody else, I would have said, 'don't worry, I'll stick a fiver in for you. Pay me back tomorrow.' I wouldn't do that with Bill. I shouted down the full length of the Street: 'Bill Waddington, we are sending Bryan champagne and flowers. If you don't put owt in as a contribution, I'll buy a bloody big card and I am going to write on it Bill Waddington never signed this because he never put anything in the box.'

You can imagine the scene with the fans on the Studios tour and those waiting outside the studio gates for a glimpse of their favourite stars and an autograph: Poison Ivy chasing Percy Sugden, calling him all the names under the sun.

I told them he was Percy Sugden in real life too, not Bill Waddington. 'You're not getting away with it this time,' I shouted to him. 'Blow the cobwebs off your wallet and get your bloody money out.' It was Monday, the weekly filming day. This little charade wasn't in the script. But the look of fear on Bill's face was the same as if the cameras had been focusing on his character Percy. He was scared to death of having to part with his cash.

He was furious. But not as mad as the fans who'd been watching from the gates when I shouted to them: 'Mean, mean, Percy Sugden has got nothing on this man. He won't give a penny towards Alf's flowers, can you believe that? He never gives anything to anybody – and he's a millionaire.' Suddenly they all started booing him. 'God forbid if anything happens to you. You'll have a poppy on your coffin and that's your lot.'

For the first time ever, I saw a look of shame creep over his face as he walked towards me, reached into his pocket, fumbled round for a few moments and handed over some cash. 'There you go, you bloody swine,' he said and gave me his contribution – a measly thirty pence.

We all had our bugs to bear. Mine was the drinking, Bill's was the meaness. But actors are naturally cruel and it was a standing joke among the cast that Bill was tight. In all fairness it was something he probably played on. We certainly ribbed him as much as we could get away with. I used to say he'd be just like Paul Getty, with payphones all over his house.

When he had his seventieth birthday party, in true Bill style he bought the first round and we had to fork out for any more drinks. It was that kind of do – and a far cry from the lavish parties I used to throw. Then there would be the best bubbly, caterers in for a slap-up caviare and smoked salmon buffet and as much booze as you could sup. I was the first person to hire out a hotel suite for a party, and it cost me a ruddy fortune. Bill of course got a discount.

Jill Summers was staying at the Portland Hotel in Manchester and had booked a small room for a private knees-up at a discount price because she was a resident. There were about fifty people there and after our one complimentary drink bought by Bill, we all sat round chatting away. There wasn't a great deal of room to sit down, but I spied a chair – empty apart from Bill's flat cap.

Just like Percy, he never went anywhere without that hat. He even used to keep his lines written on a piece of paper inside his cap for when he dried up in rehearsals. Once he took it off to have a peek and the whole script had been duplicated on his head in red felt tip pen.

It was hilarious. Anyway, at his party I thought I'd park my bottom on the chair and promptly sat on his cap – only to bring the whole gathering to an embarrassed silence. The mound I'd thought was just a bit of cloth turned out to be ... his birthday cake, in the shape of his beloved cap. It looked so bloody real, I had no idea.

'You'll have to replace that,' he stormed as I tried to pick up the squashed pieces from the carpet. I got him another cake the very next day. I'm sure he'd been hiding the cake on that seat so that he didn't have to give anyone a slice.

A couple of days after the party the joke going round was that Bill was actually seventy-two and not seventy. People reckoned he thought it was a more special occasion, and more special occasions get better and bigger presents. If the story was true, he was a crafty swine.

Bill had a photographer from one of the newspapers there to take some pictures of the party – but just as he had finished the role of film, Julie snatched the camera out of his hands and ran off with it. She returned triumphant a few minutes later with the exposed film hanging from her fingers. She didn't like having her picture taken unawares, she liked to vet everything that had the chance of getting into the papers – unless of course she had orchestrated the whole thing. Bill was furious, but as usual Julie was unrepentant. She was tremendous and I loved her dearly, a great pal.

Everyone had got used to the fact that since Doris Speed had retired, Julie Goodyear was the queen of the Street and liked everyone to know it. But nothing seemed to daunt Julie – no matter how outrageous the story about her. She seemed to thrive on it. Whether it was tales of her lesbian affairs, being 'caught' topless on holiday, love trysts with gay men or transvestites, she just held her head up high and laughed it off. The following day after a story hit the papers, the green room would be littered with newspapers. 'I see madam's in the press again,' a few disapproving folk would say – whether or not it was jealousy, I don't know. Julie would swan round the studio as if she knew nothing about it: 'What are you talking about, darling?' she'd purr as she dragged on her cigarette when asked – not that many people dared to bring the conversation up. She was a real star – nothing ever seemed to bother her at all. And she loved to embarrass me with her antics – all of which will be revealed when I get onto the steamier side of my life later on.

But Julie was a Street veteran and she could get away with that sort of behaviour. Now the young ones, they were a different kettle of fish altogether. The likes of Kevin Kennedy, who plays Curly, Sean Wilson as Martin Platt and Michael Le Vell who plays Kevin Webster all came in as bits of kids – young and inexperienced. As we did, they learned from their elders and they had respect for those who had been in the game for a long time, just as any apprentice does.

There was, and still is, a pecking order, and they adhered to that. They knew they weren't in a position to lord it on set – or off it with the fans for that matter. They simply didn't get too big for their boots. As a result, they've turned into great, solid actors without an attitude problem where they end up believing they are bigger than the show.

But the new breed of kids, they were different. Some of them looked down their noses at the rest of us, sniggering because we'd been there so long, thinking it was easy to star in a soap and not acting at all. With them came an arrogance which used to infuriate me and many of the other cast members. Chloe Newsome, who played Alec Gilroy's public schoolgirl granddaughter Vicki, was just as high and mighty off set, which seemed ridiculous for a girl of her age.

Fans used to regularly send us gifts. Some were just small tokens of affection, worthless but sent with love. Others would surprise you with their generosity. Chloe was popular with the viewers, as were a lot of the younger stars. One man, who regularly used to send me presents, once sent Chloe, Dawn Acton – who played Tracy Barlow –and me a beautiful hand-painted trinket box. He sent us all something for Christmas every year, whether it be hand-made candles or delicate china dolls, always something a bit different. We were all sat in the green room waiting for rehearsals when we opened up the packages – and the look on Chloe's face when she unwrapped hers was a picture.

'What am I supposed to do with this?' she scowled.

'Thank the man, that might be an idea,' I snapped back at her.

'It's just not my kind of thing,' she said as she put it to one side.

I went for her: 'Some man has spent time and effort making that for you. You should be grateful, you precocious little sod. When I was a girl I would have loved to get a present like that. Not everyone is as privileged as you, you know.'

To hear her talk you'd have thought she'd been acting for years, a real pro. 'Of course I won't be in the show for ever. I want to get involved, do much more challenging roles,' she'd say flippantly. You'd never have believed the Street was her first job.

'You'd better hang on to this and stop getting so big headed,' I warned her. She never spoke to me after that – not that I lost a great deal of sleep over it.

Some of the kids behaved more like footballers than actors on the Street. They simply had too much money and fame too young – it went to their heads and they couldn't handle it. Simon Gregson was a prime example, although deep down he was a decent lad. It didn't surprise me at all when the story of his smoking cannabis and bragging about the money he earned hit the papers. He was heading for a fall because he was getting far too big for his boots. I thought he'd be in for the high jump when that story about the cannabis hit the front page of the *Sun*. But as it happened, he was more concerned about the fact that holiday makers claimed he'd said he wanted to sleep with Sarah Lancashire, who played Rover's barmaid

Raquel. To talk about fellow stars was sacrilege as far as the bosses were concerned.

Luckily, one child actor who was saved from that early stardom trap was Warren Jackson, who played my screen grandson Nicky. He was a baby when he joined, the son of a friend of Chris Quentin's, and no sooner could he walk and talk he was a real pain, and extremely bad-mannered. He would run riot all over the studios during rehearsals. 'You ought to give that boy a bloody good hiding,' I'd tell his mother but she would just laugh it off. I wanted to strangle him!

I know I'll get hundreds of letters complaining about this and I'm sorry if I offend, but I'm a firm believer that kids should get a good slap if they step out of line. A bit of discipline does no harm. When we'd be doing scenes in Alf's shop or Rita's Kabin, Warren would be there taking the sweets in front of our very eyes. He didn't care – he obviously thought he could get away with murder and do what he wanted.

I wasn't very good with children – after all I hadn't had that much experience had I? I certainly didn't have much patience. Even though I had a son, I'd spent most of his formative years working away. So kids made me feel nervous – they still do.

But Helen Worth, who played my screen daughter-in-law Gail, was wonderful with them. She put Warren back on the right tracks. She was a loving friend to them all, but she wouldn't stand for any messing about and they all respected that. She and her husband Michael Angelis had no children, but she was so natural with them. She had a real maternal streak.

If they were playing up, Helen would put her foot down and in no uncertain terms tell them to behave – even in front of their own parents. Like me, she learned to love them as if they were her own, and I honestly believe that the way she handled those children helped them cope with fame and life on the Street and stopped them going off the rails as so many child stars do.

To her they may have been the children she never had ~ to me they were grandkids I was never going to have. And that would prove a great comfort to me as I grew older, knowing I would never be a gran.

Warren turned out to be a smashing kid, really sensible and kind. He treated the other kids wonderfully and took them under his wing. In the end he became a good little friend to me.

One of my favourite people on the set was Anne Kirkbride, who played Deirdre Barlow. Apart from being a fantastic actress, Anne always had a certain aura about her, and I used to call her 'one of God's special people.' She was a beautiful person who needed lots of love and hugs. We were both very tactile like that, and often we'd just walk up to each other and cuddle. Somehow it gave us extra strength when the going was tough. I thought about her a great deal when she was battling against cancer, something I had gone through myself and I knew how devastating it could be.

It really makes you take stock of your life when you are faced with death, believe me. But I knew her new husband actor Dave Beckett would give her all the love she needed and help to pull her through that crisis in her life. She was young enough and strong enough to fight it ~ and she had something to live for. She was madly in love.

I've already admitted I was the set gossip, the real-life Hilda Ogden. To say I wasn't trusted with many confidences was an understatment. Everyone knew I was very open. So I was very touched to be the first to know about Anne's forthcoming marriage. She told me months before they went public with the relationship and I can honestly say I didn't tell a soul. Most of the cast would never dream I could keep a secret, but Anne knew me better than that. I remember when she walked into the green room, looking radiant, totally full of herself. 'You look lovely today, darling,' I said to her and she grabbed my arms and whispered: 'Can you keep a secret? Dave and I are getting married. I'm so unbelievably happy.'

The tears started streaming down my face, I was so pleased for her. But the marriage didn't come as that much of a suprise. Since Dave had started on the Street – coincidentally he played her screen boyfriend handyman Dave Barton – they had been close. It was obvious they thought the world of each other.

I was delighted for Anne, for here was a woman who had not seen much happiness in her life. She'd always been a bit of a loner and never really taken much part in the social side of the Street, keeping herself to herself. But she had always been looking for someone special to take care of her, and she'd gone all round the houses to find that person. There had been plenty of boyfriends, but she had been somehow unsettled and insecure. There were times she'd get upset during rehearsals, snapping at her colleagues, saying she couldn't cope. Of course she could cope really, she was just deeply unhappy in her personal life.

But this was a changed woman before me now. This was a happy woman. Her whole outlook had been transformed. She was in love, probably for the first time in her life – and truly happy. Of course I'd been down that same path myself with Roy Douglas, but unlike Anne I hadn't grabbed at that happiness with both hands. That was lost to me forever, except for the memories. I wasn't just weeping for her. The tears I cried were also for my own lost love.

Of course there were also lots of laughs. Bill Tarmey, who played Jack Duckworth, was the loveliest person on the show. It used to crack me up when he and his screen wife Liz Dawn were shooting a scene. Their memories were so bad, the set would be littered with cornflake boxes and plant pots covered in lines to stop them drying up in the middle of a scene. There were even lines on the bottom of tea cups and stuck on milk bottles in case they slipped up. But what a fantastic double act they were. Although Liz and I had our differences, Bill was one of my favourite people on the show – though he could be a cheeky sod when he wanted to be.

Whenever he used to talk to me, he would stare straight at my nipples. I'd turn bright red with embarrassment, but that made him worse – and the more he did it, the more they used to stand on end and protrude through my blouse. I don't know what started it, but it used to get me aroused in a bizarre sort of way. Not that there was anything in it. Bill and I were just good friends. Although my relationship with Derrick was pretty unstable, Bill and his wife Alma were solid as a rock. They had been childhood sweethearts, courting since they were just fourteen, and Bill had even recorded a song, 'You Are the Wind Beneath My Wings', and dedicated it to her. He sang it for her on *This Is Your Life* and there wasn't a dry eye in the house. Theirs was a real love story.

Bill was very down to earth and didn't let his character take over. Unlike Liz and me, who used to live and breathe our characters, when he walked off the set at the end of the night he left Jack behind. When things got me down, he would take my hand and say, 'It's just a job. Don't take it too seriously. Just keep your head down and do your work.' That's how he treated it. Most people lapped up the limelight, the money and the stardom, but to Bill it was just 'a job.'

Like our characters, Liz Dawn and I were great friends when we first joined *Coronation Street*. Ours was a friendship we had forged long before we met up on those famous cobbles. Like Ivy and Vera – and indeed like most good pals – we also rowed like bloody hell. We had known each other for years before we joined the cast and our lives in many ways were a reflection of each other's. We had a similiar Yorkshire background. We spoke our minds without thinking about the consequences, and both being the family breadwinners, we both got aggravated about keeping our husbands in the lap of luxury. It was something they had become far too accustomed to.

We had a lot to talk about and we told each other everything. As time passed by, petty jealousies and stupid arguments ensured that we drifted apart. Eventually we had such a bust-up that our friendship would be irretrievably wrecked, but that comes later. Now I'm talking about my friends, and some of my best memories on the Street were spent with her. The pair of us were like twins, even though she towered over my tiny frame. We had the same raucous accents and manners – which we didn't turn on for the cameras – the same bleached blonde hair, taste in clothes and love of a drink.

At some point both our husbands used to drive us around to personal appearances and the like. It was a kind of personal thing between Derrick and me – I didn't want him to be on on the dole. I couldn't bear the thought of him collecting benefits, not when I was earning so much. I felt very guilty, so I paid him instead. I don't think Liz had much choice because her husband lived with her and eventually became her manager.

Sometimes it did get ridiculous and some of the cast must have been sniggering behind our backs, for the similarities didn't end there. Just after my sixty-second birthday I had my hair cut short. Liz, who wore a curly wig on screen, had been growing hers for months and it was looking good, but I was fed up with my look so I went for the chop. It wasn't long before she turned up at the studio with a new cropped look.

'But you've been growing it for so long,' I said to her. 'I was fed up,' she replied.

We'd both had cosmetic surgery: I'd had a facelift and she'd had her eyes done.

When I bought my brand new Mercedes car, just a few weeks later she drove into work in hers. I told her about the fantastic new spa bath I had had installed – she went out and bought one too. Every time I was invited on a TV show, she'd come in and boast that she too had been requested to appear on telly. I would turn all offers down because I was too committed to the Street. But Liz would make sure she could fit them in, as if she was trying to get one over on me for some strange reason.

The final straw came when I confided in her that I had been approached by publishers to write my life story. No sooner said, Liz came into Granada telling everyone she'd written an autobiography.

I must admit, I began to get a little paranoid about telling her anything in case she did it first, and I developed a complex. Derrick said I was being silly, that I should take it as a compliment because Liz obviously admired me so much. I was just being daft, he said.

One thing we did share was our sense of humour and the love of a good giggle, even when we were supposed to be deadly serious. I remember when Liz was going into hospital for a gynaecological operation, and she never stopped talking about it. We were just about to shoot a scene in the Rovers and as we were walking in I compared her womb to Hilda's flying ducks – more particularly the one that never used to hang straight, it was always falling down. Liz cracked up and by the time we got on set, we were crying with laughter. Our faces were so wet the director had to send for the make-up girl to sort us out. It looked as if someone had thrown a bucket of water over the pair of us.

Liz, who was quite flat-chested, thanked me for giving her her first ever cleavage. It was the time Jack joined the dating agency as Vince St Clair and Vera found out about it. She joined up too and needed a disguise so she could surprise Jack when he turned up at the rendezvous to meet his 'perfect match'. The red frock she wore on screen was one of mine and the bust she'd acquired to fill the low-cut top was masses of cotton wool. She went berserk over her new shape: 'I'd give anything to have boobs like this,' she kept saying. Funnily enough, I never got that dress back, though I must say it looked a lot better on her than it did on me.

It is a shame my memories are not always of the good times. But Liz and I were to fall out badly and our relationship would never recover. We would never trust one another the way we had. I have revealed the first visible cracks in our relationship – the whole story is a tale to be told much later on. But we had some great fun behind the scenes.

The culprit behind many gags and practical jokes was Roy Barraclough – one of the wittiest actors I have ever had the pleasure of working with. Once I missed a call, because I was in Dawn Acton's dressing room giving her a radio. Dawn was a lovely girl who was very lucky to have Anne Kirkbride playing her mum, because she's such a terrific actress. Anyway, I was sat nattering to Dawn in her dressing room, and unbeknown to me they needed me to do a scene. It was filming day and you just don't disappear on take day, but there was no Tannoy anywhere near so I had no idea they were frantically searching for me.

One of the assistant floor managers eventually found me and rushed me down to the set. We were filming Tina Fowler's leaving do in the Rovers and the cameras were already rolling so I had to sneak into position without being noticed. Of course there were a lot of actors crammed into the set, so there wasn't a great deal of room for manouevre. I had to climb over everyone, whispering 'Sorry, oops, sorry luvvie,' and disrupting everything. I got a bit nervous when everyone kept asking where I had been been and was convinced I was going to get in trouble.

Without thinking, I picked up a sausage roll and pretended to eat it. But everything kept going wrong – either someone messed up or the director didn't like the shot, so we had to keep re-taking. In the meantime, not realizing we were going to do so many takes, I'm still stuck with this bloody sausage roll in my hand. The thing started crumbling and suddenly I couldn't stomach it any longer and had to take it out of my mouth without anyone spotting me – least of all the cameras. I thought I'd got away with it until I saw Roy smirking. 'Put it back on the plate,' he kept mouthing to me. But I couldn't because I was worried someone else would pick it up and eat it.

The director: 'Let's try once more. This will be a take,' so I pretended to eat it, and suddenly as I was talking to Vera the whole lot crumbled and the flaky pastry went everywhere – up my nose, down my frock and all round my mouth! I was coughing and spluttering so much, I didn't want to ruin the scene again so I grabbed a drink to prevent my coughs which I duly spilt down the front of my dress.

Liz Dawn was staring at me in disbelief and I burst out laughing, unable to control my hysterics. As my shoulders shook, I tried to stay out of the way of the camera, if I managed to escape that, then maybe I would escape the wrath of the producer.

Then from the back of the bar I heard a rendition of 'Ivy's pissed at the party, Ivy's pissed at the party ...' Behind everyone's backs that naughty boy Barraclough was singing and pulling funny faces. Now that set me off laughing even more, which made it appear as if I was actually drunk. Of course I hadn't even had a drink, but in those days my reputation went before me. And who was going to take my word for it?

CHAPTER TWELVE

Life's a Gamble

The Bible says money is the root of all evil. But my husband Derrick worships my wicked way of earning lots of it. Filthy lucre is a precious commodity in his book. His attitude to cash has made me spend, spend, spend as fast as pools winner Viv Nicholson.

If I'd been careful I'd be a millionairess today. But I'm not careful. I have no respect for pounds, shillings and pence. My unhealthy disregard for money has grown from my husband Derrick's miserly ways. As far as I'm concerned he is the tightest man on two feet. Always has been, always will be. He saves his cash, he calls it 'us' money, but it isn't in 'us' names. Derrick Barksby is the only name on that bank account.

There was a time he didn't trust banks. He was that careful and so clever with his cash that he stored it in tins in the garage roof. But those days are long gone ... ever since the garage caught fire. Derrick thought he'd lost the lot. I'll never forget him jumping out of bed at the smell of smoke. He was hysterical when he saw it was the garage. I swear he put both his legs down the one leg of his trousers As he bounded through the door. I just rolled over and went to sleep.

I started the fire accidentally with a discarded match.

I knew that the firemen who arrived in next to no time would soon put it out. But I never knew Derrick kept thousands of pounds on beams in the garage roof. He only told me that when it was almost too late. He rescued his St Bruno and Elastoplast tins with the charred notes inside. He had about £3,000 – a fortune in those days – but he sent the notes off to the bank to get them replaced.

When he got them back he deposited them in a much safer place. Or so he thought. He buried nearly £3,000 in a biscuit tin in the back garden. I kid you not. I made the big money find one afternoon when he was out. I saw a fence panel with a pale blue dustbin bag underneath. The plastic bag was pegged at each corner. I wondered what Derrick was cultivating, so I lifted it up and hidden underneath was this tin containing all the cash wrapped in cellophane. I dug it up, took the money out and then put the tin back. I thought, I won't say anything. I'll wait to see how long it is before he notices. I was trying to find out how regularly he added to his pile.

Shortly afterwards I was doing a show with Liz Dawn in Hull. We were billed as Ivy Tilsley and Vera Duckworth in big letters on the billboards. I said to her, 'They don't want Lynne Perrie and Liz Dawn. We'd better go home and get our sewing machines.' This was the first time we'd ever appeared on the same bill. And Liz was nervous. She insisted on going on first and went down a storm.

Her first line to the audience, however, astounded me: 'I don't know what you've booked me back here for, because I died on me arse last time you had me on.' Now that's something I believe you should keep quiet about. She kept saying things to the audience and leaving people waiting for the punchline. She said to one woman with a big bust, 'Are they your own or are you smuggling coconuts?' The woman was left there looking down at her chest. But the punters were always left up in the air – there was no close to the gag.

Having said that, she did a bomb. She was very, very funny. A big part of it is the fact she is so gormless. She was rushing round the stage, dashing everywhere. Now Liz was plastered on that night. She was so nervous that she'd had a great deal to drink. She had seen my act before and knew what I was like. I asked her husband Don if she always moved about so much, but he said it was the first time he'd seen her do it. She couldn't keep still – it was like she had ants in her pants – and it was obviously so alien to her. That just served to make her look extra funny.

I was up next, and the organist came along to tell me. I gave him my music, but he said I was down as a comedienne. And that's when I told him, 'I've got three religions – coward, more coward and devout coward. If them bastards don't like the gags then they can enjoy the songs.' I went down really well, they loved the whole act.

They wanted us to do two spots each, but we agreed to do one apiece then finish off with a duet. After my act I bent over and put the mike behind my back and whispered to Liz, who was sitting on a front table with Don and Derrick, 'Have you got the medley?' I didn't want the audience to know what we were doing. But Liz ignored me and turned the other way. I coughed and made out that it was a little gag. Liz turned round very slowly and said to the audience, 'Is she talking to me?' She was well oiled by now. When I mentioned the medley again she remembered what I was on about and nipped off to the dressing room. When she returned she put the music in front of the organist and in so doing nearly knocked him off his stool. She started kissing him and everyone else must have realized by then, if they hadn't before, that she was drunk.

I was getting very panicky, because I wasn't sure what she would do next. When she got up on the stage we were just like Little and Large. By this time I had kicked my shoes off and she was standing in front of me. I asked her what the first song was, but didn't get a reply. So I then lifted her arm up and poked my head under her armpit and asked again. It got a great laugh. That's when it dawned on me that it looked like a rehearsed double act.

The act was going down great and we followed it up by singing 'If You Knew Suzy'. I was still standing behind her and lifting alternate arms up every now and again. When we got to the end of the song the audience went mad they loved it. They really thought we'd worked it out.

Then someone at the back shouted, 'Sing, "My Way".' I said, 'No way. I've had a funeral pyre and the music of "My Way" was on it because it's been done to death.' The chap would not give up. He said I'd had everyone crying in the club when I'd sung it there two years earlier. So I relented and said to Derrick, 'Go and get the music to "My Way",' but he refused. I couldn't believe it ... I thought Liz had infected him. I asked again, but he was adamant. In the end a lady sitting next to him went and got it from my bag. She gave it me and I handed it to the organist.

Liz had now wandered off to the back of the stage and was flicking through some papers and humming to herself. I thought, I'm going to have some problems here with her. So I said, 'Come on, Liz. We're going to sing "My Way".' She looked at me puzzled, and said, 'I don't know it.' I said, 'Don't be so bloody silly. Everyone knows "My Way".' So we sang it and once again it was hilarious. The audience erupted and were shouting for more.

But I'd had enough, so I went back stage and Derrick came after me. I told him to get my gear so we could get off home. He walked past me like a hurricane and said, 'You are disgusting.'

I said, 'What do you mean, I am disgusting?'

He said, 'You've gone out there and deliberately shown that girl up. You know you can sing better than her, you know you do gags better than her and you knew she was so nervous.'

I just hit back immediately and said, 'It was a good job one of us was sober.'

When we got in the car he was still going on at me and his pal John was with him in the front. He was going on and on. So all of a sudden I tapped him on the shoulder and said, 'Guess who's got your money?'

The car swerved and he tried to call my bluff. 'Okay,' he said. 'It's in the roof in the bungalow.'

'No. Light blue dustbin bag, four pegs on the corners,' I told him.

Derrick paled visibly. He pulled into the first layby. He said, 'You've found it. What have you done with my money?'

I saw he was sweating and turned up the heat. 'I've got the biggest diamond ring you've ever seen in your life in my safety deposit box in the bank.'

Beads of perspiration appeared instantly on his forehead. 'You haven't,' he whimpered.

'I have,' I said.

And for the first time in my life I saw him speed. He put his foot down, he was that anxious to get home. Derrick was a tortoise when it came to motoring. I often said to him: 'Derrick, don't look now, but we've just been overtaken by another moped.'

I was the opposite. Two days after passing my test I was stopped by two policemen for doing 40 mph in a 30 zone. I told them: 'It pulls a bit if you go under 40 – it jerks a little.' The policemen looked at each other and started laughing. I told them I'd only passed me test on the Friday and they thought I was so funny that they let me off with a caution.

But I digress. Back to Derrick hurrying home. He dropped his mate off en route. As we pulled into our drive he leapt from the car and ran into the garden to check. His secret hoard had, as I said, disappeared. I carried on the pretence. On the verge of tears he begged, 'Where's me money?'

I wouldn't tell him anything else. I left him stewing for ten days. He was physically sick with worry about that blessed cash. He was so upset that he couldn't eat his breakfast. Come to that, he couldn't eat anything for days. He lost over a stone in weight. All the time he was pestering me for the money. Not a day went by without my forlorn husband quizzing me about his beloved loot. If I offered him food his stomach would turn. To me that showed just how unhealthy his attitude on savings was.

In the end he looked so unwell that I couldn't stand it any longer. I went round the house and found it for him. I'd put little piles of notes everywhere – in the Horlicks jar, in the pans, in pockets of clothes in the wardrobe, in the back of the wireless and pinned in the curtain lining. It took me quite a while to find it and even then I never retrieved the lot. I was £500 short and he was convinced I'd spent it. I hadn't – I just didn't know where I'd left it. That little bundle turned up several weeks later when my cleaner Mrs Hastings was sorting through the kitchen cupboards. She came up to me with this £500 and said, 'Look what I've found between the cake tins.' She was a real angel. I can't recall her first name, but I know she was a Pisces. I'd forgotten I'd put some of it there. The problem was I'd hidden all the loot when I was drunk. But Derrick was very happy when I handed it him back. He almost orgasms at the sight of sterling notes in neat wads.

His cash-conscious behaviour made me more and more of a spendthrift. I reckon I've blown over £250,000 on gambling. That started when I was unhappy with Derrick. I would go straight from doing my act to the casino and put all my wages on the tables. I'd play Blackjack and roulette without any logic, putting piles of chips down all over the place. I'd get lucky and win, but rarely more than my stake. I'd stay at the tables until I'd lost the lot ... all my wages. It was a habit that infuriated careful Derrick, so I did it all the more.

Some people gamble and it's a catharsis that drives them on. The only thing I really did it for was to punish Derrick for being a meanie. Money didn't matter to me and that was my way of showing it. I was a chancer who never knew when to stop. I describe myself as a fatalistic gambler – it wasn't in my make-up to quit when I was ahead. When I did have a mountain of money in front of me I'd go wild throwing chips all over the table and I'd only finish when I lost the lot.

The only remarkably lucky streak I ever hit was when I was staying with my brother Keith's father-in-law Fred in Inyanga. I persuaded him to take me to the gaming tables despite the night-time trip being fraught with danger because of guerilla raiding parties and bandits. I was going to go on my own, so Fred reluctantly had to join me.

Now at this time the authorities in Zimbabwe would not let you take more than £2,000 out of the country, so Fred used to provide my spends at an exchange rate of about 10 to 1. I'd put £100 into his bank account in Jersey and he'd give me $1,000. He was looking forward to the casino because he imagined I'd lose a fortune and top up his offshore account.

But this night I could not lose. The tables were up a spiral staircase and I kept coming down telling Fred I couldn't lose. I even started putting the chips on one single number at a time and they came in paying 35 to 1. I was coining it in. It was a great windfall, and the only problem was that I would not be able to take it out of the country. I won over $18,000 that night – the biggest win of my life and one of only two occasions when I walked out of a casino richer than I went in. Fred was stuffing the brass all over the house when we got home – in the speakers, in the wireless, in the bread bin ... everywhere.

It was my second lucky break out there on the trot. Shortly before, I bought a winning state lottery ticket. The first prize was $25,000, but because I was a visitor I was only allowed to collect ten per cent. Still, I was happy, and gave Fred's house boy $250 as a tip.

But most nights were losers, and even if it took until 5 am in the morning I wouldn't leave till I'd lost the lot. Many a time I had to borrow the money for petrol to get home, because I'd be that skint. And Derrick would be so glum. I'd be losing at least £200 a week, and it went on for years. The gaming clubs who put my show on were always delighted, because they knew they'd get the wages they shelled out back through the tables.

Miraculously, one night I came home with £250. I had decided not to gamble all week, so my fees were intact. But as soon as I stepped through the door Derrick asked, 'How much have you lost this week?'

'I haven't lost anything, clever clogs,' I replied smugly.

He said, 'I don't believe it.'

So I got the money out to rub his nose in it. Then he started nagging me about my easy come, easy go attitude. He was banging on about money, money, money.

'Derrick,' I said, 'you're making me hate money. You've got an unholy respect for it and that's giving me a unhealthy disregard for it. Just look at this.'

And I started tearing up the £250 in front of him. He went crackers and started scrabbling about on the floor picking it up. I grabbed as much of it as I could in my hands and stuffed the lot in a great big pile of sand outside the back door. I dug it all the way in and mixed it up. He was out there for about three hours with a torch before dawn trying to find it all and piece it back together. He found some, but the builders who were doing our extension got a great bonus the next morning.

I said, 'Derrick, I hate money. You and money have spoilt my life. I'm sick of it.'

In those days Mervyn O'Hara, who was based in Doncaster, was my manager and I'd be borrowing off him all the time. He manages Paul Daniels these days, but I bet he wished he had a magic hat to pull the money I was after out of back then. It reached the point where he would come with me and collect my wages to stop me gambling it all away.

I was regularly three or four years behind with my income tax as a result of my frivolity. I had to send the taxman post-dated cheques at one junction to clear the mess up.

A girl called Carol who worked on the tables at a casino in Doncaster helped me give up gambling. My biggest win in Britain of £400 came at that place, but I was destined to be a loser. Carol knew how hard I worked and hated seeing me cleaned out every night.

One night she explained how I was playing cards regularly with some real high-rollers and I couldn't win. I had a fellow who owned a string of garages on one side of me and somebody else with buckets of money on the other. I could never match them and they were able to price me out of the game. I quit gambling in casinos a couple of years after joining *Coronation Street* full time, because I'd stopped getting a kick from it. I just gave up going and never went back. I am very proud of that, it shows how strong my willpower is. Years later, when I resolved to stop drinking, this was to stand me in good stead.

But when I was on *Coronation Street* I got hooked on another money-wasting habit – one-armed bandits. Fruit machines were like a crutch to me when I was drinking. If there was nobody to talk to in the bar I could stand by the fruit machine and drink till I dropped. I'd fill a machine with £30 or £40 just before closing time and stay on it for ages. David Haddock, the bar manager in the Old School, once threatened to chain me to the machine overnight if I didn't stop playing and let him go home. I'd regularly be glued to the machine at midnight, an hour after last orders. Everyone else had gone home, but I was lonely and hated going back to my empty flat.

I became seriously addicted to them at one stage. I just couldn't walk past a machine and would lose as much as £90 during a night. It all started with watching other people win on them. Most of the time you don't give a fruit machine and the punter attached to it a second glance. The only time they attract your attention is when they are paying up, so they give the impression that it's easy money. Every time you look at them, coins are dropping out. But that is definitely not the case.

The only time I ever had any real luck on one was when I was in Australia over twenty years ago. I won a hundred $100 jackpot, but almost missed that because I didn't understand the machine. I was jumping for joy after winning $25 when this kind Aussie told me not to let it go, because I'd netted a share of the jackpot. And sure enough $100 tumbled out in a minute or two.

The habit was terrible. I was monotonously blowing hundreds of pounds a week on one-armed bandits. It was ridiculous, but I couldn't stop. In those days you used to be able to load £70 or £80 into the machines and play until it was gone.

Then one night I decided I had to pack it in. I put £98 into a machine and then jumped a taxi home which cost me another £30. Suddenly I realized playing that machine had cost me nearly £130, and I made up my mind to stop. Next day I wrote a promise on the back of one of my publicity photos to pay Bill Podmore £1,000 if I played the one-armed bandit again. I told him to hang on to it and, if he ever caught me at it, I would pay up. But later I asked to see the photo, which he kept in his wallet, claiming I needed a copy. Then I ripped it up in front of him – just in case I fancied a gamble on the fruit machine again.

My enthusiasm for a gamble got me involved with my horse-mad Street co-star Bill Waddington. Bill bred race-horses and he sold me two foals that might have turned into winners. But these animals were only a few months old and

I'd have had to wait a couple of years to get them on a racetrack. I only went down to see them in the stables near Cholmondeley Castle in Cheshire once. I got so bored waiting for them to run that I sold him one back, losing out on the deal.

I was cursing Bill, but I ended up having the last laugh. I decided to sell the second one off and discussed it with him. I told Bill it looked a bit sickly, so he suggested sending it off to the Doncaster sales as it was a well bred colt. I was a bit disappointed, because I'd been hoping he would have bought it back as well. After putting it in the sale I got pangs of guilt in case it went off cheap and ended up as dog meat. So I gave Derrick instructions to go along and buy it back if the price was no good. Derrick got into the auction against another bidder and banged the price right up. In the end he let the other chap have it at a profit of over £400. I was working away in Wales and was delighted when Derrick gave me the good news.

When I got back to the studios Bill came up to me and said, 'That horse you sent to Doncaster sales – I paid a lot more for it than I thought I would.' 'Hang on,' I said. 'What do you mean, you paid a lot more for it?' It turned out he had sent a friend along to buy it for him and that was who Derrick was bidding against. He obviously thought he'd pick it up for a song. He should have asked me straight and I'd have let him have it cheap.

Another time my brother Duggie, Derrick and I went to the races to watch one of Bill's nags run. Derrick wore a trilby and a crombie overcoat. He looked just like the racing commentator Peter O'Sullevan. Duggie was videoing the race, so I set about fixing up the tripod. But by the time I'd done it the action was over. Duggie said, 'It's all over. Bill's horse might get first place ... in the second race.' The horse finished a long way last, but I can't remember it's name. And I wouldn't dream of asking Bill, because he wouldn't admit to owning a racehorse that never won.

Duggie had managed to video the race by resting the camera on his shoulder. He was a dab hand with a camcorder and gave me some great hints after I made a meal of my first video. I'd bought one in time for the Street's 25th anniversary bash at the Dorchester Hotel. I succeeded in taking lots of shots of the carpet and people's crutches, but not a lot else. And my running commentary of the big night made me cringe. All I could hear was my voice. Duggie told me to overcome that problem by switching a Sony Walkman on and putting the headphones beside the camera's mike.

It worked a treat when Derrick and I went on a Safari holiday in Kenya. Elaine Paige's record 'Cinema' captured the flavour of the trip. I got a great shot of an eagle soaring as the song 'You Are the Wind Beneath My Wings' was playing.

Hand in hand with my big spending was my generosity. It was legendary round Granada. Whenever a story about my generous nature appeared in the press I'd be inundated with begging letters. Some would be for very deserving cases, but there was no way I could check if they were genuine.

When my big pal prop man Vinny McNally left the show the story got out that I'd presented him with a blank cheque to take his family on the holiday of a lifetime. He took his wife Linda and two young sons Darren and James to Disney World in Florida. He wouldn't discuss it when approached by the newspapers. He simply said, 'Lynne is a sweet kind lady who only has friends in this world.' It was a very touching thing to say, but that story sparked thousands of begging letters.

The backroom boys gave Vin a great send off. They made a coffin for him for his leaving do, because he was that thin faced he looked like someone had dug him up. He was one of the technicians I really missed after the waves of redundancies swept through Granada in the early 1990s.

They could never replace him or all those years of experience. Many similarily gifted stalwarts were thrown on the scrapheap by the company's redundancy policy.

I always bought the technicians presents at Christmas. There were bottles of champagne, brandy, whisky or vodka for all the lads and a couple of bottles of spirits for the directors. One year I had a dozen bottles of Dom Perignon as presents stored in the Old School. I cut a picture of myself up and divided it into a dozen chits, which I handed out to my pals. I told the bar manager David to dish out the bottles to those who had bits of the photograph. I only did that once. I gave one to Johnny Briggs, but he kidded on he had another that he'd lost and waltzed off with two bottles. I suspect Geoff Hinsliff saw him do it and pulled exactly the same stunt. My Christmas presents were cleaned out in double quick time. I didn't mind. The expensive booze only cost money, after all.

Splashing out on outrageously expensive outfits was another penchant of mine. Derrick would have dropped dead if he'd seen some of those price tags. Despite my spending serious dosh on my dresses, they very rarely met with Derrick's approval, and that was really all I sought.

I'll never forget a real knockout chiffon number with a hint of pale pink, covered in diamantes and lace. It was a dream dress, but Derrick despised it. Every time I wore it he'd describe it as insipid and suggest I change. I'd bought it in a Bond Street boutique in London and it cost £1,200, but Derrick never knew that. One night in Scunthorpe after I'd had it about three months he started moaning about it again. A woman in the audience had said she loved it, so I went back stage, took it off and handed it to her. Derrick didn't like it, but he liked me giving it away even less. It was only after I handed it over that I told him the cost. He's six foot tall and he almost hit the dressing room roof when I told him. He said hopefully, 'You're joking?' But he knew I wasn't. He could have said that was the price of a terraced house, but he didn't. It was my money and he knew better than question how I spent it.

Another time I blew a packet on a posh frock was after flying back from Zambia to attend my first Lady Ratling ball at London's ultra-exclusive Grosvenor Hotel. I went straight into Harrods in Knightsbridge after getting off the plane at Gatwick. The price tag on the dress I adored was in the region of £1,000. It was five inches too long, but I bought it all the same and snipped the extra length of myself later with a pair of scissors. I was in my travelling clothes and when I asked the girl on the counter to wrap it she haughtily pointed out the price tag to me. I plonked my Gold American Express card in front of her and said, 'I don't care how much it is. I want it. Now will you please wrap it up?'

She couldn't believe it. Here was a woman with a thick Yorkshire accent, dressed in a crumpled trouser suit and with no make-up on, buying the most expensive dress in the department.

Pat Phoenix had proposed me as a Lady Ratling, the female equivalent of the Water Rats, and Jill Summers had seconded me, and this was my initiation. Jill and I had splashed out several hundred pounds a piece for the table and we both invited half a dozen guests along.

Before the ball I slipped down to Jill's room for a drink with Derrick. Now Jill knew about fashion. She spotted I was wearing a very costly outfit. And the wicked swine decided to wind Derrick up. Everyone on the Street knew about his mean streak. I had made it common knowledge among the cast. Jill winked at me and said, 'My God! I bet you didn't get much change out of £400 for that.' Derrick, who had no idea of the price, was shocked and spluttered: 'How much?' I played along a bit, but he'd have passed out if he'd known the real price.

Later that night Derrick's cash-conscious ways were to give us all another good laugh. Whenever we went out socially I would slip him a couple of hundred pounds to make sure he had enough to buy a round. But he'd always hang back and hardly ever put his hand in his pocket. I wasn't going to let old tightfist get away with that on my big night. I niggled and nagged through the evening to get him to buy a drink. All to no avail, so I took the initiative and ordered some champagne for the table. Derrick's eyes lit up as he gazed at me and whispered, 'Look, someone's splashed out on the bubbly.'

Knowingly, I nodded my head and said, 'Derrick, I'm looking at him. I ordered it on your behalf, just in case it slipped your mind.' His complexion rapidly changed to chalk white as the realization dawned. It had done the trick, he was shamed into putting his hand in his pocket.

Now at this point I must explain he looked ever so dashing in his dinner suit, complete with bright red cummerbund. Resplendent as he was, the last thing anyone expected to see was Derrick's famous wallet. The wallet used to be my dad's, and Derrick used to boast that as long as he'd had it we'd never been short of money. I tried to point out that we'd never ever been on our uppers anyway, but he wouldn't have it. The wallet was very old – that ancient, in fact, that it had to be held together by twelve elastic bands. And on my big night it made a guest appearance at the table. Everyone stopped and stared when it emerged from his tuxedo. Chris Quentin broke the spell by starting to laugh. He said, 'Lynne, you've always said he was tight, but that wallet hasn't seen daylight for years.' Chris cracked up as Derrick unravelled the elastic bands that held the worn leather together. It was a hilarious sight, but at the time I was a bit embarrassed by it.

I was the exact opposite of Derrick and would tip all the waiters and porters in the hotel, given the opportunity. Derrick loathed the habit, so I'd do it all the more. We went on holiday to Jamaica a few years ago and one waiter got $118 in one tip from me. That was more than he earned in a week, and he stayed at our beck and call for two weeks. I'd tip him whenever Derrick wasn't looking. Manchester cabbies know I'm a good tipper. I think you should tip, because it signals your appreciation.

Another thing Derrick hated was my insistence on flying first class. He'd look at the savings we could make by going economy, but I would only use British Airways premium cabins. I was happy to pay the extra to get me away from the hassle of having to sign autographs for hours during the flight, because that is what happens if you travel economy or even club in my experience.

Unfortunately my policy backfired on the trip to Jamaica when some drunken colonel insisted on making small talk with me. He was a fan of the show and he just wouldn't shut up or go away. He was a real drunken bore. His wife was dripping in jewellery and about half his age. She looked as fed up with him as I was, but that didn't stop me putting my own sparklers on to match her.

He invited us to his villa for a meal when we touched down and true to his word, sent a limousine across to pick us up. It turned out that he'd made a fortune in Jamaica. We spent a fortnight over there at the sumptuous Jamaica Inn, but I never left the balcony of our luxury room. Derrick would go down on the beach with his knotted hanky on his head or a daft hat, but I didn't see the point of getting sand in my toes when I could enjoy the sunshine without having to walk. If I did venture on to the beach I rarely went into the water. But I could always spot Derrick swimming ... he'd still have the hanky on his head.

When we were in Antigua in 1984 the pair of us went along to a nudist beach and stripped off. It was a lovely stretch of sand. There wasn't a soul in sight when we got there in the morning. But as the day progressed people started to appear, and one particular couple with a camera terrified me. They came walking towards us and I could see this holiday snap of me naked finding its way into the papers back home. I put a towel over my head and this girl said, 'It's Ivy Tilsley, isn't it?' I said, 'Yes it is, but you're not selling my nude body to the newspapers.' I sat with that towel over my face for ages. They must have thought I was a funny one.

I loved holidaying in the sunshine. So when Johnny Briggs was arranging a golf tournament in Portugal and invited his pals from the Street over, Derrick and I decided to go along with Bill Tarmey and his wife Alma. The only problem was, the tournament was called off and Johnny hadn't told us. He said he'd put a standard letter up on the notice board in the green room, but none of us had seen it. We ended up in an awful hotel on the Algarve that Johnny recommended. Apparently at one time it was a good hotel, but it had become run down over the years. Derrick didn't much care for that holiday, because in the end we had to pay for it.

My frivolous spending might shock some people. And I'm not really proud of having thrown tens of thousands of pounds away in my lifetime. But my big-spending streak did have a saving grace. I was great at raising cash for charity. Ask me to support a good cause and I'd throw my all into it. I am an energetic fundraiser and naturally big hearted. I have helped thousands of worthy causes over the years.

I'll never forget the night I went to a charity dinner as a special guest and imagined I'd be invited to sit on the same table as a weathy aristocrat. Far from it. I was stuck on another table at the furthest extreme of this magnificent baronial hall. The aristocrat, like myself, was a patron of this charity. I'd taken Bill Waddington along as a guest, and he got stuck on another table. The chap next to me was a real bore, who had never watched *Coronation Street*. He said, 'I believe you're on television?' Instantly I disliked him and replied, 'No, I never sit on it.' The rest of the table were old folk and a couple thought that was quite funny.

These other guests were supposed to buy the drinks for the privilege of being in our company. When this toffee-nosed twerp asked what I'd like I requested my usual – Dom Perignon. Now the fellow looked at his lady friend and squirmed, but he stumped up.

After about an hour with this pest beside me I went off to find the organizer to ask why I wasn't on the same table as the aristocrat. He made some weak excuse about not having enough room, but it didn't wash with me. I saw straight through it and went to chat to Bill Waddington. He groaned, 'This lot are boring me stiff.' I said it was outrageous that we'd been dragged along for nothing more than a glorified PA.

On the way back I spotted Les Dawson, who was one of the funniest men I've ever met. He started pulling daft faces and told everyone I was one of the best club acts ever, something Bernard Manning said when I popped into his World Famous Embassy Club in Manchester. Les was so sweet, but I had to tell him to button it because I was still playing the clubs at night after filming at Granada. I told him I was sick of the two pillocks I'd been sandwiched between. He was so unpretentious and we had a great giggle together. I went back to the table for the meal with Mr and Mrs Miserable, but as soon as the plates were cleared I was off.

The highlight of the evening was a charity raffle with a ladies' Cartier watch as the top prize. I saw a string of numbers pulled out and as the queue went down I decided to take the plunge and buy some tickets. I had about £500 in my handbag and reckoned that was enough to buy all the remaining tickets and collect the watch. When I expressed my intention to the two women doing the draw they went grey. I'd already spent about £70 on tickets before I said I wasn't going till I'd got the watch.

At this one of the women dropped her handkerchief and rummaged in her handbag. I saw her take the number thirty ticket out of her handbag. The watch wasn't meant to be won. And she'd made it so obvious that everyone queuing up behind me knew what was going on to. And the next second she pulled number thirty out. But the fiasco wasn't over. Not only didn't they have a winning number in the barrel, but they didn't even have a Cartier watch.

I was outraged. I was also pretty sloshed after the bottle of Dom Perignon and a few large brandies. I had planned to auction the watch off to raise more cash for the charity. It was well after midnight and the people on the dance floor could hardly stand up, because they were so drunk. It was the best time to auction off the watch. But the organizers didn't like the fuss I was causing because they hadn't got a watch. In the end they brought out a Cartier box with a Burberry watch inside, but I caused so much mayhem they wouldn't let me raffle it off. They were literally dragging me and my coat out of the dance. They bundled me into a car and I was off quicker than Superman, screaming about the injustice of it all on the way. I asked them to take my name off as a patron after that and told them I was writing to the aristocrat to tell him about the shambles.

I often raffled off prizes I'd won to raise yet more cash for the charity I was supporting. In Brighton recently for a showbiz charity gala with my pal Kevin Horkin, the animal expert on ITV's *This Morning* show, I won a luxury weekend in Jersey. I auctioned that off at this glitzy do and raised a further £600 for the cause. Another time I raffled off a tiny teddy bear for £75. I sometimes think I should have been an auctioneer.

Years ago at a charity auction at Bredbury Hall in Stockport, Cheshire, our Duggie saved me from forking out £238 on a snooker cue that once belonged to Steve Davis. I was that plastered that I didn't know what I was doing. I had already spent £415 on the bell Colin Crompton used to ring on the Wheeltappers and Shunters Club. I've even got one of Hilda Ogden's famous ducks somewhere upstairs. In fact I've got the most famous one – the bird that wouldn't hang straight on her muriel, as she always refered to the landscape on her living room wall.

A few years since I went to the Isle of Man on a SPARKS charity golf weekend with Johnny Briggs. The organizer, Paul Gascoigne – not the Geordie footballer, another one – was so impressed by my fundraising that he invited me back any time. Lionel Blair, Richard O'Brien and Robert Powell were there and I got a fiver off each of them, despite them protesting that they were playing in the match for nothing. I told them not to be so mean and to get their wallets out. Johnny disappeared when I started shaking the collection boxes. I filled eighteen of them and after that started putting the donations into pint pots. I went all round the Palace Hotel, where we were staying, and knocked on every door. I was tipsy and didn't care who I was waking up, but I insisted they all made a contribution.

The following day I took a bucket down to the golf course and did another collection. Everyone was throwing their coppers in and my arm was stretching to orang-utang proportions. I got so carried away that I ran off the golf course and onto a picnic area nearby where a family were having lunch. I dashed over with this bucket and told them I was collecting for SPARKS. They looked at me as if I'd walked off a UFO. He said, 'Pardon,' and I told him it was a children's charity. He said, 'Hey Mabel, look who's here.' I apologized for being in a hurry and unable to talk. But he told me not to worry and that even though he didn't play golf he'd contribute. The smashing fellow slipped a fiver into the bucket and shouted after me, 'Ivy, why don't you ditch that Don Brennan?'

Now that was something that had been praying on my mind, but before I tell you that, let me tell you about some real heartache.

CHAPTER THIRTEEN

Double Whammy

Stephen lay on a bed in the middle of the hospital ward, his skeletal body draped with a sheet. He was slumbering, his chest was rising and falling irregularly. I was convinced this was almost the end.

The sight was heartbreaking and all around him other young men and women lay dying. It was like a scene from Belsen – wasted bodies seemed to be everywhere. Many of the victims were abandoned by their families, because of the awful stigma still attached to their disease.

Derrick and I were facing the trauma together. The prospect of losing our only son left us speechless. We looked at his prone body and into each other's eyes. We didn't have to speak. The look said it all.

I feared the worst, but was hoping against hope everything would be okay. We asked the nurses not to wake him, because he looked so sick.

When the doctor came to see us I was already in shock. He calmly walked into a side room, on the Charles Bell ward at London's Middlesex Hospital, and I immediately blurted out: 'Just tell me has he gone from HIV positive to full-blown AIDS?'

The doctor laid it on the line for us, saying: 'Yes, he has AIDS. Nobody knows how long it might be before he gets more symptoms.

'It was touch and go last Wednesday whether he would live or die.

'He could have a couple of weeks, months, years or even longer. Nobody knows.'

Derrick and I just stared at each other. We had dreaded hearing those words. Derrick was very upset, and I was so stunned. We held hands for the first time in years.

We walked the corridors of the hospital in a trance. It was a muggy day and we needed fresh air. The traffic was heavy and noisy as we stepped outside, but we hardly noticed. No parents expect to outlive their child – it's simply not natural. Losing a child is the most devastating thing in the world, and we were both facing that prospect.

The hardest thing to face is not knowing when it could happen. Four days later one of Stephen's friends died in his sleep, out of the blue, after making plans for a weekend trip.

As we walked, tears streamed down Derrick's cheeks and glistened in the sunlight. It was the first time in nearly fifty years together that I'd seen him cry. My husband – the hard-bitten Yorkshireman – was weeping for our only son.

I'd cried myself to sleep hundreds of times since I discovered Stephen was HIV positive. But seeing his father weep moved me beyond words.

The spell was broken as Derrick's grip on my hand became tighter. I said, 'Stop squeezing, you're hurting me.' The hypnotic effect of the awful news was broken for a short minute. We went back to Stephen's North London flat by taxi, the unhappiest people in the world.

That night, for the first time in our forty-four year marriage, Derrick asked me for a cuddle – but I was too upset to respond. I should have hugged him, but my own terrible pain over Stephen had made me want to be alone.

We stayed for a week in Stephen's flat, visiting him

every day and every night in the hospital. I cooked him a casserole to cheer him up, he hated the NHS food.

He had gone into hospital on 1 July 1994, with stomach pain, violent sickness and dizzy spells. The doctors did not know what was wrong with him, and that made it even more worrying.

He was in tremendous pain twenty-four hours a day and was on constant morphine injections. His bad turn on that Wednesday was a result of all the drugs he had been given building up in his body and sparking an adverse reaction.

He began vomiting from the pit of his stomach. People who saw him were shocked at the violence of the retching. That, and the constant nausea, spurred the doctors into emergency action to stabilize Stephen's condition. By this time he had collapsed with pain.

They feared he would suffer blood poisoning, and that could have proved fatal coupled with his reduced blood pressure. He was also very dehydrated.

For the visits I deliberately dressed down. I took three brown outfits and left all my jewellery at home. An AIDS ward isn't the place for glitz and glamour – particularly when your only son is lying in one of the beds.

Stephen had asked me to make my visit low key. Now it still hurts to admit this, but he initially barred me from the hospital and instructed staff to throw me out if I appeared on the ward.

We had rowed over my larger than life personality. Stephen believed at that point that he was close to death, but told nurses: 'My mum is persona non grata – I don't want her here. If she turns up on the ward I want you to throw her off.'

Stephen banished me for fear my star status might upset the other terminally ill patients. He had heaped extra pain and anguish onto my shoulders. I was absolutely heartbroken when a nurse told me my son didn't want to see or hear from me. Until that moment I hadn't realized just how strongly he felt about me. I was distressed when the male nurse answered the phone and told me I was persona non grata. It was terribly upsetting and humiliating to know that my only son was so angry with me.

Eventually he relented and allowed me to visit when I promised to come 'disguised' ... as his mum plain Jean Barksby.

I cast aside all my soap star trimmings – the diamond encrusted Nina Ricchi sunglasses, the sequined Bruce Oldfield gown, the Gucci handbag, Galiano stilettos, Rolex watch and sparkling jewellery – at his request.

I hurried onto the ward hiding behind Derrick with my famous face partially obscured by a head scarf. I wore a plain dark brown trouser suit.

Stephen wept when he saw me. He hugged me and movingly said 'Thank-you.' When he was feeling better he told me: 'For the first time in over twenty years I saw Mrs Jean Barksby – my mum – not Ivy Tilsley, Ivy Brennan or even Lynne Perrie. It meant the world to me seeing you there dressed down instead of up to the nines.'

At the end of three days visiting he'd said he had never seen me looking so awful. I'd worn no make-up at all. I hadn't planned to enter as a star in the first instance. I just didn't want to enter the ward looking like a washer-woman.

He told me he'd been searching for Jean Barksby for years and me visiting like that was a real tonic. People still recognised me, despite the drab outfit, but that didn't matter. What counted for him was that I was trying to be his mum.

Afterwards I promised myself that Stephen would see a lot more of his real mum. And we both agreed that, whatever I wear, I am first and foremost his mother.

For months I'd been worried about him losing weight.

Every time he got a cough or a cold I prayed that he wouldn't deteriorate. I saw him in March, only a few weeks after my departure from *Coronation Street*, when I went along to support an AIDS charity night at the Victoria Hotel in New Brighton on the Wirral. Stephen was in great form that night and sang to a packed house under his stage name Stevie B. I joined him for a duet and fought back tears as he sang 'The Power of Love'.

Granada writing me out of the show at least gave me time to be with my son – for probably the first time since he was a toddler. In his early years I occasionally took him to clubs with me, but as I became more famous my career took me further afield. Now I want to spend as much time with Stephen as possible.

I've put my £170,000 house in Manchester on the market, and plan to buy a smaller cottage where he can come and visit me. I've learned a lot about my son since his illness and I want to know more.

For too long I'd been a soap star on a pedestal – now I'm back to earth and can be a good mother again. I aim to be by Stephen's side through his ordeal.

Having a famous mother meant Stephen's predicament would make the newspapers. We decided to sell the story to raise some cash for AIDS charities.

'TV Ivy's Son Dying of AIDS' the headline on the front page of the *Sun* proclaimed. The headlines were harrowing, but the newspaper dealt with the subject sensitively and sympathetically.

If the coverage of Stephen's experience helped just one AIDS victim or their family to cope with the anguish ahead of them, then telling the story will not have been in vain.

Our nightmare started years earlier when, in one fell swoop, the world discovered my son Stephen was gay and suffering from HIV. He'd kept the diagnosis secret from me for over two years, because he feared the truth could have brought on a heart attack and killed me.

I was staggered when I found out. I am convinced he would never have told me had he not been forced to after receiving a phone call at my flat from a friend in Brighton.

Exhausted, Stephen was staying with me in Manchester for a break from the pub he'd been running with two business partners in Hove, on the coast near Brighton. These chaps, as far as I could see, had him doing most of the work. A couple of weeks earlier I'd gone down and done a cabaret slot to officially open their boozer.

It was a massive old building on three floors and, while I was there, Stephen spent all his time running up and down the stairs from top to bottom. He was looking really worn out and I wasn't happy that his partners were doing their fair share.

On the opening night Stephen had organized a keyboard player and a drummer and I was going to sing 'My mother's eyes' and do a short spot. There were a few members of the cast of *The Bill* in that night and the pub was pretty busy. Stephen introduced me on stage by saying: 'Ladies and gentlemen we've managed to secure the services of a lady you know as Ivy Tilsley, but I know better as Lynne Perrie.'

I was on the stage and half way through the song when I thought Lynne Perrie – he should have said mother. So at the first opportunity I went up to him and asked why he hadn't said 'mam.' He said he hadn't mentioned it because he was thinking about my career and the fact that I had a gay son hadn't been in the papers. He had tears in his eyes. But I thought 'I'll tell them'. I told the audience that Stephen was my son and that he was ashamed of me.

Two weeks later he came to Manchester for a visit. He looked really ill and told me I was right about his partners not doing their share. I thought it was stress, resulting from problems with the pub, that made him look so haggard. On the Wednesday he got this phone call from his friend in Brighton.

As soon as he put down the receiver, I knew something was wrong. Call it a mother's intuition, but I knew he was in trouble. I asked: 'What's the matter?' He declined to answer, but I pushed and pressed him. So Stephen stunned me with his revelation: 'Mam there have been reporters at the pub. They've found out I've got HIV.'

I'd only just found out myself. I panicked. I immediately thought HIV equals AIDS and that means death. I imagined he had only weeks to live. I asked him straight: 'How long have you got?' These days I know a lot more about HIV, but back then I was ignorant and hysterical.

I only knew what I'd seen in the papers and so much of that had been terrifying. In those days the man in the street simply thought HIV was AIDS. I now know there is a wealth of difference between the two. Not least of all the difference between life and death.

But, when he told me the heartbreaking news, I asked him a string of silly and stupid questions. The pair of us were in tears in each others arms. We were just crying and comforting one another. I cried all day.

I kept hugging Stephen all the time. Despite what he'd said I still thought he was going to drop dead at any minute. He kept saying 'mum I'm not dying.' But I'd have taken a lot of convincing then. Fortunately Stephen had undergone counselling and was able to explain things quite well. He'd collected lots of literature and was very well read.

He also got a counsellor, called David, to call me at the flat and he did a very good job as well. He told me he'd seen Stephen's blood count and he was doing very, very well. He explained how you could have HIV for a long time before it developed into full blown AIDS, which is the real killer. Before all this I knew nothing about HIV

– just what I'd seen in the papers about the horrors of people dying from AIDS.

Then Graham King, *Coronation Street*'s publicity expert, came round to the flat. He told us the Sunday newspapers had got hold of the story and that we might as well sell the story to one of them. He did a deal with a reporter called Alan Hart who works for the *News of the World*.

But when Hart called on the Saturday I'd changed my mind and wasn't letting him in the flat. It was 21 October 1989 and I had this stupid idea that if we didn't do the story then it wouldn't come out. Graham King came round and went mad having fixed up the interview. Hart waited outside for an hour. I was just coming to terms with what Stephen had told me and I didn't really need the added aggravation.

In the end I decided to go ahead and do it. But not before I called on my friend Kevin Horkin, who runs a chain of opticians, to supply us with some heavy glasses to disguise Stephen. I knew what prejudice and ignorance there was about HIV and didn't want Stephen to suffer extra trauma, just because he had a famous mum. All I actually managed to do was make Stephen look about twenty-five years older than he was. We gave every penny of the £7,500 we were given by the newspaper to AIDS charities.

The feedback I got from the newspaper article was phenomenal and very moving. I had a postbag full of letters wishing us all the best, some from mums in the same boat as myself, and lots from lads who had been disowned by their families for being gay. They said how lucky Stephen was having a mum who would stand by him. Some of those letters were heartbreaking. Only a handful were nasty, but when you are in the public eye it is sadly inevitable that cranks latch on to you and send hate mail.

I also got a very warm response from my pals on *Coronation Street*. I thought of Pat Phoenix and her saying: 'When you cut one of us, we all bleed.' Liz Dawn, in particular, was really lovely when she found out about Stephen. She knew he was gay, but was really upset by the news.

I once cried my eyes out in her dressing room. She was talking about her daughter and her grandchild and I broke down. I said 'Liz you are so lucky – I'll never be a grandmother.' It was heartbreaking. I can't remember now if she was showing me photographs or if we were just talking. But when I started sobbing she just came over and put her arms round me to comfort me. It was really sweet of her. She felt it because her kids are so important to her. They mean the world to her. Mothers feel empathy for one another in a situation like that. It is a case of there but for the grace of God go I.

Stephen, I later discovered, had found out he had HIV back in 1986. He discovered the news on 28 December at 4.32 pm – he knows, to the precise minute, when he was told. He was living down in Lowestoft and had decided to go and work in the States.

When he had the test there were only about 600 HIV cases in the whole of Great Britain with a population of 53 million-plus. He was confident he would be negative. He must have been totally bewildered and heartbroken with the news he was positive. But he is a gutsy little devil and decided to go to the States all the same for six months.

He was only over in San Francisco for three weeks when he telephoned home to let me know how he was getting on. I'd known he was gay for years but the thought he might have HIV never entered my head. I didn't know anything about AIDS, let alone HIV, back then. The initials horrified me, but only because I knew so little about it and that it was associated with dying.

During the course of this phone call I guessed something was wrong. Call it telepathy, but mothers can pick up the slightest hint of a problem. He'd told me that the city had suffered a power cut and all the files on the company's computer had been wiped from the memory. He was spending over twelve hours a day in the office, working his socks off to input five years worth of information back into the computer system.

But I thought there was more than just his work weighing heavy on his mind. The next day I went into Granada and asked for the two weeks off, I had coming up, to be extended to three. I had this compulsion to go over and see Stephen. My passport had run out, but I asked Granada's travel people if they could sort me out with a new one complete with a US visa. They did it in double quick time. The company can be very good like that. At Easter I was able to jet straight over using a new British Airways link.

Stephen was gobsmacked when I told him I was flying across. When he asked why, I told him it was because he sounded ill and I fancied seeing the States. He told me I didn't have to come, but I said I was already booked and would be there. Derrick was also surprised, he thought I was over-reacting. But how could I explain my gut instinct.

When I arrived Stephen, as ever the dutiful son, met me at the airport. He walked me across a freeway to get a bus, and we were struggling with my five bags between us. He was dragging three cases and I had the other two. There was no porter and we had to go across three streets in total to reach the bus stop.

Now I'm the type of person who'd take a taxi to the loo, but he wouldn't let me call a cab. He wouldn't let me spend any money. I thought, 'good God it's like his dad all over again.'

We finally got on a bus and when I was getting off I

tipped the driver. Stephen went crackers and said the twenty-four dollars I had given him was way too much. I told him to stop looking at me. He was unhappy for the duration of my stay, but never once told me why. He seemed determined not to have me spend any money.

His apartment was above an Italian restaurant and was awful. I didn't like garlic back then and the smell of the stuff was everywhere. The bed was built into a cupboard on the wall, the television was on the blink, the oven didn't work, and he didn't have a wireless. The place was driving me mental. When I asked why he was living there, I never got a proper explanation.

The next day I went out and bought him a microwave oven. The day after I bought him something else for the flat. I bought him a couple of other bits during the week, but he kept telling me not to buy him anything. The next day I thought, 'I can't have him in a house without a radio,' so I bought him one. He came home and went beserk. He picked the radio up and threw it against the wall. He was crying: 'Will you stop buying me things.' He was in a dreadful state.

Initially, I thought: 'What an ungrateful sod. The awkward little devil doesn't want me interfering in his life at all and all I'm trying to do is help him.' I ended up getting an abcess under my tooth and, because of all the medication I am on, the dentist over there wouldn't treat me. He gave me some antibiotics and told me to see my own dentist in England. I ended up returning from the trip three days early, because I was in such pain.

All the time Stephen knew he had HIV, but he kept it from me. I couldn't work out why he was so off-hand with me. We only laughed a few times during the whole visit and I'd gone over hoping to cheer him up and have a good time.

One of the funniest things to happen on the trip was when we were on one of the famous San Fransisco trams.

An American lady sitting opposite recognized me from *Coronation Street* and squealed: 'Oh my God! It's Ivy Tilsley.' It was incredible because they don't show it over there. She very politely asked for my autograph and I agreed. Stephen had a photo in his pocket and as I was signing it she started chatting.

She explained that she was married to an Englishman whose mother lived in Chester and adored *Coronation Street*. I told her that was nice and she said 'I hate my mother-in-law and she's going to be so jealous when I show her your autograph.' I was dumbstruck – what do you say in a situation like that?

Years later I found out that Stephen might have got HIV from a student of about twenty-three he had a relationship with years earlier. The lad, called Keir, is dead now. God rest him. They had visited us up in Maltby, but there was no way Derrick would let them share a bed in the bungalow. Even when they came to my flat in Manchester I wouldn't let them share a room. I tell Stephen he can bring boys to my house, but they must sleep in separate beds. Whilst I'm not discouraging it – I'm not encouraging it either. I can't take to the idea of him bringing a man home and sleeping in the same bed as him.

I hope these days that Stephen isn't having sex. I don't believe there is such a thing as safe sex, so to save him spreading the virus I'm sure he has stopped. He does his best to help AIDS charities and I've promised to help whenever I can. He helps Crusaid, FACTS – the Foundation for AIDS Counselling Training and Support – and Food Chain, which provides one hot three-course meal a week for between 130 and 160 people with full-blown AIDS. He also supports the London Lighthouse and Body Positive.

Stephen has, for the last few years, manned a tent at London's Gay Pride rally. In 1993 I had hoped to attend with a crowd from *Coronation Street*, but I collapsed in June and was later confined to barracks by Granada. He was very disappointed when only Debbie McAndrew, who played Curly's lodger Angie Freeman, turned up. He'd called his spot the *Coronation Street* tent when half a dozen of my pals in the cast promised to go along and sign autographs for charity. I was very glad that Debbie showed up, and I've no doubt if I'd been in the studios I could have persuaded a few of the others to go along as well.

Only Julie Goodyear and Thelma Barlow wrote explaining why they couldn't attend. Big hearted Thelma sent a generous donation, which was very sweet.

For months after Stephen told me he was infected with HIV I was not myself. I went into a sort of trance. I lost weight, lots of weight, with all the worry. I kept trying to put it behind me. But it was like having a giant piece of concrete in my stomach – I felt laden down. The burden was immense, but it did bring us closer as a family.

After the story appeared in the *News of the World* we went off for a family holiday to the Seychelles to escape the reporters camped on the doorstep. It wasn't much fun, but we enjoyed it as best we could.

When we got back home I started going out more, which was pretty difficult to do as I was already out nearly every night. I began going over the top to enjoy myself. If I pushed the boat out before – this time I went at it like a hurricane.

I went on incredible benders. I spent all my time trying to enjoy myself in bars to wipe away the heartache I felt inside for Stephen. But all the time this big concrete lump was weighing me down. No matter how hard I tried I couldn't get Stephen's predicament off my mind.

I drank to blot out the pain, but when I woke next morning with a hangover the ache in my heart was still there.

In life there is a natural order and that is that children outlive their parents. When someone dies tragically, at an early age, it is so heartbreaking. I've seen families ripped apart by the loss of a child. When you get to the position I am in and know your only son is dying it is too terrible for words. But Stephen has come to terms with what he has got and is living his life to the full. I admire him more than words can say.

Stephen referred to the newspaper revelations about him as a real double whammy. The Tories coined the phrase to describe Labour's tax plans, in the run-up to the general election. But for Stephen the double whammy was the world discovering one Sunday that he was both gay and suffering with HIV.

He had revealed his sexuality to me eight years earlier – when he was thirty. I had been travelling round the world and everywhere I went the bands I worked with would give me cuddly toys. I had a tremendous collection of teddy bears. I was saving them up for when Stephen got married, so I could give them as presents to my grandchildren.

Working as hard as I had been I never saw that much of Stephen as a child. I was pretty out of touch with the type of presents a young lad would like from my trips round the globe. My gifts weren't perhaps as good as they could have been. There were always lots, but not really the type of things he wanted. I used to molly-coddle him a bit, but that was probably through the guilt of not being at home as often as other mums.

I asked him when he was going to start courting. But every time he'd dodge the issue. He'd never had a girl-friend, but I just thought of him as a slow starter. Then when he was thirty I said: 'When are you going to get bloody married? I want some room here. I want to get rid of some of these toys.'

He was going out to a nightclub in Doncaster when

he snapped back: 'Mother I think we'd better get something straight.' But by the time I asked 'what' he was already on his way down the road. He never did tell me.

I waited up for him to return that night. By this point I had some sort of instinctive feeling, having worked among gays in the clubs. But, I'll be honest, it was still a terrible shock when I found out he was gay.

That night I just asked him: 'Stephen, do you meet girls in these clubs?' And he replied: 'Mam, I'm getting a bit sick of you asking me all the time. I'm gay.'

Straightaway I said: 'It's me isn't it?' He looked puzzled and said: 'What do you mean?' I told him that I'd worked all these gay clubs and was always coming home raving about the warm receptions I received. I had a big friend who was gay and I'd brought him home lots of times and Stephen had seen me make a fuss of him.

It seems ridiculous now, but I thought he'd seen me making a fuss of gays and had turned homosexual to get my attention. I felt I had neglected him and that had some way altered his sexuality. I was very upset to tell the truth. My only son was never going to give me the grandchildren I craved. And I blamed myself.

I was from a traditional working class background and homosexuality wasn't talked about in families like ours in those days. It was still not an accepted thing, society has thankfully become more open to it these days. Back in the late Sixties free love was okay between a man and a woman. But two blokes, now that was a tricky one. Only in the most liberal circles would it have been acceptable.

To this day I still think, deep down, it is my fault. If I'd stayed at home and not gone on the stage, perhaps he'd be different. He never had the childhood he should have had. There are a whole host of perhaps and ifs that I run through my mind, despite reassurances from Stephen. Mothers will always blame themselves if something isn't quite right.

Stephen has assured me it is just the way he is. He told me he realized when he was about eleven or twelve, that he wasn't the same as the other boys. He was never a Georgie Porgie, pudding and pie type of boy. He'd never gone for girls at school, but he also told me he'd never gone for boys either. He simply never has had a sexual feeling for a girl.

Only after his AIDS diagnosis did I discover that Stephen's first sexual experience happened when he was 12 in a Doncaster cinema, where he was molested by a man. Stephen did not view it as sexual abuse, but he knew it was wrong. The little swine went back to Saturday matinees on a regular basis for more of the same.

Derrick didn't discover Stephen's sexuality until after me – we both knew it would upset him terribly. His automatic reaction was to blame me. He said the way I glorified the things that went on in the gay clubs had turned our precious son that way. It was a lot harder for Derrick to come to terms with it. He was angry and told Stephen straight 'you want to be gay, well you are not being gay in this house.'

At the time Stephen was working in the local KP peanut factory. But he later moved away and spent years travelling round from job to job abroad. He worked for a spell in the Far East and in Holland, where he used to watch me on *Coronation Street*.

I never told our Keith or Duggie that Stephen was gay, but they must have known. He always had a flat on his own.

I did my best to persuade Stephen that he wasn't gay – of course I now know nothing I could have said would have changed him. That is the way he is and we have to accept it.

Even though I worked gay clubs and loved homosexuals I didn't want my son to be one. I still don't like him being gay. But now I'd rather him be gay and happy than suppress it and be desperately unhappy with his life. He's only got one life, and if he's happy with it then that's all that matters. God made us all and he must have had a plan in mind.

But I still went wild after Stephen revealed he had HIV. I had enjoyed a swinging sex life for years and had strayed from the marital bed dozens of times. Derrick living seventy miles away, and being as cold as he is, didn't help my fidelity one iota. I eventually took an AIDS test myself, but I'll tell you all about my life as a promiscuous pensioner later.

Up until Stephen's health hit the headlines I had been making them myself with a string of medical problems. Of course with my pharmaceutical knowledge I can be an awkward patient. I remember one doctor trying to fob me off with a placebo for a stiff shoulder. I told him it was no good and would never cure it. After I told him I'd studied pharmacy at Nottingham University he was very wary of me.

In the 1960s I collapsed on stage at the Ace of Clubs, during a cabaret performance, and was rushed to hospital. After tests, doctors discovered I had a dodgy heart valve. I was later told I had mitral stenosis, which is narrowing of the mitral valve in the heart. It causes the left side of the heart to work harder to force blood through the narrowed valve.

Medics told me it was probably the result of scarring of the valve during a childhood bout of rheumatic fever. Mother always told me I never had it as a child, but I did get yellow fever so perhaps that caused the problem. Women are four times more likely to suffer from the condition than men. I had a lot of tests before they diagnosed it. ECGs, chest x-rays the lot. They didn't rush into it.

I collapsed a total of four times as a result of angina attacks brought on by the condition. One of them happened on Manchester's Piccadilly railway station. That was the time I was in hospital the day my screen husband Bert died. After one of my collapses I spent a week at Helen Worth's cottage with her and her charming husband Michael Angelis. She's a brilliant actress and, in later years, we'd grumble together about the disappearance of all those great Ivy and Gail scenes we had when Brian was round.

I was so worried by these attacks that I paid £8,000 to have valvuplasty, where a balloon is inserted into the heart valve, through a catheter, to stretch the opening. It appears to have done the trick, although I still go for yearly check-ups to a heart specialist called Colin Bray.

When I was in Africa I was a novelty in one of their hospitals when I went in for treatment. They had not had a case of mitral stenosis in and I had all these young doctors round listening in to my heart with stethoscopes. I quite enjoyed that. They had to turn me on my side and lift my boobs – it was a very pleasant experience. I thought, 'I've clicked again', but all they were interested in was science.

I'd been rushed into hospital as an emergency after picking up a tropical illness, when I fell off a boat into a stagnant pond. I was on a safari trip with a belly dancer friend called Syringa when the boat overturned and we plunged into this gunge. I lost two stones in weight and suffered awful diarrhoea and vomiting after picking up a bug in the slimy green water. I went down to under six stone and friends were very worried for me. But it didn't get the better of me and I battled back to fitness.

Yet I very nearly met my maker years later outside the Granada studios. I was walking over to the Old School bar after a day's filming. There was a fair on the lawn and a horse box between me and the bar. I walked past the box as the nag was being led out. Just as I did so someone patted the beast and it flicked its hind leg straight into my side. The pain was incredible.

It felt as if it had kicked a hole right through me. The bruising that followed was phenomenal. I was still going to the doctor two months later, because the bruise hadn't subsided. Thelma, who plays scatty Mavis Wilton, suggested I use arnica cream to take the bruise out and it worked. She's probably the furthest removed from her screen character of all of the people on *Coronation Street*. She is a really sensible lady and a great actress. She has a knowledge of homeopathic medicine and loves organic gardening. She must be an expert on that, because she's written a book on it.

On the Street my wealth of medical knowledge often came in handy and I became an agony aunt for some of the cast. In 1979 Julie Goodyear came to me when she discovered a smear test she'd had was positive. She was really frightened. I told her there was nothing to be scared of, because I had a hysterectomy a couple of years earlier and it had saved my life.

I showed her the ruddy big scars I'd been left with on my stomach from the hysterectomy and from Stephen's birth – with hindsight they would not have cheered her up much. Although I did explain that the operations were routine and thankfully they didn't leave massive scars anymore.

Julie needed surgery after her smear and, following two operations, was given the all-clear. She then put her heart and soul into raising funds for cancer research. Although that led to a run-in with the law when Julie was charged with conspiring to defraud after a charity raffle. Somebody had allegedly rigged it to raise more cash for the cause.

She told us that something had gone wrong with a section of the charity that she knew nothing about. She had to work with the strain of the court case hanging over her for about a year. But when she appeared at

Manchester Crown Court she was aquitted. The judge completely threw out the case against her.

As a result of her tireless campaigning she raised enough money to set up the Julie Goodyear Laboratory, at Christie Hospital in Manchester, which analyses smear tests taken in the North West. A tremendous achievement that everyone in the cast admired.

My own cervical cancer was only detected when our Keith's wife Judy came over from Zambia and persuaded me to go for a smear test with her. I'd been on the pill for nine years, but never had a smear and Judy was shocked. In Zambia the American doctors insisted women on the pill have regular smears. I went with her to the clinic on a Wednesday and thought nothing of it.

The next Monday I was up in Sunderland preparing for cabaret when Derrick rang to tell me there was a social worker at the door who wanted to talk about my smear test. My heart sank, straight away I guessed something was wrong. The woman on the phone suggested I get back as quickly as possible and have a second smear, because there was something not quite right with the first. After the second I was called to see a gynaecologist called Mr Balantyne who told me I needed to have my uterus removed.

I asked him why there was such a rush and he explained there was a lot of cancer and if I'd waited another three months it would have spread. It would have killed me if they hadn't performed the operation.

I'll never forget regaining consciousness as the anaesthetic wore off. An Indian lady doctor was at the bedside and said: 'Mrs Barksby you had a lovely clean operation, the womb, the fallopian tubes and the ovaries all came right away.' As soon as she said it I screamed at the top of my voice 'No, no you haven't taken my ovaries away.' The doctor asked what the problem was. I explained that after my Auntie Bessie had it done she had grown a moustache. I said: 'You'll turn me into a man.' I was hysterical. The tears were flowing so much that my nightdress got damp.

Our Duggie and his wife Jackie came to visit me during my fourteen-day stay in Moorgate Hospital at Rotherham. He brought me a little telly in and cheered me up with his good humour. He noticed my doctor, a lovely Pakistani chap, and said 'I hope he's not operated on you with a knife and fork.' I didn't know what he was on about until he pointed out the doctor's name ... Cutlery Walla. He also told me I'd really become a star, because it was admission to my bedside by ticket only. I was only allowed two visitors at a time. Each pair had to pass the tickets over when they left to the next visitors.

For about six years after I never had hormone replacement therapy – HRT. But during the years I wasn't given HRT I developed osteoporosis in my knee – it's like having a sponge in the joint. But as soon as they put me on HRT that stopped deteriorating. A lack of oestrogen, the hormone produced by the ovaries, brings the condition on. My life changed for the better after I was given HRT, or at least my sex life did as I shall divulge later.

But for now I take twenty-one pills each day just to stay alive. I take two Betablockers called Monoco 5 a day to slow my heart; one Nicoumalone anticoagulant to thin my blood; one digoxin to keep the membrane in my heart pump steady; four water pills called Neonaclex-K; two ferrous sulphate iron tablets; two Thiamine vitamin B tablets to help my liver as a result of my drinking days; one Prem Pack hormone replacement pill and eight other pills to help me withdraw from the sleeping tablets I was using.

I don't believe in going into £1,000-a-night clinics to help me beat addictions – like the sleeping pills, which I was using like Smarties when I discovered about

Stephen's condition. I believe if you have a strong will you can beat most things with that.

I managed to get myself out of the dreadful drinking habit without resorting to a clinic. I never used Alcoholics Anonymous either because, although I polished off pints of sauce, I was never an alcoholic. My resolve not to drink to excess since my collapse last year has proved that. I'm proud of myself for what I've achieved through willpower. I know those close to me are proud of me too and that is important to me.

A specialist once said to me: 'You have one of the finest livers I've ever seen in someone who drinks too much – you don't deserve it.' I've given that liver of mine a hard time, so now I'm treating it well. I have no plans to go back on the boozing benders that were destroying my life. I have been there and done that, as they say, and don't need to do it anymore. If I hit the bottle again I will be dead and I don't want that just yet. I've tried suicide. It doesn't agree with me.

CHAPTER FOURTEEN

My Strange Marriage

Derrick was with me constantly when I was ill. To any by-stander, he was my guardian angel, a tower of strength who spent night after night at my hospital bedside. But that was just a front. To the public we were a devoted couple who'd commendably survived the ups and downs of a showbiz marriage. He was there when I was laid up in hospital, when I was at death's door. But there were hundreds, no, thousands of lonely nights when I came home at the dead of night to an empty shell of a house with no-one to talk to.

Unbeknown to the public, Derrick and I had lived apart for almost twenty years and hardly ever saw one another. Our relationship was a sham that we kept secret from everyone. The public face was one of adoration and unity. In private, it was sheer indifference.

While I spent most of my time alone in my plush home in Salford, Derrick was seventy miles away living a bachelor's life in the run-down Maltby bungalow which was once our marital home. I'd given up all hope of getting him to move in with me. He'd simply refused. I don't really know why we stayed together – apart from the fact that for most of our married lives I had supported him financially because Derrick hated work. I was his meal ticket to a life of leisure. But I honestly believed he never walked out on me because he loved me in a strange kind of way, and he feared I'd kill myself if I was totally alone.

He was probably right. My life had become an utter shambles during the traumatic months after discovering our only child had a death sentence hanging over his head. Suddenly my world was falling apart and I realized how meaningless life had become. I would never be a grandma, my career had reached a stalemate, and after seeking some much-needed affection in the arms of other men, much younger men, my marriage had crumbled around my ears. I wasn't sleeping or eating, and my weight plummeted to under seven stone. I found it difficult to concentrate on my lines and work was undoubtedly suffering. My only escape, I believed at the time, was to numb the pain with booze. Then because I was drinking like a fish and felt so wretched I'd convinced myself I had cancer. I was, in effect, worrying myself to death.

Of course, this didn't go unnoticed at Granada. To give my bosses their due, they could see I was going off the rails and tried to help me out – by offering to send me to a psychiatrist! I was outraged when Mervyn Watson first suggested it: me need help from a shrink! It seemed absurd. The thought went over and over in my mind and I almost told him where to stick his ludicrous idea. My son was HIV positive and I wanted to know why it had happened to him. Why, when there were only 600 people in the whole of the country with HIV, had he been stricken with it? Stephen wasn't promiscuous, he'd only had two relationships, and we knew who he'd got it from because the lad died. What good would it do talking about it? Would it prolong Stephen's life? Would it allow him to out-live his parents as children do?

But Bill was persistent and asked me to give it a try. He said Granada would pay for the sessions, and convinced me that anyone going through such a time would need some sort of help. It was true. How much longer could I take comfort from the bottle? Even in my hazy, confused state I knew that the drinking would eventually kill me. So I agreed to go along.

I felt apprehensive as I made my way to the pyschiatrist's surgery in well-heeled Altrincham, a posh suburb of Manchester. It was a beautiful priory house with ivy creeping up the walls. Inside, it was tastefully carpeted and decorated. I imagined walking into a waiting room full of nutcases, rocking from side to side in their chairs like a scene from *One Flew Over the Cuckoo's Nest*. If it had been like that I would have run a mile.

I walked into a waiting room with half a dozen people sitting round, and I felt a tremendous sense of unease as everyone turned their gaze to me. Many of them had recognized Poison Ivy, others just wanted to check me out, to see if I was mad. The question in fact had crossed my own mind. No-one said a word, but I could see them taking sneak glances. I was shocked when I took a good look myself as I waited for the pleasant-looking receptionist to call my name. None of them looked troubled, or mad – they were just ordinary people like me. They were probably just people with troubles that needed a helping hand to sort them out.

The doctor was lovely – a kindly-looking gentleman with greying hair and glasses in his mid fifties. He put me at my ease at once. I didn't know whether he watched the Street, or if he even knew who I was. If he did recognize me, he certainly didn't let on. For a start he called me Jean, or Mrs Barksby – and that threw me. To the nation and the Street's army of fans I was Ivy Tilsley. But to him I wasn't even Lynne. For the first time in years I was Jean, and I was forced to face up to what was really happening in my life. My real life. I didn't like being called Jean at first, it seemed alien to me – but the more he said it, the more it gave me comfort.

That comfort came in the fact I was able to shake off Ivy. It made me realize that I had become Ivy. My character had taken over my life, even though we were two completely different poeple. I ate and breathed my TV part. There was never any escape because everyone knew her, so I could never leave her at the studios when I left at the end of the night. She came home with me. Yet here I was, and Ivy simply didn't get a mention.

After my first visit I came out thinking, What a waste of time. All he did was show me pictures of his second wife and four kids. When I got home I realized he'd actually got me to talk about quite a lot, mostly Derrick. That had been spurred by the fact he called me Jean. It made me think of the past – and Derrick was the only person, apart from my brothers, who still called me Jean. It was something he had always been adamant about.

I went along every week after that and found myself talking more and more about Derrick. 'It's about time I met your husband, Jean,' the doctor said after my sixth visit. 'He seems to hold the key to what's locked up inside your head. Bring him with you next time you come.'

Derrick was furious. 'No way. Absolutely no chance. They might think you're crazy, but count me out because none of this is my fault.'

I told Derrick it takes two to make a mess of a marriage and that Granada probably wouldn't waste any more money sending me if I wasn't prepared to get to the root of the problem. The thought that I might have to pay myself, which meant that indirectly it would come out of our money, made a difference. Reluctantly he agreed to give it a try.

Once there, all hell let loose. Everything started pouring out of us both, and we both found years of pent-up anger rearing its ugly head. We began talking about Stephen at first, then he steered the conversation onto the marriage. Derrick surprised me by talking openly about all the things I'd done. He said life hadn't been easy being Mr Lynne Perrie. He kept nothing back, and told the doctor about all my affairs – at least the ones he knew of! I snapped back: 'If I'd been happy with you I wouldn't have been having affairs would I?'

The doctor was taking it all in. Then when Derrick was in full flow, the doc asked him why he hadn't left me. 'Because I loved her,' he muttered in whispered tones, as if he were ashamed of the fact that he felt any emotions at all. I hadn't heard him say that more than a handful of times in all the years I had known him. Once I would have given my right arm to hear him say those three little words. But it was too late now.

To my amazement, and to Derrick's, the doctor said to him, 'Well, you can't just sit there and blame her for everything. It seems to me that you have had a pretty good and easy life being married to Jean. I'm afraid if you stood by and accepted what she was doing, then you condoned it.' That didn't suit Derrick very much. He dried up, refusing to discuss further the problems of our long-suffering marriage.

On the way home we had a blazing row in the car. He was furious that the psychiatrist had suggested the break-down of our marriage was his fault as much as mine. It didn't help that I piped up, 'Told you so,' which rubbed even more salt into his smarting wounds.

The psychiatrist had scraped the surface, but nothing had been resloved between Derrick and me. He refused to make a return visit. And that was that.

Of course we talked about lots of other things. Liz Dawn's name came up frequently, and we discussed our relationship. It really was amazing how similar our lives had been – but with that came a sort of resentment for each other's success. Her life mirrored mine, and for a long time I had been in the position that she'd found herself in, earning the money and being the boss.

One day I'd fallen out with Derrick and Liz had had a row with her husband Don. 'I'm not going home tonight,' she said defiantly. 'I want to go out on the town.' It was before I'd bought my place in Manchester and I said I'd join her for a night out. We booked into a hotel and got our glad rags on.

We supped brandy and Babycham all night in a city centre bar and were getting rather tiddly when I spotted two blokes staring at us. The pub was a real knocking-off shop, but Liz said she knew one of them as she'd been introduced to him as the owner of the bar. 'I don't fancy yours much,' she giggled about the other fella, but she was only joking.

We ignored all the men who tried to give us the eye – to be honest, I think we scared them half to death, and no one would come anywhere near us. 'Bugger our husbands,' was the toast and we didn't go home. We had a good moan about what bloody fools we were not just for keeping our fellas in a life of luxury, but for putting up with the constant arguing on top!

It was refreshing because we both understood each other's gripes. Don was driving for Liz and Derrick was driving for me. Liz had left Don just as I in the past had left Derrick. I remembered how ill that made her at the time. She moved into a tiny flat on her own. She was in a real mess when I went round to see her. I cried, I felt so sorry for her. She was just sat there, miserable as sin, in the middle of the day with her dressing gown on. She had lost all her spark, and like me she was drinking heavily.

I suppose it made it easier for me to talk about Liz to the psychiatrist: that way I was not admitting my own failings, my own problems. Of course he saw straight through that!

But it turned into a happy ending for Liz. Don came to live with her and they sorted out their problems. He became her manager and now they enjoy a wonderful happy family life with their kids and grandchildren, which is more than I can say for Derrick and me.

When the papers found out I had been seeing a psychiatrist, I felt dreadful, like a freak. Even though I had only been receiving counselling sessions, a helping hand in a time of crisis, there was such stigma attached to going to see a shrink. Of course everyone does it in the States, it's the fashion – but not here in civilized England. I'd used every precaution to prevent the press from finding out. They already had me down as a drunk, and the last thing I needed was for them to think I was nuts as well. After my first visit I'd made sure I was allowed in through the back entrance and never sat in the main waiting room. I sat alone in a side room while I waited for the doctor in case anyone recognized me and contacted a newspaper. I had covered my tracks there.

So someone had obviously let it out at Granada. I couldn't blame the cast and others who worked on the show for gossiping – I would have been a hypocrite because there was no one worse for tittle-tattle then me! But it hurt to think someone had gone behind my back. While I was a chatterbox, I was never malicious. But it didn't stop me thinking about who could have told them. I went through all the names, all the possibilities of who had let the cat out of the bag, and even suspected my friends. But no one ever owns up and, as they say, there's no crying over spilt milk because the truth always surfaces eventually. And how could I blame anyone when I never really made a secret of my treatment myself? I used to tell everyone what was going on in my life, and kept very few secrets.

Ironically, my visits stopped a few weeks later – because my psychiatrist was taken into hospital with his nerves! I'd called for an appointment when his secretary told me he hadn't been too well. So that was the end of that. I just hope it wasn't anything to do with me.

My life apart from Derrick continued. I'd see him for the occasional weekend – usually when he needed some washing doing. He'd turn up with his little plastic carrier bag full of clothes. I'd feed and water him and then he'd drive back to Maltby in the Mercedes I'd given him. There was no question of sex. That had stopped a long time ago and I didn't even bother trying to get him worked up any more. As far as I was concerned, he just wasn't interested.

At one point, though, I'd actually wondered if he had another woman because his washing load was getting less and less. I wouldn't see him for two months and there would only be one pair of underpants for me to wash and just one sheet. 'What's her name, then,' I'd ask, but he'd play dumb, pretending not to know what I was talking about. 'You've either got another woman or you've been sleeping in the same bedding for the past two months,' I joked.

I wouldn't let him sleep in my bed when he stayed over sometimes because he smelt so bad. I have a nose like a bloodhound, and when he hadn't changed his clothes, I could smell it a mile off. I bought him all kinds of smellies – I tried everything to encourage him to rid himself of his little hygiene problem. One Christmas Stephen, Sandra and myself all bought him toiletries to drop a hint. Sandra even wrapped each item individually – including talc, deodorant, aftershave and even a pack of Odour Eaters for his shoes. But nothing seemed to shame him into making an effort.

When he'd climb into bed I'd say, 'For Christ's sake, Derrick, you stink worse than the dog.'

Grumbling, he'd roll out of bed. 'I'll go and put some smelly stuff on then.'

I simply couldn't drum it into him that he had to wash and use it every day at home to get rid of the smell, not just when he visited me. But he couldn't be bothered. I was totally the opposite. Every week there were fourteen pairs of knickers drying on the line. I'd wear a pair during the day, then I'd take a bath and change them for the evening.

Derrick had forgotten what it was like being looked after. He lived like a bachelor and he cared little for cleanliness. The only thing that mattered in his life was his greyhound Sally, and I'd often pull his leg that he was having an affair with her because he paid her much more attention and far nicer compliments than he ever paid me!

It was 1978 when I started to spend less and less time at home. I'd just started getting regular slots on the Street, but there was no permanent part for me in the script at that time so I busied myself with cabaret spots in the evening, driving up and down the country working the clubs. It was a hard slog. Sometimes I was doing *Coronation Street* in the day and going up to Newcastle to sing in three clubs in the night, then driving back for filming the following day. I used to work so hard I couldn't muster the energy to make a special effort to see Derrick and spent most nights in Manchester.

That set a precedent, and after that I rarely visited Maltby, preferring that Derrick visit me in the comfort of my neat little flat. At least there I knew the beds were clean, the fridge was always full of fresh food and it was modern and tidy. Going back to Maltby was like being in a time warp because the bungalow had been so neglected. It wasn't through lack of cash – Derrick had plenty of my money stashed away for a rainy day, he just didn't like to spend any of it.

Once, after a stint away, I got the shock of my life. I returned to find the house in Maltby like a pig sty – absolutely filthy. I knew I had to hatch a plan to get him out so that I could give it a damn good clean.

I'd already bought myself a ticket for a trip to Switzerland. I'd planned to go away on my own to get away from it all and have some fun, but instead I convinced Derrick to go for a much-needed holiday. 'Go and have a nice break on your own,' I said. 'You've never been abroad before.' And off he went.

I couldn't wait until he was out of the house so I could get to work chucking out all the rubbish he had collected over the years and stored like a magpie. As Derrick left on the Friday afternoon, a skip had been delivered by that night. In just a few days my skip was more full than next door's – and they were building an extra front bedroom and a new kitchen! I went through every room with a fine-toothed comb ... and a bottle of disinfectant.

I cleared the shed, the loft and the cellar, and I can honestly say I have never seen so much junk in all my life. Things I hadn't seen for years, useless items I had no idea were still in existence, had been neatly stacked and saved – 'just in case.' To my utter amazement Derrick had even saved the top off an old sewing machine which I had chucked out years earlier when it had seized up on me. What good that was supposed to do, I had no idea. There were still building materials left over from when the house was under construction – and we had no possible use for them at all. There were bits of drainpipe, old tiles, decrepit furniture and stinking clothes stashed away in bags. I called two burly blokes round and said, 'Right, we've got a week to clear this lot out.'

By Wednesday I needed another skip. In his shed at the bottom of the garden I found old newspaper reports on dog racing dating back twenty years which he'd been saving. The whole lot was chucked out. Then I had to start cleaning – another mammoth task.

Derrick went berserk when he came home. 'What have you done with all my stuff? We could have used most of that.'

I was bloody fuming. I said, 'I've been on my hands and knees cleaning that little lot out, and I am going to tell you something else. Don't you ever let it get like that again. When I picked up some old floorboards which were neither use nor ornament, I was almost sick when hundreds of woodlice crawled out from underneath.' He stormed out and took the dog for a walk.

Derrick's incessant tightness inspired me to introduce him into my stage act. While the likes of Bob Monkhouse and Bernard Manning were doing gags about how fat their mother-in-laws were, I was ridiculing my husband's obsession with money – and he loved it. It was probably the only time Derrick received any attention from me. During my act I'd go down into the audience, pick up a fella's pint and knock it back in less than five seconds. It was my party piece and it went down a bomb. Then I'd ask the audience: 'Have you ever seen a miracle?' They'd always say no and I'd reply: 'Well, you're going to see one now. My husband is going to go to the bar and he is physically going to open his wallet and buy you two pints back. Aren't you Derrick?' Derrick would look at me and gasp: 'Two, two?' 'Yes, Derrick, two. That fella's either got a red tie on, or he's gasping for a pint. Now get to that bar.' He loved it because he felt part of the act, part of my life, though he'd never admit that.

My singing was something I never gave up, even when I became permanent on the Street. I'd do personal appearances, and as I've said I couldn't resist getting up and doing a turn at the show's parties. Derrick resented my career. He would have liked to have had me at home, to be the proud and efficient little housewife. He liked his home-cooked food, he enjoyed being pampered when I'd had the time to play house, but he knew it was always short-lived and soon forgotten by me.

Sometimes I wondered if I would have liked that too, to have been settled, to live a normal life. When I was on stage, one song particularly used to move me to tears: 'I Miss the Hungry Years'. Every time I sang it I dedicated it to Derrick because it reminded me of the time we had before fame played havoc with our lives. The tears would stream down my face as I sang those magical lyrics: 'Once upon a time, that lovely long ago, when we didn't have a dime. Those days with me and you, we lost along the way. How could I be so blind not to see the door closing on the world I once had before? Looking through my tears ... I missed the hungry years.' It took me back to the days when we had nowt. I'd always worked, so we never went without food in our bellies, but we certainly knew nothing of the luxury we would later take for granted.

I remembered the fun we had when we bred pedigree dogs and entered them for Crufts. We reared twelve beautiful Wirefox puppies in our tiny back yard and won a second prize with a seven-month-old pup. We had a darling dog with a little beard – we thought he was timid until he bit Derrick. I couldn't believe my eyes when without thinking Derrick turned round and bit him back, right on the nose. The dog never left his side after that.

Then we got into the greyhounds after he 'acquired' a dog that had jumped over a friend's back wall and he started breeding it. It had a litter of twelve pups, three of which died at birth, one we gave away, sold two and reared the other six. Then we started going to the tracks together.

They were never glamorous days, but they were fun. Derrick left me to feed them with a strict diet of Vitabrite, which he swore by. But unbeknown to him, I was so taken with the little mites I'd buy them fresh meat, steaks and mince. As he was proudly prancing around with his litter of hounds with their fine shiny coats, little did he know they were eating only the best – with tins of rice pudding to follow every meal. They ate better than we did.

I helped out with training the dogs for the tracks. I bought Derrick a bike and he attached a dummy rabbit to the back so the dogs could chase it. Then he asked me to cycle, which was a dead loss because I'd get less than four yards and they'd catch up with me.

I knew that our marriage might have stood a chance had I not pursued my stage career. But I was not one for regrets. Derrick often said, 'If only we'd done this, if only that would have happened.' I told him I'd have IF carved on his gravestone when he died. And when it came down to it, Derrick was just as happy to live with the money as without it.

He knew I'd had affairs, he accepted that. He'd taken me back when most men would have thrown me out and called me all the names under the sun. I was a fiery little bugger, and it's a wonder I'm still alive because a lot of men wouldn't have put up with me, I would have sent them over the edge. But I still contend that if he'd been so dissatisfied, he wouldn't have stood for it. And I suppose I lost a lot of respect for him because he didn't take me in hand. In a way it was showing me that he didn't care about me as much as I'd have liked him to.

The trouble was, I could never get into Derrick's head. I thought I was in charge, I earned the money and called the shots. I'd go away, have affairs, tell him what I had got up to in bed – and he would still take me back. I always knew he was going to be there for me, regardless of what I did. If I wanted to do anything I did it – I didn't care a damn about Derrick or anybody else. I know that was selfish, very selfish of me. Now as I'm getting older, I'm a bit more considerate. But in hindsight, Derrick never did anything he didn't want to do. When we rowed, and it got a little too heated for him, he walked away without resolving anything. I liked a good row, to get everything out in the open, but he always left me feeling frustrated. In a way that gave him an edge over me. And he never left me, so I never knew exactly where I stood with my darling husband. One minute I'd feel as if I was trampling all over his feelings, taking him for granted and manipulating my position as breadwinner. The next I felt as if he was laughing on the other side of his face at me, totally hoodwinking me into a false sense of security.

No matter what I said or how much I threatened him in my moments of madness, he wouldn't leave Maltby and come to live with me. He said he had no intention of spending all day hanging around for me. 'I won't know a soul. I was born here in Maltby, I know everyone and do my shopping in the morning and take three hours talking to people. They all want to know what you are up to, find out how you're getting on. All my friends are here, my dominoes partners, my life. What would I do in Manchester?' I was mad as hell, and told him if he wanted to stay put he'd have to start paying the bills and keeping himself. Of course that never happened.

Six weeks after my sixtieth birthday I mentioned to Derrick that I hadn't been sent a free bus pass or my pension book. 'You have, actually,' he told me. 'But I have been collecting your pension for you and using it as out-of-pocket expenses.' He was a cheeky bugger because I'd never stopped paying him a 'wage' just to keep him off the dole. In a bizarre kind of way, that made him the boss – he wouldn't give up his bungalow, his friends, his dogs and his privacy in exchange for my lifestyle. As long as the money was still pouring in, he was happy on his own.

They say distance makes the heart grow fonder, but I don't know whether I believe that. If Derrick had moved in with me as I'd wanted, then we would probably be divorced by now after finding out we simply couldn't live with each other. But we'd probably be a lot better off than we are now, because Derrick would have had tighter controls on the purse strings. He was always planning for the future while I flitted away every penny I could lay my hands on. But the more time we spent apart, the more we got used to our own independence, our own way of living.

And you get more set in your ways, it becomes more difficult to compromise.

I didn't fancy the idea of having to break my routines, making allowances for Derrick's dirty underpants and socks lying round the place. I liked living alone. If I'd been stuck at home doing his washing and ironing it would have driven me crazy. We would never have gone out to dinner or done anything glamorous because that simply wasn't his scene. It took me all my time trying to get him out of his overalls. He never wore a suit because he never went anywhere. He wasn't fond of going out and so never had to make the effort, though when he did he looked tremendous. But he never felt comfortable in fancy clothes. The number of times I'd bought him fashionable gear, sophisticated jackets and shoes – and they stayed in the wardrobe untouched for years. Johnny Briggs used to beg me for some of the clobber I'd got for Derrick when I'd tell him how the moths were getting more wear out of it than he was. Especially a beautiful white leather jacket I'd bought for him on a trip abroad.

I can't be blameless in all this, of course. Derrick would say that Ivy took over my life, that everything I did was a mirror reflection of the antics of my screen character. At the time I thought the suggestion was ludicrous. Now I strongly suspect he was right. Today I can see that Ivy was taking over my life and I had stopped thinking about myself as even being Lynne. As I've said, Derrick was the only person, apart from my brothers and the psychiatrist, who called me Jean. He'd always refused to bow down to my fame. I look back and I think maybe I resented that. I didn't want to be Lynne or Jean, because Ivy's life was a lot easier. She didn't have as many problems as me.

I should have left her behind every night when I finished at the studios, but foolishly I allowed her to come everywhere with me. Derrick would taunt me, saying it was like being married to Ivy – that I *was* Ivy. He said, 'You never escape, and if you've a minute off, you're learning your lines or talking to your fans who want to speak to Ivy.' I suppose I couldn't think about anybody else – I was Ivy, and Derrick was right. Even the scripts eventually seemed to reflect my own sorrow, and I'd sit in bed reading them crying myself to sleep every night. I couldn't distinguish myself from the character, and that depressed me a great deal.

But through thick and thin, Derrick and I are still together – and Ivy has now been removed from our lives. Where it leaves us now, I really don't know. It will be strange for us both not having her round. It makes me wonder if we are soul mates, if we are ever meant to be apart. We can't seem to live with each other, but we can't live without the comfort of knowing the other will always be there. We must still be in love – after all, we've been through hell and high water together. Or is it just the need for security, a habit which allows us a little familiarity in our bizarre lives? Maybe neither of us can bring ourselves to say goodbye and instead have clung together, hurting each other enormously along the way – him by starving me of emotional commitment, me by having endless affairs behind his back. But neither of us is young any more. We are both getting on in years, both needing comfort and company. As my mother always said, 'Better the devil you know.' That was all right for her. She had met and married the man she loved and spent the rest of her life with him. Fate, it seemed, had always played its part in our lives and whether we like it or not, we remain somewhat reluctantly tied together.

CHAPTER FIFTEEN

My Toyboys

Tied by fate we were, but Derrick and I had come to a mutual understanding that while he was preoccupied with my pay packet I was far more interested in what lay waiting for me in the guise of other men. Let's say that when I reached sixty my husband picked up my pension – and I was busy picking up toyboys.

It sounds terrible, doesn't it, a woman of my age still lusting after extramarital affairs? But as the psychiatrist had said, by virtue of the fact that Derrick had never walked out, he had condoned my behaviour. Subconsciously we both knew his lack of emotional commitment and physical love had forced me to seek solace in the arms of other men. That's apparently the way he wanted it and why he stayed with me. I had the shrink's report to back that up. As far as I was concerned, I couldn't lose really. Of course, that didn't prevent the endless vicious rows about my infidelity when Derrick caught me out. But I'm afraid we'd both come to realize that faithfulness never seemed to play a part in our relationship.

Even as I write this book, I've dabbled again. I confess I've had a brief affair with a toyboy lover twenty years younger than me, and I've enjoyed every minute of it.

I'd not been anywhere near another man for a couple

of years when I stumbled across an old boyfriend, and we rekindled the flames of passion. I tried to fight off the urge to go headlong into a relationship. I really wanted to stay faithful, to give my marriage to Derrick a chance. Putting my life onto the pages of a book was making me take stock. I'd resigned myself to being a one-man woman for the first time in my life. But I knew what pleasures lay before me when I bumped into my old beau on a night out, and I couldn't resist.

He all but moved into my house during our short romance. He was a terrific lover and kept going all night long. I'd be forced to spend the whole of the next day in bed through sheer exhaustion after experiencing orgasm after orgasm in his skilful hands. For about three weeks we got caught up in the bliss of it all. We'd spend all our time at home at my house, cooking, sensually massaging each other's bodies with exotic oils, sharing baths and making fantastic love. Well, we couldn't exactly go out for nights on the town together, could we? He could, literally, make love all night, and he knew how to treat a woman. I once had seven orgasms in one night. Ralph Halpern, eat your heart out! He simply wasn't happy until he'd satisfied me.

To be honest, I was grateful it ended – I couldn't keep up, and that's the first time I've ever admitted that. No matter how many tablets I was taking to slow me down, that man was no good for my heart condition. There was no animosity when we broke up. We both knew there was no future in it, the sex was just a bit of fun. Even so, I couldn't resist testing the water. It's the story of my life. I suppose old habits die hard.

The latest lover was my twentieth illicit encounter during my marriage – at least the twentieth that Derrick got to know about. It may come as a shock for him to learn there were more, many more. Too many to mention individually. Even I have lost count of exactly how many men I have bedded over the years. I suppose that's a shocking admission for a woman of my age. But no one was as shocked by my behaviour as the nurse who did my AIDS test for me just after my sixtieth birthday.

But first let me tell you about my passion for young men. Toyboys are a phenomenon that still mystifies people. Why do older women prefer younger blokes? Well, look at Joan Collins, look at Cher, look at Kate O'Mara ... they're not randy old women out for a good time. We've simply rediscovered our sexuality and our appeal. And of course, apart from a reputation for bedding toyboy lovers, our other common denominator is ... HRT, Hormone Replacement Therapy.

I have no doubt that HRT increased my libido tenfold. Suddenly after a long stretch in the sexual wilderness with Derrick I rediscovered sex and I never looked back. The HRT gave me the confidence to enjoy and exploit passion properly. After years of lying back and thinking of England, I started thinking of me. I began to experiment and explore – to find out what pleased me. I felt like a woman again, it filled me with vitality, youthfulness and a lust for life, as well as lust for the other.

Before I started on the HRT, I hadn't much felt like sex. That's not to say I didn't indulge. Many a morning after the night before I'd wake up to find a stranger in my bed and have no idea how he'd got there. Let alone who he was. It was a bad habit. A pal wrote a song for me entitled 'Ships in the Night', and I always thought about the futility of those one-night stands when I sang it. But for a long time I just didn't fancy sex.

I've talked about my hysterectomy, so we won't go into any more gory details. That period was a strange time for me. For some women, the menopause drags on for years as their bodies slowly come to term with the fact that the reproductive days are over. Me? I crashed through the menopause overnight and got the whole bloody lot at once. That meant of course that one minute I was full of hormones, the next everything had been removed. Nowadays, I would have been put on HRT immediately, but at the time my quack didn't believe in meddling with nature. So I struggled on without them. It was six years later when I changed doctors that the new GP told me I could have been put on the HRT straight after the op. I had no idea what it even stood for, let alone what a difference it was going to make to my life.

I was put on a course of testosterone and oestrogen – the male and female hormones. But they soon took me off testosterone because as my ovaries had been whipped out too I didn't need them. I felt a little dizzy when I first started taking them, but I could feel the difference. Apart from feeling as randy as hell, my complexion improved no end. And that was without the aid of the expensive creams I have since become a sucker for. I'll buy anything that promises to make me more youthful, even if it's a tiny pot of lotion costing £500. I'm a marketing man's dream.

Roy Douglas had awakened my sexual desires without the aid of drugs, but HRT was something different. I became rampant. After Roy had unlocked my ability to orgasm I became a skilled lover. I realized he wasn't really so magical in bed – other men could do as well, with guidance. Of course I can't blame the HRT for all my dalliances. I was playing round behind Derrick's back probably before the scientist who invented the stuff was a twinkle in his father's eye.

My first-ever affair was with a man who lived in a big house. He was very well-to-do. He was a professional man, fair, stocky and not so dishy. But I was still impressed that he was interested in me. It was the start of the swinging Sixties. I'd been married about ten years and realized from early on that Derrick didn't have much of a libido. So when I plunged headlong into my first extra-marital affair, I was completely overawed by the whole thing. Not that it was a big love job, far from it.

My lover had a beautiful home where he lived with his wife. This really does sound awful, but she was an invalid. So whether they couldn't have sex I don't know. It wasn't something we discussed. We just, as they say, got down to the business in hand. But I felt sorry for him and could understand why he was carrying on. He was only a young man and had been prematurely robbed of his conjugals. I was thirty-one, he was three years younger, so my very first experience of being unfaithful was with a toyboy.

We first got chatting in the local club. I was there with Derrick, and he was on his own. In those days everyone knew who their neighbours were, and I had seen him round about. It wasn't like today where everyone keeps themselves to themselves. People were literally falling over each other to dig into other folk's business – and to be honest, most had nowt to hide anyway. Kids of today laugh when you tell them how everyone left their doors open and talk of how different life was then. But it was.

I was working the clubs at the time, so it was part of the act to mix with the punters. You had to mingle with them – they were your bread and butter, the difference between making it and drifting into oblivion. If you had a chat and seemed amiable enough, they'd be back time and time again. If they didn't like you, you could fall flat on your face. It was all part of the scene. And as I've said, so was being the target of almost every man's lust.

Steve bought me a drink, we got chatting and he asked me out. We'd go out for a drink and a meal, then he'd drive me home – stopping off at Clumber Park round the corner first for a quickie. He'd back his car into the bushes and we'd do our gymnastics in the back seat. I was an energetic young woman, eager to learn.

When I think back, it was boring as hell. But at the time it gave me a thrill. The affair lasted only a couple of months before I decided I was playing with fire and called it off.

It's funny how I can clearly remember my first affair, and my last. But don't ask me to fill you in with every encounter in between. Some happened during my drunken years when I could hardly remember who I was, let alone the names of any of my conquests. But there always seemed to be a similar pattern in my approach to getting young men into bed. I have always had a penchant for younger men which has simply got stronger as I've grown older. There have been dozens of occasions when I have rolled over the morning after the night before to find a stranger lying flat out in my bed. I'd be stunned, staring at the hair on the pillow next to me, thinking: Jesus Christ, what the hell am I doing with that in bed?

Slowly, through the haze of the fifteen brandy and Babychams I'd had the night before, it would come back to me. Of course, during the evening he'd seemed attractive, a young Clark Gable. I'd have to have him. But in the cold light of a sober morning it was a very different story. It's the kind of sexist joke a blue comedian would tell in his act: 'She looked slim and gorgeous after fifteen pints, but she'd put on ten stone and had a pig's head transplant by the time I woke up next to her the morning.' I've told you, sometimes I was worse than any man – and I could relate to that feeling.

Sometimes I'd try to creep out of bed. If they woke, I'd make some excuse about not having time for breakfast, give them their bus fare and get them out.

Of course my one-night stands weren't all quite so unmemorable. Some were wonderful – nights of joy and lust, a young lover wanting the knowledge and experience of a mature woman. It was strange, but regardless of how young they may be, I could always manage to tire them out in my quest for sexual satisfaction. My favourite chat-up line was to ask a man I fancied how much I could buy him for: 'Come on, everyone has a price. How much are you?' I would tease and offer to take him on a cruise. I had no intention of paying, and never did. But that way they got the message from the start that I was the boss, and would call all the shots.

I'd go for anything as long as they were a bit younger, and I didn't even have to fancy them. I was horny all the time – and to be honest I think it frightened Derrick off. He stopped feeling like a man, he wasn't in charge and that dented his sexual pride. It's understandable that he stopped wanting to make love to me. I scared him.

The drink combined with my HRT was a lethal enough combination, but I was also on Royal Jelly which contains a natural aphrodisiac, which further heightened my sex drive. Apparently I was very noisy and enthusiastic in bed – always had been, so there was no change there.

When I lost my driving licence in the early seventies, I hired a chauffeur to drive me around the clubs. He was gorgeous, a bronzed Adonis in his early twenties with long blond flowing locks, just the way I liked them. I suppose he was more of a groupie really. He was impressed with my act and the lifestyle I led. He was in total awe of everything I did, including in the bedroom. He fell for me in quite a big way and actually wanted to marry me. He took me to a club in Newcastle where I was doing a show and I was so proud parading this God on my arm. But the next time I went to that club was with Derrick and the barmaid took one look at him and said to me, 'He's a sight better than that thing you had hanging off your arm last time you were in here.'

One night on my travels I stayed in a guest house and Tony Christie and his band, who were topping the bill, were booked into the same place. Obviously me and my young chauffeur were at it hammer and tongs, and Tony Christie was in the room below mine. The next morning

I went down for a leisurely breakfast – and it turned into a scene from *When Harry Met Sally*. The dining room was packed full of pensioners getting tucked into their eggs and bacon with pleasant music being played in the background. Suddenly the music from the loudspeakers was interrupted by a strange noise. It was the sighs and groans of a woman obviously in the throes of wild passion. The voice was building to a crescendo as the orgasm approached. And that ecstatic voice was mine.

I nearly died. I looked round the room and everyone was choking on their food. My face went a deep shade of purple and my toyboy turned beetroot red. Tony Christie couldn't contain his laughter at the table he shared with the other twelve members of his band.

I confronted him: 'What the hell do you think you're playing at?'

He said, 'Well that's what I have to listen to every night. So while you were out yesterday we taped a microphone under your bed so we could get a record of it. That way, you could listen to it too.'

He'd put the microphone under my bed and hidden the wires down the side of the carpet and out through the door so I wouldn't notice them. The affair ended when I got my licence back the following year. Derrick was anxious for me to get rid of him because he had an inkling of what was going on. But to this day I don't know what happened to that tape.

My affairs stretched through my club years and my days abroad. But it was my *Coronation Street* years that saw my sex drive go through the roof. Once, after a boozy night in the Old School, I took a bloke home to the flat after he'd told me he had nowhere to stay. I didn't tell him I only had one bedroom. He was the spitting image of Chris Quentin, my screen son. He was a weightlifter in his early thirties with a fantastic physique – and the first man ever to tire me out. I had the reputation of keeping men awake all night. No sooner had they rolled over and gone to sleep, I would be poking them in the back asking for more. But this one was different.

During the session I had to go to the bathroom to freshen up and go to the loo. I noticed he'd left his overnight bag in there and when I peeped inside I found every type of vibrator you could possibly think of. Jesus Christ, I thought, he comes prepared. I marched straight back into the bedroom and told him there was no way he was using any of them on me. He started laughing and said, 'You don't need them.' We made love all night and I was exhausted. He'd have gone on all the next day had I not kicked him out in the morning. I didn't even have the strength to cook him any breakfast.

My activities were renowned by the time I was a regular on *Coronation Street*. But it wasn't all a greed for gratuitous sex. One affair I had was very different, and the man concerned was very special. He was a fellow member of the cast. The romance went on for about nine months and no one ever found out. Obviously we had to keep it top secret because not only would it have ruined our careers, it would have devastated our families. Ours was not a mad, passionate love affair. It was simply brought on by loneliness and in a way despair. His relationship was on the rocks, going through a very unstable patch, and I was available – it was as simple as that. We were both far away from home, both in need of stability, comfort and attention. From our drunken nights together we tried to salvage a semblance of normal life. But what we found in each other was no substitute for what we both secretly yearned for – to be surrounded by a loving family. I can't name the person involved, who is still in the Street, because they are happily married now with kids. But I will say he was another toyboy. At the time I was euphoric – I thought I was having a wonderful time being wined and dined by someone in the same business, someone who understood the pressures and stresses of stardom.

People don't realize the difficulty of being famous. You couldn't cry on anyone's shoulder if you weren't happy, you couldn't go out with just anyone for a night. You couldn't really sleep with just anyone if you didn't want to suffer the consequences of your actions. Let's just say my friend thought more about that than me. He was a little more discreet, more careful. And it paid off because nobody ever found out. But we both knew it was shallow, and a poor substitute for the lives we should have been leading with our families. Eventually it fizzled out. But to this day we remain friends. I have to admit there were other little indiscretions on the Street with a few men I would never dream of naming. But it was always me who did the running. I'd invite them for a drink and then put the pressure on once I had them inside my den. There are not many men who turn sex down when it's handed to them on a plate. One thing would lead to another and Bob's your uncle. But it was never anything heavy, always a bit of harmless fun with no repercussions.

I was a terrible flirt and I got a bit of a name for it. I loved teasing men and getting their undivided attention because it made up for the lack of attention I received from my husband. But it only added to my reputation and sometimes I found myself in hot water.

One date that sticks in my mind is Thursday 20 November, 1989, when the whole cast appeared at the London Palladium for a Royal Command Performance. We were put up in a top hotel for the night. We all had a few drinks after the show – some more than others. After we'd retired in the early hours, there was a knock on my door and a fellow member of the cast was stood there begging to come in. I was worse for wear at the time, and he was smashed too. I invited him in, and inevitably we got down to having sex. He left and about half an hour later there was a tremendous banging on my door as he screamed at the top of his voice: 'Lynne, I have come back – I want some more.' Again, I can't tell you who it was. The toyboy in question would never forgive me. It was hilarious. I had to let him in, just to shut him up, but I'm sure all the cast knew exactly what had been going on as we travelled back to Manchester in silence on the coach the next day.

Coincidentally, I met up with Freddie Starr again that night because he was also appearing in the Command Performance. He joked with me: 'Stay away from me. I know all about your reputation.' Well, he'd experienced it at first hand, hadn't he?

I also met Hinge and Brackett, and Sir John Mills was the Master of Ceremonies. Johnny Briggs went crackers because he took a picture of me and John Mills and it came out beautifully. But I took one of the pair of them and it was so blurred you couldn't tell who the hell was in it. He was furious.

Somebody else with a big reputation for being randy was my co-star Ken Morley who, after only four years in the show as Reg Holdsworth, won an award for being the best actor ever in British soap. That got up a lot of people's noses and turned the new boy into a big bad wolf.

But I loved working with Randy Reggie and his side-kick Curly Watts, played magnificently by Kevin Kennedy. The pair of them could be described as the Street's thinking woman's crumpet ... in as much as any woman with half a brain would rather toast them on a red hot fire before even considering jumping in bed. Yet Kevin and Ken saw things differently and lampooned themselves at every available opportunity. I loved Betta-buys scenes with them, because they always had a grasp of their lines and there was no messing about when it came to the takes. On the way to the supermarket that pair would serenade me with some of the bluest songs imaginable. I couldn't even repeat a line, they were that obscene.

Ken had a wonderful sense of humour and caught a lot of females out with his lascivious ways. He obviously enjoys a practical joke like most actors. But when he switched the ladies' toilet sign onto his dressing room door and I stepped inside he soon found out he had bitten off more than he could chew.

He was sitting there in the dark and as I entered he said lewdly, 'Come here, little girl.'

I was shocked at first, and said, 'This is not the ladies. What's happened?' But as he chortled away I knew exactly what to do.

'Ken, you're all gong and no dinner,' I said, 'because if I started on you, you'd run a mile. I'd show you what being randy is all about.'

It stopped him dead. What could he say? He certainly didn't fancy sampling a clinch with a female maneater.

The girls in the cast soon got wise to Ken's little trick. It was ironic that the powers that be had put Randy Reg's dressing room adjacent to the ladies' loo. Only a clown like Ken could get away with swapping the signs.

My reputation for passion often passed before me, and men were wary. The unsuspecting ones often ended up in the sack with me, because when I want a man I let them know. Streetwise blokes at Stage One knew all about my prowess in the bedroom. Boys talk about those kind of things among themselves, as I'd found out years before. At one time a story got back to me at Granada about my sexual exploits, so I stopped performing for a spell to kill the rumours off.

During my cabaret career I was in a hotel when I heard a group of lads talking about me. One was boasting how he'd enjoyed an amazing session with me, so I thought, I'll stop this little game. I marched across to the huddle in the hotel bar, dragged this boy to one side and announced, 'He's never had me. If he'd had me he'd keep quiet about it. Most people know when they've got someone as good as me in their bloody bed that they'd keep it to themselves.'

I never liked men heckling me or getting me down. Derrick did more than enough of that for the whole male race back at home. But when you are up there on the stage you do become a target of male desire.

I'll never forget the time I slipped off for a quick legover with a fellow who owned a big hotel in Rotherham. He took me out to his motor and produced a giant piece of sticky plaster. When he told me what it was for, I got a surprise. He said, 'I've heard you can be very noisy, so I'm taking precautions.' I told him not to worry, I wouldn't be too noisy for him. I do become very vocal when I'm making love – I think it is only right that you should indicate your appreciation in one way or another. But that proved my reputation had gone before me. I didn't know that blokes talked about how loud I was in bed.

It got to the stage where chaps were queuing up to bed me, and I became very fussy. I turned a hell of a lot down. The energetic stage act had them all thinking that I must be just as hot between the sheets. They were right, but only the chosen few found out. I wasn't the type of girl who was happy to take things lying down, if you get my drift.

Of all the young male stars on the Street over the years the one with the most sex appeal for me has always been Nigel Pivaro. Sadly, I can't say that I ever bedded him. He was so different from all the others. There was always that undercurrent of sexuality with him. I called him the Mean Machine. And he'd go crazy when I said every morning, 'Here come's the Mean Machine.' He'd say, 'I'm going to kill you.' When he'd been away for ages and came back the first thing he did was come up to me and give me a great big hug as he said, 'The Mean Machine's back.' He's much more attractive to me than Phil Middlemiss, who plays bookie Des Barnes, the number one sex symbol in the cast at present. With Nigel the sex appeal is simmering under the surface all the time. I think he's absolutely gorgeous, and if I could afford him, I'd buy him.

But it wasn't just men I had to watch out for while I was living it up on the Street. Julie Goodyear was larger than life, she really was. Full of fun, and great company, she used to get up to some real tricks. She was without doubt an exhibitionist. She made no secret of the fact she'd had relationships with men both straight and gay, women and even transvestites. Julie simply relished shocking people – and as you can imagine there were some very prudish characters in the show and not just in the scripts.

When newcomers, boy or girl, came onto the set, she'd give them the once over and joke: 'I'll have them first, thank you very much.' That was just her being mischievous – anything for effect. But she would regularly say she was going to have me. Julie plagued me with her attentions and told everyone she wanted to marry me. Time and time again she proposed to me – usually trying to embarrass me in front of other people.

Once when I'd gone shopping with her in Kendal Milne, a posh department store in Manchester, she gave me the shock of my life. I went into the wine section to buy my next-door neighbour a bottle of sherry. As the assistant wrapped it up, she stared down at my feet in disbelief. I turned round and there was Julie, down on her knees, holding a huge bunch of flowers and asking, 'Will you marry me?' When I opened the first gay night at Peter Stringfellow's London club, he interrupted my act to present me with a basket of flowers from Julie. He read out her card and it said, 'Now will you marry me?' The gays loved it.

She did it all the bloody time – even in front of Derrick, which I'm sure he found more offensive than when I was chatted up by men. One night in a Granada bar, Julie spotted Derrick walking through the door. He was only there to pick me because we were to spend a rare weekend together in Manchester. I hadn't seen him, but Julie, quick on the uptake, threw me over her arm and started to kiss me. It was like a proper kiss, or at least that's how it would have looked to Derrick. It all happened so fast I didn't have time to protest. My husband stormed out in disgust. I ran out after him, trying to explain it was a joke, just her way of winding people up, but he wouldn't discuss it.

Promiscuous I was, but a lesbian – never. I knew that simply because I'd tried it and decided it wasn't for me. So I was never tempted by Julie's come-ons, be they wind-ups or serious. To this day I still don't know what to make of her. When I was doing the clubs, I had a huge gay and lesbian following. I don't know why, but they were always attracted to me. Derrick used to get worried when I worked some of the clubs around Huddersfield and Bradford because I had a huge lesbian following there. Funny he seemed more concerned about other women fancying me than other men!

I am not a lesbian and I could never tell you today if a woman was a lesbian even though I should have learned my lesson. For when I first started in cabaret, I paid a young hairdresser to do my hair before I went on stage. Funny thing was, she was married at the time so I never thought anything of it. I just wanted the company when I was doing bookings around the country, I hated driving on my own.

One night I booked us into two single rooms in this hotel up in the North East somewhere. We arrived at the dead of night after the show only to find there was only one double room left. I never thought anything of it:

'Well, we'll have to double up, no problem.' But there was a problem. That night Yvonne, who was about thirty, two years younger than me, confessed that she loved me. I was gobsmacked.

'Don't be so daft. How can you love me?' I asked. 'I'm a woman and so are you.'

Before I knew it, she was undoing the buttons on my dress. We'd obviously had a few drinks and I was used to being in this situation with a man, but being seduced by a woman – never.

'You hardly ever see Derrick,' she said as she slid her hand underneath my frock.

'I'm not that bloody lonely,' I retorted nervously.

'How do you know until you've tried it?' she asked . . .

The next day, I crawled out of the bed and felt nothing. I had not enjoyed my sexual experience with Yvonne one bit. 'I don't want you travelling with me any more,' I told her as we packed our cases. 'Our "friendship" is over.' Well, I thought, I've tried it, and now I know I'm not a lesbian. So I knew I wasn't going to get in that situation again, no matter how much Julie tried to ridicule me.

They say you can't catch AIDS if you're a lesbian. Well, as you can imagine, because I had been so promiscuous, I had no such security. I had slept around and never used a condom. There was no need. In my heyday AIDS didn't exist, or if it did nobody knew about it. Safe sex then meant not getting pregnant, and I had no fear of that as I'd had a hysterectomy. I simply didn't have to bother with contraception. Of course there were venereal diseases, but I was fortunate never to have caught a dose. If you did, it was no big deal – a course of tablets usually sorted it out.

But AIDS, that was different – it was a killer. And for all I knew, I could have been a prime candidate. And when I discovered my son had the HIV virus, I was shaken and worried for my own future too.

So I was sixty years old when I decided to have an AIDS test and see if I was to be repaid for all my little indiscretions. I had read Stephen's literature on the condition, and had had counselling when I was coming to terms with the fact that my only child might one day die from it. So I was prepared.

Which is more than I can say for the nurse who carried out the test. She stared at me in disbelief when I walked through the doors of the tiny clinic.

'AIDS test?' she asked.

'That's right,' I replied. 'I want to know one way or another.'

The astonished nurse, who was a fan of my Catholic Street character, asked, 'Good grief, Miss Perrie, what the devil have you been up to?'

Damn cheek, I thought, as I explained to her that it wasn't my recent behaviour I was worried about. I hadn't had sex for over a year. But the last decade or so, when the disease may have lain dormant, that's what worried me.

It was a tense three weeks waiting for the result to come through. When that envelope dropped on the doormat I recognized it immediately. My heart skipped a beat as I ripped it open and scanned the page for either word, positive or negative. Thank God, it was the latter, and I vowed there and then I would be careful, that my promiscuity would now be a feature of the past. Somehow I felt cleansed, wholesome and as if I'd been given a new lease of life. I would never put myself at risk again by sleeping with a stranger.

Now I have my blood checked every month – not because I've turned obsessive like a Howard Hughes type figure, but because of the anticoagulants I take for my heart. But it lets me know if there are any peculiarities.

I'm not expecting any change. My casual sex life is no

more. I aim to make a fresh start in life. To stick with one man. For now the plan is to make my marriage to Derrick work, so he's in for a lot of sexual surprises in the future. I hope he finds it pleasant. I've been told I'm very good.

CHAPTER SIXTEEN

Anguish – On Screen and Off

The last thing Ivy Tilsley needed as far as I was concerned was a cold eel for a husband. But that's just what she got when she walked up the aisle with Don Brennan.

In those days hopalong Don had two legs, but Geoff Hinsliff, the actor who played him, made it plain from the start that he wasn't a fan of mine. His opening line when we met was a virtual insult. He told me his daughter had said, 'You can't go in as her boyfriend, she's a grandmother, she's too old for you.'

I couldn't believe my ears. I looked straight at him and said, 'Well, that's a very good start to a friendship, before we've even done a scene together.'

He tried to backtrack, but the damage was already done. He said he hadn't meant it like that, but in my book if you don't mean something then you don't say it.

He is in his mid-fifties, but obviously felt he looked younger. With all that grey hair he's only kidding himself. We've had rows in real life as well as for the cameras. I confess we don't see eye to eye. But then again not many actors and actresses forced into such a situation do hit it off straight away. On many occasions there are teething problems.

With all the aggravation in my relationship with

Derrick I loathed having an unhappy screen marriage. I hated playing out all the problems for Ivy that were mirroring my life at home. And working with Geoff was far from plain sailing, as I discovered soon enough.

Yet the wedding itself was a fabulous affair and all the more poignant for me as it took place in a church. It was the posh wedding that Derrick and I never had. Memories of our hurried hitching at Rotherham register office came flooding back. The tears I cried during the recording of those scenes that hit the screens in June 1988 were real enough, so much was running through my mind.

At the time of writing this book Geoff featured in a second-rate tabloid newspaper and told its readers how well we got on. To tell the truth and put the record straight, I am compelled to say we didn't. He suggested his character Don could be turned into a psychopathic serial killer. Now that just isn't *Coronation Street*. It's also pretty sick, and in very bad taste as at the time he made the suggestion they had been digging up bodies of victims of a mass murderer in Gloucester. When I saw it I wondered whether he thought about the relatives of all the poor girls who were slain. I know he was suggesting a storyline for a soap, but it doesn't fit into the comfortable *Coronation Street* mould.

Geoff and I worked together for six years, but I only began feeling comfortable with him in the final six months. He is not a man you can get close to. He was always a bit of a loner, although latterly he started knocking round with Johnny Briggs. Geoff now even drives a flashy Jaguar just like Mike Baldwin's in the Street. I'd often drink with the pair of them in the Old School. Maybe I am partly to blame for our rift, because I secretly hankered after another Peter Dudley, a wonderful person as well as an excellent actor. I wanted Ivy's second marriage to have warmth and love, but that wasn't to be.

When he first came in Geoff was a typical luvvie, looking down his nose slightly at those who were not trained actors. I'd never heard of him before he arrived on the set. His biggest part as far as I knew had been in *Brass*, the hit Granada comedy, but I'd never watched that so I didn't recognize him. He initially told me he wasn't staying in the show, because he didn't want to get typecast. There are a lot of people who say that – then stay and are very content to plod on for the pennies. I just told him to wait until he'd had his first year's salary.

From an early stage I noted that Geoff had some irritating habits. When you play a married couple in a soap you get to know your screen partner pretty well. One of Geoff's foibles was dashing off to chat with scriptwriters or directors at every opportunity. I once told him at lunch in the Old School, 'I can sit here with my back to the door and I know when a scriptwriter, or a director or anybody who is anybody walks in, because you'll excuse yourself for a minute and stay away for the rest of the day.' I regularly asked him why he was so keen to find out what was happening to his character in three months' time.

I'm the opposite. Carolyn Reynolds, the Street's current executive producer, would bear that out. She'd tell me I had a lovely storyline coming up and I'd insist she didn't tell me. She used to say I was funny. I explained to her I didn't mind knowing next week's script, so I could put this week's into context. But I didn't want to know what the final line was, because I liked it to be a surprise. Geoff often tried to tell me what was happening to Ivy and I didn't appreciate it. I don't know if he did it deliberately to wind me up.

The last disagreement I had with Geoff was described in places as a blazing row. It wasn't, it was just another annoying, petty argument – another Lynne and Geoff niggle blown out of proportion. We were in the Old

School when Geoffrey told me that people thought Ivy was looking a bit too good. I said, 'Well, you can talk. You've been doing nothing but poncing around with your hair lately. Treating yourself to a hair-do and buying new clothes.' In my mind he always thought of himself more as Don Johnson than Don Brennan.

I asked him, 'What's up with you? Are you jealous because I'm getting dressed up? Look, if you think about the story, for four or five years I have looked a shit on that box. Now according to the script I am trying to get you back and I'm going to play it right. Of course Ivy is going to doll herself up a bit. Any woman would if she wants to win back her husband.' I was an expert on it ... I'd been there myself with Derrick.

The row only lasted that lunchtime and he didn't storm off. It was a particularly boring disagreement, but many of them were. I walked off before him. I always reckoned that Geoff hoped for too much for himself. He came into *Coronation Street* knowing he was coming in as a Catholic woman's boyfriend and then husband. Then suddenly he wanted to change the whole cosy atmosphere. He wanted to turn into dirty Don Brennan the philanderer.

His playing away was pathetic, because the character should have been morally upright. He should have strived to make the family unit tight. It might not have been as exciting, but it would have been more in character. But it is fashionable in soap these days to wreck marriages of major characters to grab the ratings.

I'm a big believer that soaps should not show all these extramarital affairs. I suppose with the shennanigans I've got up to I'm a fine one to talk. But *Coronation Street*'s charm is its cosiness. All the characters can't be off chasing pretty girls. The show has its Romeos in Mike Baldwin and Ken Barlow – I don't think the viewers want a one-legged Lothario. That stretches the imagination too far. It's not *Dallas*. It doesn't need a sexy image. It should remain as down to earth as a Lancashire cobblestone. As Wendy Richards, who plays Pauline Fowler in *EastEnders*, once said, 'EastEnders is a stiletto compared to *Coronation Street*'s slipper.' The viewers know which one they are comfortable tuning in to. A soap character losing a leg in a dramatic car crash should send ratings shooting upwards, but because Don isn't a popular figure with the viewers it never happened.

My opinion that he is unpopular with viewers is supported by the number of times I've been called Ivy Brennan by the fans. It has happened five times in six years. On every other occasion the fans have always referred to me as Ivy Tilsley. She made an impact. As Bill Podmore always said, Ivy and Bert were the backbone of *Coronation Street*. He'd say, 'The couple might never make the headlines with leading storylines, but you are always there and we can throw anything at you.'

I expected Don as a minicab driver to be a working-class man, enjoying family life. I was probably expecting too much. I must admit that during the confrontations over Don's role as the telephone terrorist I had some of the best scenes I'd had in the show for years. But I don't think they had the same effect, because the character had been eroded, having already accepted an adulterous husband back. A strict Catholic woman like the old Ivy would never have done that.

I know for a fact that it was Geoff who went up and suggested Don should start having affairs. I think he was frightened of getting stuck in a rut. Perhaps you can't blame him if he couldn't foresee any exciting storylines for his character in future.

Our off-screen squabbles revolved round a personality clash between the pair of us. We had a series of minor confrontations before I left over how I looked. If you are going to work with someone on a long-term show you've got to have some sort of feeling or rapport. It is an essential ingredient in any screen relationship if it's to be really convincing. Don and Ivy were an odd couple from the start, and I was unhappy with that.

Another of Geoff's annoying little habits was what I term 'doing an Annie Walker' – in other words, manoeuvring to get full face on with the camera. I realized at one stage that Ivy was becoming the back of my head, but I never let that get to me.

The one time I did get upset was when I went back onto the set and heard Geoff instructing a director on how he felt a scene should be done. I suddenly realized he was manipulating the situation to make it his scene. He wanted Don to finish the scene, instead of Ivy as it was in the script. I was shocked and outraged. Instructing a director on how he should be doing his job is entirely wrong as far as I am concerned.

I have worked with some fantastic directors over the years. There is nothing that instills more confidence in an actor or actress than a real expert in complete control of their craft.

When kids today watch telly, I'm sure they imagine that we actors make up our own lines completely off the tops of our heads and instinctively know what to do.

What they don't realise is that we have a brilliantly talented team of people behind us who are all dedicated to making every production slick and professional.

Even the best actor is lost without a great scriptwriter and on the Street we have some of the best in the business.

Julian Roache won critical acclaim for his sex triangle plot in the Eighties involving Ken and Deirdre. Along with the Street's John Stevenson, he is one of the finest of them all.

My favourite director on the cobbles of Weatherfield has to be Brian Mills. He understood just what was needed in every scene and pinpointed the highlights with his trained eye. Having an actress as a wife helped a lot.

He was an expert at filming the famous Mike Baldwin and Poison Ivy rows in the factory.

As shop steward Ivy, I would take the girls' pay claims and complaints about conditions to Mr Baldwin – the far from benevolent boss. Brian would make me look granite-faced by filming from the floor straight up my nose. And he would make Mike appear ten foot tall by instructing the cameraman to stand on a chair from across the room to shoot his scenes. It made for great television.

My old pal Peter Dudley was a great fan of the back-room boys – on their advice we made Bert and Ivy's on-screen relationship as close as possible. Peter always used to touch my hand and was very loving during filming. Little touches that lots of husbands and wives have between them. If he was reprimanding Ivy he'd grasp my hand and say, 'Listen, lady'. It was very realistic, and people related to that.

The one time I tried to kiss Don he pulled away from me. He said, 'People our age don't do that.' I was just trying to introduce a little realism into the situation, but he wouldn't have it. I got upset and said, 'Good God, what are you like with your wife?' By all accounts he is devoted to her, so you'd imagine he might have been a bit more loving on screen with Ivy if he was well practised at home.

As I mentioned earlier, it was only in my last six months on the show that Geoff started to appreciate me. We decided we were quite good together, and he'd put his arm round me and take me to the Old School for dinner. We both thought our roles were coming on smashing at one stage after he was unmasked as the telephone pervert giving hairdresser Denise Osborne, played by actress Denise Black, a hard time. It took Geoff two years to explain to me why he used to walk away from me before we filmed. It was because he likes peace and quiet, so he can concentrate on his lines. Some people are like that, but Liz Dawn and myself can yak, yak, yak like hell right up until the last minute. We once walked on to do a scene and we'd been laughing that much that it looked as if someone had just chucked a bucket of water over us. We'd been crying with laughter.

When it comes to crying on screen, it should go without saying that the tears shed are real. It is a pet hate of mine when actresses say, 'I cried real tears' – what are they going to cry? Banana milkshake mixed with vodka? Of course the tears have to be real. They have to come from deep down. I can't be doing with actresses smudging their mascara and messing up their make-up. It puts me off right away.

I believe that if you are really sad you don't get made up in the first place. I looked awful on the TV for four or five years, and that was because the character was going from crisis to crisis. I let the roots show in my hair in real life, because I wanted to be authentic. I don't think wigs are suitable in situations where you are supposed to be crying, they never look natural enough for my taste. It might be just me, but I can tell when it looks like crying from the heart. It is no disgrace to say that you can't cry – some actresses are unable to turn on the waterworks for TV.

When Peter Dudley died I wept buckets, and when Bert passed away on screen I had no problems crying for the camera. The memories just brought the tears flowing out. I cried when Brian died on the show as well. I am naturally an emotional person and can be moved to tears if I'm watching a good movie. Thinking about my mam and dad is also guaranteed to make me sob.

I have my mum's musical jewellery box upstairs and occasionally it makes a note without prompting. It's like she is still around watching over me. After Pat Phoenix died I was thinking about her when my answerphone just clicked on and off. It was incredible, because the damned thing wasn't plugged in.

But talking about tears I felt like having a right go at Liz Dawn when she told a newspaper she'd cried for real. The industry has had women who'd been crying for years and she goes and talks about it like it is some new innovation. I was furious. How bloody ridiculous, I thought. What will people like John Mills think of us. No wonder *Coronation Street* can't collect a BAFTA award when people behave like that. I never told Liz my feelings at the time. I just did not speak to her for about a week I was that mad.

I have had some ding dongs with Liz in the past. Once when she made a comment about the way I was looking I hit back straight away at her for wearing curlers. How many people do you see these days with their hair in rollers? The answer to that is none. They leave their hair shaggy. Liz was trying to do a Hilda Ogden and said as much when she replied, 'Well, it's a tradition in the Street.' I thought, do me a favour. We have had some real fiery rows over the years because we have similar temperaments. We are both very passionate about what we believe is right.

We even very nearly came to blows on one occasion. She is a great hulking woman and towers over me. On this particular day she was so bloody furious that she threatened to hit me. I was terrified, but decided the best way to deal with her was to brazen it out. I told her if she touched me I'd call the police. Fortunately she saw sense before she ripped me limb from limb, as I've no doubt she'd have been able to.

The argument started after I'd been cancelled from a club, because I was told that the week before Liz had been on and hadn't gone down as well as usual.

I was hopping mad. People were saying, 'We don't want another *Coronation Street* star.'

The people on the clubs at that time didn't know anything about my cabaret experience. I am not being egotistical when I say that my cabaret act had a format. It was sophisticated. I didn't just go and sing a selection of songs.

I had done cabaret all round the globe. I even did one spot for American GIs in Paris who had started watching the show lying down on sofas in their concert hall. Many of them were big black blokes and the act in front had been molested by one of them – this chap ran on the stage and bit her bum. But I did a lot of blues and got them up on their feet. I thought, Their lethargy ain't killing my act, and it didn't.

So I was fuming when I found out clubs were cancelling me because they decided I was just another *Coronation Street* star.

When I saw Liz at rehearsals I asked, 'What sort of bloody act are you doing?'

She said, 'What do you mean?'

I told her a club had just cancelled, and that's when she erupted. She told me to shut up and went beserk. She screamed, 'You and your big hotels and your flying all over the world.'

I said, 'At least I don't take me teeth out and try to bite a fellow in the audience.' That used to be part of her act and I was getting as personal as she was.

There were never any holds barred in our rows and this was the real thing. It got nastier and nastier. We both know how to snipe.

There was a couple of other actresses – including Helene Palmer, who played Ida Clough – watching open mouthed as we laid into each other with insult after insult. The director Gareth Evans hit the roof about the row and sent the pair of us out of rehearsals. He told us to come back when we'd finished arguing.

When we got outside I started it off again when I said to Liz, 'You call yourself a professional? I have never been sent off set before in my life.' The row erupted again and she threatened to thump me.

I can look back now on it and laugh, but at the time I was terrified. She is a big woman and it would have made a hilarious comedy script. I was cowering there with my hands up in the air yelling, 'I'll call the police if you touch me.' And she was towering over me screaming: 'I'll bash your teeth down the back of your throat.' But my yell seemed to do the trick and the director came out to check everything was okay.

I thought afterwards it had been stupid, but we still didn't talk to each other for a couple of weeks. I am sure that Liz has told the story many times and laughs about it as well.

In the run up to my leaving the Street I had another blazing row with her. The newspapers suggested we had an argument, but the true story never came out. With hindsight I blame myself for bringing the situation to a head. I should have minded my own business, instead of worrying about what Liz was doing. Derrick had warned me not to open my big mouth, but I've never been one for taking his advice, no matter how sensible it may be.

On the Monday Liz had come in and she looked really unwell, full of flu. She said she only had four scenes to do and wanted to get them done. But she went home. The next week we found out she had done a rehearsal for the Michael Barrymore show during the week when she'd been too ill to come to work. Because she was off a lot of us had to change our schedule and come in on the Wednesday morning of the following week, which some of us had been given off. There was quite a few in, and they were playing hell. Alison Sinclair, the new press officer, came in and I told her I didn't believe what was happening with Liz.

Once I've decided an injustice has been done, I don't care a bugger about anyone. So Liz was for it next time I saw her – putting us all out just so she could appear on *Barrymore*. The next morning she was in and now I'd gone down with flu myself. We were doing a scene together and she was reading her lines off the back of her purse.

Well, that was the final straw. I just blew up. I said, 'You are bloody indescribable. Liz, *Coronation Street* is your work, so why are you always chasing all these other shows? You know I've been asked back on the Des O'Connor show and to go on the Wogan show, but I turn them all down because *Coronation Street* comes first. How could you go down to London as ill as you were? I've got flu and I've had to come in and rehearse my scenes with you.'

Now this row took place in front of everybody, but none of the people who had been moaning about her backed me up. I was very hurt by that afterwards.

Liz was very quiet and just said, 'You're mental, you're mental, you're going funny.'

I said, 'What do you mean, I am mental, I'm going funny? I'm telling you the truth, Liz. You've been doing your book, driving all over promoting it, then coming in here shattered day after day. You know you've not put *Coronation Street* first. If you want to go off and do all these other shows you shouldn't be on *Coronation Street*. You're doing too much and you're looking ill.'

I never gave her that tongue lashing through jealousy, because I've been offered all the shows myself. Derrick had said if she died on the Michael Barrymore show then it was nothing to do with me. I told him it was something to do with the rest of the cast when it affected the show. I affirmed it was something I would never do. He said it still wasn't my problem – it was Granada's.

I was carpeted after that row and called upstairs to see Carolyn Reynolds. She told me I shouldn't have said what I said in front of the cast. And I admitted she was right, but that I should have given her a right bollocking in the dressing room.

My rows with Liz were no big secret and, despite the

ferocity of our disagreements, everyone knew we'd
be mates at the end of the day. That's just the way it
always was.

I apologised to Liz afterwards. I don't want people to
get the impression that we were rowing all the time,
because as I've already explained earlier we had some
great laughs together. It was often great fun behind
the scenes.

But you can't escape from the truth of the matter that
actors and actresses can be quite temperamental people.
I know of rows between other members of the cast, but
workmates in whatever job have run-ins from time to
time. They wouldn't be human if they didn't.

Many times people keep their feelings hidden, and I
don't think that's right. I'm a Yorkshire lass who believes
you should call a spade a spade. Although I'm really easy
going, I don't put up with people who take advantage of
my generous nature.

I remember once giving a taxi driver a right earful.
This presumptuous devil was one of the lads from the local
cab firm who regularly popped into my house for a cuppa
and a chat, should they be passing. But, on this occasion,
I had gone out for a few minutes and left the door
unlocked.

He let himself in, which was pretty cheeky when you
think about it, then wandered upstairs and caught one of
my friends lying half naked on the sunbed.

To her horror, instead of apologising he offered to give
her a massage. She told him to clear off in no uncertain
terms. He thought it was funny – but I was furious. I
complained to his bosses and made it very plain I would
not tolerate that type of behaviour.

Julie was just like me in that respect – she didn't suffer
fools gladly. I loved that down-to-earth streak in her and
we got on so well. She has been a great friend to me.

I remember her telling me of her plans to get engaged

to Jack Diamond, the drag artist. Now I used to work at the Viking club where Jack played, and I thought he was bloody gay. Julie used to do a lot of things to shock people – to give them something to talk about. As old as I am, I am still confused about Julie. Deep down I suppose she simply liked causing a furore.

I was generally happy on *Coronation Street* and can't stress that enough. Yet just before the end of my time there things had started to go sour.

Something I dreaded was the way they were turning Ivy into a drunk. Off screen I was having my own battle with the bottle as a result of all the stress in my life over Stephen and the loneliness of having a husband seventy miles away. The last thing I needed was to have my real life mirrored on the telly. But it happened. I remember watching an actor's master class with Michael Caine and Sir John Gielgud instructing young actors on how to play the part of a drunkard. Caine stressed it was one of the hardest jobs to do and shouldn't entail a lot of falling over. He suggested that you should try hard to concentrate on walking in a straight line and then you'll stray off it like a drunk. He stressed you should never play the part as someone who is absolutely sozzled.

Now I'd had a lot of practice at that and was trying very hard to do it the other way. I had some belting stuff to do, but I thought, Oh God! Why are they turning Ivy into a drunk? There was a suggestion that they may have done it to help me stop boozing, but nobody ever told me that was the case. And if it was it didn't work.

So many things were going through my mind at that time that the last thing I needed was to play the demanding role of a drunk on screen. I think I did it well enough simply drawing from my own personal experience.

CHAPTER SEVENTEEN

From Lip Job to No Job
– the Kiss Off

Those lips of mine had the nation talking, but contrary to popular belief, they were not the reason for my departure from *Coronation Street*.

To this day I don't know exactly why I was placed in a position where I had to tell my soap bosses that I wanted out for good. I still don't know why my contract was not being renewed.

It happened on a Monday afternoon. I was summoned to the producer's office, on the fourth floor of the main Granada building. Now getting called up there generally fills you with dread. If it's good news you don't get instructed to attend a long way in advance – it's more an informal 'come up and see me some time'. But this was a rigid appointment.

I'd known producer Sue Pritchard for years and suspected something unusual was afoot – just how unusual, though, I never imagined. I walked in my usual bubbly self that afternoon and said 'hello' to my pals on the security desk. I was unsuspecting. That is how they wanted me to be ... a lamb to the slaughter. I stepped out of the lift and started the long walk down the corridor. My mind was racing. What was all this about? I walked somewhat hesitantly towards the end door on the left-hand side. As soon as I saw her, executive producer Carolyn Reynolds took hold of my hand and gave me a kiss. I knew it was going to be a different day. She had returned especially for the meeting from her maternity leave to give me the news – my contract was not being renewed.

I sobbed. It was the news we were all supposed to dread. It was an inbred fear hammered into the whole cast that leaving the show was not a good thing. But, as I wept, I realized my over-riding emotion was one of relief. After twenty-three years I had been set free. The sobbing subsided as the relief welled up inside me. Carolyn was saying that I should have a break for a few months and, although they didn't want to give me a new contract, they'd like to leave it open for the future. She told me my work had been absolutely fabulous, but they had nowhere for my character to go. How ironic, for the Street was full of characters going nowhere. 'I'll have a hotpot Betty luv,' must be the most frequently spoken line in British soap over the last quarter century. But the character of Betty Turpin just plods on, surviving on the strength of that.

Yet Ivy had been involved in some superb storylines in the past. Real battles in the family over the grand-children, over anything she got her teeth into. No character has anywhere to go until the scriptwriters produce a storyline for him or her. Carolyn told me I wasn't happy and hadn't been for a long time. She was dead right, but I was shocked when she told me how she knew. She said people had told her I was not happy and at times I didn't look well. I thought 'some fine mates I've got in that cast'. I knew who had been upstairs, but I won't embarrass them by pointing a finger. She also asked me if I'd been drinking again. My drinking had been a concern to everyone, not least of all me. But I hadn't. I was very proud of the fact that I had given it up. It proved

I was not an alcoholic as some people had implied.

The company doctor had done a check on me and found alcohol in my blood after the festive season, but that was from the brandy in a Christmas pudding, the spirits in a Yuletide cake and some Bucks Fizz I'd downed on personal appearances. I told Dr Glenn the Bucks Fizz was mostly orange, but he told me it was alcohol. They never have Perrier water at those dos. I'd also had the occasional sip of my friend Sandra's cider if she called round to the house for a chat and a game of dominoes or cards. I told him I'd been to the Old School and Johnny Briggs would say I was boring, because I drank nothing other than mineral water. I told Johnny I was better for not drinking. I could listen to what he said, speak coherently and understand what was going on. I told Carolyn that I hadn't touched a drop since Dr Glenn warned me to steer clear of alcohol – including sherry trifle.

Carolyn and myself were always very friendly. We never rowed, despite what appeared in some newspapers. I respected her and she was my boss. I went to the last Christmas party in the Victoria and Albert Hotel, near the studios, and had a cake I'd baked presented to her. It was in the shape of a child's cradle with a baby and teddy bear tucked into it, topped with an iced patchwork quilt. It was beautiful, but she didn't thank me – I'm sure she thought it was presented to her compliments of the hotel.

She once admitted to me: 'Before I got this job, I'd see you getting drunk night after night in the Old School. I used to feel so sorry for you and think that's one very, very lonely lady. She is obviously very unhappy.'

It was true, and sometimes the truth hurts. But at the time I would never have thought I was anything other than deliriously happy.

When the character of Poison Ivy was on the slippery slope, Carolyn told me they didn't want to kill the old battleaxe off. But I didn't think that was good enough for

Ivy. Pat Phoenix's favourite phrase came to me: 'If you are going to do anything do it with panache.'

'That won't do, if she's going, she's got to go out with a bang,' I insisted. The poor dear had suffered enough down on those cobblestones. Now was the time to put her out of her misery and lay the ghost of Ivy Tilsley to rest once and for all. She, just like me, had never been happy since she married Don.

I walked out of that office and a weight lifted from my shoulders. I felt light headed. At last I was free. Unchained after twenty-three years tethered to Ivy. I remember asking for a week off to take stock of the fact that, after so long in the show, I wouldn't be around much longer.

I wanted to be killed off. I can't stress that enough. They would have prefered to have kept me dangling on a string with the possiblity of a comeback – the chance of a guest appearance here or a guest appearance there. I didn't want that. They'd asked me if I was sure, and I told them straight. I knew my own mind – nobody else did.

The public suspected I'd been sacked because of the cosmetic surgery on my lips. I admit they were quite swollen when I went back to work. With hindsight I should have taken another week off to let the swelling subside. But I didn't. I went in because I felt it was my duty to Granada to carry on with the show. They had already given me a lot of time off sick. They had been very good to me and I didn't want to take advantage. It was a big mistake.

As I have already explained, I had been rowing with people on the set and perhaps those rows contributed to Ivy's downfall.

My favourite astrologer, Justin Toper in the *Sun*, had predicted on that day, 7 March, 1994: 'This is a time of recovery and reward for you. You can look forward to plenty of pleasant surprises, starting from today. If you don't believe in fate now – you will after this week.' I couldn't believe it. At first I wept, convinced he couldn't be more wrong. But Justin was to be proved right and it was a very pleasant surprise. People expected me to be devastated and distraught. I was – for a few hours. I'd been Ivy for too long to let go without a little grief. But my overwhelming emotion was relief. In the end I knew what was happening was for the best. As Justin so rightly predicted I was a believer in fate by the end of that week.

The next day the news was splashed exclusively all over the front page of the *Sun*. My son Stephen had spoken to the newspaper. He was angry about the way I had been treated. He was set to meet a reporter on a totally unrelated matter, but fate gave the nation's favourite newspaper a page one story.

I couldn't believe the response to the news. There were dozens of journalists camped outside my house the next morning. Some of them, I swear, must have been there since dawn. They were well behaved and well mannered, but what must the neighbours have thought of all those cameras and pads and pens?

ITN even carried the news on their lunchtime bulletin. It was like watching a televised obituary of my big pal Ivy. I was honoured that the television news, which generally dismissed soap stories as trivia, deemed my screen character popular enough to deserve a prime slot. I was to be even more stunned by the overwhelming show of sympathy from the public. Thousands of letters flooded in wishing me all the best – and the inevitable stream of crucifixes and rosary beads followed from all my Catholic fans.

It was as if the country was praying for Ivy. I was starting to adapt to life without her. Fabulous offers of work popped through the post continually in those first few days. I thought it was too good to be true. It had to stop somewhere. I could have taken some of the offers up, but Granada were paying my wages until August, so I felt obliged to be at hand for them if they needed me.

Friends kept ringing saying how sorry they were. It was as if they had suffered a death in the family. My emotions began to fuse and the inevitable confusion came over me. I was happy it was over. I was unhappy at the way they had treated me. I was happy to continue filming. I never wanted to set foot inside Stage 1 again. I can sometimes be too fickle for my own good.

I stupidly rang the *Coronation Street* office and told them they could kill me off without me being there. Carolyn called: 'Don't you think you are being a bit silly? With your acting ability you could have the country broken-hearted.' 'Bugger them,' I thought. They are only thinking about their precious ratings. I stood firm.

I suggested somebody should run into the Rovers and announce that Ivy had had a heart attack in the street. I just didn't want her to die in a car crash – everyone seems to go out that way. Stephen rang me and helped me get my act together. He said I was being a moral coward and even my husband Derrick said I should go in there and die for the cameras. After much tooing and froing the professional actress inside me got a grip of the situation. I wrote a letter to the producer, witnessed by my friend Sandra, assuring Sue that I would return to film any scenes they required. I was quite happy to co-operate in Ivy's grisly end.

But some rather enterprising journalism scuppered my return. After much of the fuss had died down, there were still the odd two or three reporters hanging round my house. This particular day a note dropped on the mat from Cavendish Pictures in Manchester explaining that their photographer was round the corner and eager for a snap. I didn't want him to waste his time because there was no way I was posing for a picture for anyone. I rang up to call them off. Please remember, on that very day, Sandra had witnessed my letter to Granada promising to co-operate. Anyway, I started chatting with the nice man who answered the phone. He seemed concerned about my future. I've always liked photographers and this fellow was very pleasant.

He joked with me about how I could assassinate the top half dozen characters in the show if I wanted to. Laughingly, I agreed but explained that if I did I'd have to do a Salman Rushdie and disappear. I couldn't do it because I'd never be able to walk round the streets of Manchester or look my friends in the eye again. And I wanted to work again! It was a jovial chat.

The next thing I was making headlines for all the wrong reasons – the chap I'd been talking to wasn't a photographer, but a crafty freelance journalist who ran the top news and picture agency in the country. A down-market Sunday newspaper bought a story from him and everything that had been said appeared very different in print. Things look awfully harsh in black and white.

It gave the impression that I was gunning for Granada and my old pals on the Street. Nothing could have been further from the truth. I was hurt and upset.

I had to get a message over to my friends in the cast that they should take the story with a giant pinch of salt. Aggrieved by the article I rang my long time pal Julie Goodyear, the woman who had assumed Pat's mantle as Queen of *Coronation Street*.

Julie is a larger than life star that I trusted as a friend. But on that day she disappointed me more than words could say. I told her to let everyone in the cast know there was no way I was going to lift the lid like that. I asked her to tell them for me. Julie said: 'You know it would be no good me telling them. You know what they are like in there. They don't listen to me. They wouldn't believe what I say.' I was puzzled. 'So you won't help me then?' I asked forlornly, as it dawned on me. I'd rung her at home and asked a favour. She told me not to be silly, but the damage was done. They would have taken notice of her — that's why I'd telephoned her. If anybody could have done it she could. I was gutted.

After that I asked Geoff Hinsliff if he would tell them. To this day I don't know whether he did or not. But Julie really surprised me. I was so shocked.

That article proved a real headache. As a result of it I was sent a letter by Granada telling me they took it that I didn't want to come back. I got a letter from the head lawyer trying to put the frighteners on me and I was not happy with that. I'd worked at Granada long enough to understand my contract.

I could do a lot of damage and hurt a lot of people, but I never intended to do that. I've not named the members of the cast I've slept with to save upset and stop them getting into trouble with their partners. The people concerned know who they are and they have all played a part in my life.

Bill Roache did a series of newspaper articles containing some very scathing comments about other members of the cast. And people find things like that hurtful. Those who were close to me in the cast know I would never do anything like that.

Granada TV's chief executive Charles Allen knows me well enough to realize I don't bear any malice. He was ever so good to me during his time there. He sent me a lovely message when I was recovering after my collapse at the studios. And, at the Christmas party, he'd been very charming and even asked me to sing. He is a fantastic man and that night he made a bee line for me and requested the first dance.

He said that before the next year's party they would have a band call and I could do a proper routine. There was no intimation at all then that I wouldn't be around in twelve months time. He probably got as big a shock as the fans when he learned that Ivy's time on the Street had come to an end.

Latterly, I have to say the character of Ivy was not all that I wanted her to be. Even so I was paid some tremendous tributes after the scenes in which she took Don back as her husband. I didn't like the way Ivy had become this smarmy woman. I watched a scene depicting her and Don and I cringed. I knew Ivy wouldn't stand for that one-legged philanderer. The old Ivy would tell him to hop it. Instead I played the lovey dovey wife, so happy with him coming home. I played it wheedling and whining and I am ashamed of that scene. Yet people thought it was great, including my brother Duggie. He rung me and said: 'You did a beautiful scene last night. God, you had us crying – the pathos.' So you don't really know how the public will react.

But I hadn't been putting 100 per cent into Ivy. I was taking the easy way out allowing Ivy to behave out of character. I knew better than the writers how she should act – I'd lived her life for twenty-three years. And that gave me one hell of an insight. For the cameras, though, I acted as if Ivy was in love with Don. That was the way the scriptwriters wanted it. They'd lost their way a little as far as I could see. The lines that had Ivy noseying in and out of all the houses in the street were the ones I enjoyed doing. She was snappy and a bit of a tougher Hilda Ogden. The character of Ivy could have played a major part in *Coronation Street* in that role, but they decided to water it down.

As a company Granada must be one of the best to work for. Yet it has changed a lot over the years. At first you were able to go and do personal appearances without anybody saying anything, but that changed as people realized they could rake in more from them than from acting. Look at Ken Morley. He makes a fortune, and thousands turn out every time he makes an appearance.

Even Sarah Lancashire, who plays Raquel Wolstenholme so brilliantly, brought a town to a standstill in June.

People used to stay with the Street, but now they look to moving on. The superb young actress Eva Pope, who plays temptress Tanya Pooley, gave in her notice in less than a year. I wish her all the best. She has a tremendous talent and she's done the right thing. Eva should spread her wings while she's young, before she gets trapped in a role as the Street vamp. She could always return, and with a few years under her belt, could even make the new Elsie Tanner. That is a hell of a compliment to her ability, as I admired Pat Phoenix enormously as an actress.

But someone leaving after such a short spell would never have happened at one time. Now Granada are broadcasting three episodes a week, the work is seven days a week and very gruelling. In the old days there were only about twenty odd regulars in the cast – nowadays it's nearer forty. You can do runs of up to twenty-three weeks without a break.

You might finish on a Friday, and you would have Saturday to learn your lines, before you are back at work in Bettabuys on the Sunday. And in the week you are expected in the studio for 10 am, but might not be used until the afternoon, if you only have the one scene. Another major change was when Ken Morley proved that one character can be bigger than the show. His holding off signing his contract until he got the deal he wanted was a remarkable turning point. In Bill Podmore's day I tried that trick and told him I was unhappy. Now Bill was a pal, but he'd said: 'I don't want you here if you are not happy, so you know where the door is.'

I was shocked, but he pointed out: 'I can't allow one person to become bigger than the show.' But that's not the case anymore as Ken showed. Julie Goodyear was also allowed to do pilots for a chat show. The maxim that *Coronation Street* comes first has been lost somewhere along the line. In the old days we all had an equal standing, but that has now obviously gone. If the newspaper reports about Ken's contract negotiations are to be believed, one of his big grumbles was about the Granada press office. He didn't like the degree of control they try to exercise over every aspect of your life and I'd agree with his feelings on that one. It is the only complaint I've got about Granada that the press office tries to exercise supreme control over the cast.

After I was ill they, not the doctors, instructed me to stay indoors. They even told me not to go and visit my son Stephen in London. I lived like a prisoner in my house for eight weeks, with every curtain drawn tight. It was like living in a crypt. Derrick got so fed up that he returned to Maltby moaning: 'I'm not staying here, it's like a funeral parlour.' Not going down to London really let Stephen down. He said it was a terrible infringement of my civil liberties Granada telling me to stay indoors. I told him they had been good to me, paying all the clinic bills and I would be doing what they wanted. He stopped talking to me for two months after that.

When I was eventually allowed back to work, they organized a big press call for the Monday morning. But without any notice, they brought it forward to the Friday. It was complete chaos. The way they treated me on that day was appalling. A new press officer arrived at my house with a burly driver in his car. It was the first time I'd met him – and the strangest introduction of my life. Within minutes of saying hello, he'd put a coat over my head and guided me out of my kitchen door into the back of this car.

The engine was revving and we made a getaway like something from the Sweeney. I was being treated just like a criminal at court. 'I wonder just how long the judge will give me?' I asked. I wasn't joking at the time.

There were only a couple of newspapers in attendance

at the photo call at the studios. It had thrown them all into disarray because they'd planned to use the pictures on all the front pages the following week. But it had all been changed at the last minute. When I eventually walked out onto *Coronation Street* for the press call, it was cordoned off and there were thousands of fans cheering and waving bunches of flowers. They went crazy when I stepped on to the cobbles. It was a remarkable home coming – the fans were that delighted to see me that they were kissing my hands.

I can honestly say that I have never had a reception like it. Ian Howarth, the head of the publicity department, said he'd done personal appearances with most of the artistes on *Coronation Street*, but had never seen anything like it. He told Carolyn Reynolds afterwards: 'It was like walking down the street with the Queen.'

I only wish the photographs of my lips after the collagen implants had been given the same sort of low key publicity. But when the *Sun* found out I'd paid £2,800 for cosmetic surgery, they slapped my new face all over the front page. The photographs were fantastic and proved to me that it was money well spent. The ones they used were taken on my first day back after the initial op.

The problem arose a few weeks later when I returned to the private clinic for a top-up operation to have more fat from my thighs implanted in my mouth. The first time I'd had it done, my face was battered and bruised like I'd been in the ring for ten rounds with Frank Bruno. But on the second visit, that never happened. My lips simply swelled up. More accurately, they ballooned. I had a couple of weeks off work and was confident the swelling would subside. Sadly they didn't go down enough. Television can be a very cruel medium. Pat Phoenix always said the cameras saddle you with an extra four or five pounds in weight. The way the cameras had emphasized the creases round my mouth made me determined to do something to rid myself of the unwanted lines. Watching the programme and seeing those lines used to cause me pain. Even people older than me in the Street didn't have the facial lines I had.

I knew they had been brought on by the years of worry over my son Stephen and the years of excessive boozing. The first time I went to the clinic, I was frightened to death they'd take the character away from my face by pumping in too much collagen. The operation is simple enough. They syringed the fat from my thighs and then inserted it into my lips while I was under a local anaesthetic. The second time I asked the surgeon to pump in a little more. He frowned – but I was paying the bill. I should have heeded his advice and settled for less, but I'm not generally one to listen once I've got an idea in my head. The whole thing took about an hour and a half.

The swelling took just seconds to appear. My lips puffed up almost immediately. For days after I was applying packs of frozen peas to my face at home in a desperate bid to reduce the swelling. I didn't dare step foot out of the house. I was like something from the Black and White Minstrels show. I could not bear to look at myself. I stopped people from visiting with all manner of spurious excuses. I put cubes of ice in rubber gloves and bashed them with a hammer to make them more pliable before wrapping them round my swollen kisser. Even my voice was affected. I was mumbling. I couldn't bring myself to look in the mirror. I was eating and drinking through a straw and could only manage food that had been liquidized.

They had gone down a lot when I finally left the house for a trip to London. Cheeky *Sun* photographer Jim Clarke snapped me at the railway station and they carried a picture of me in the paper with these slightly puffy lips. It didn't look too bad at all. I went down to London for a guest appearance on the SKY satellite shopping channel

QVC. I am a big fan of the show and have spent thousands buying gifts and items off the screen from the comfort of my living room. *Coronation Street*'s press office had approved the trip weeks earlier, but on the day the station was bombarded with calls from Granada. John Roe, the man in charge, was astounded by the number of interfering phone calls, but I told him that it was not out of the ordinary.

When I got back I was carpeted over the appearance. It was pathetic to have been given approval for it and then to find myself in trouble. I returned to work with my lips still slightly swollen. This was a sad time for *Coronation Street*, because Bill Podmore my old pal had only recently died. He passed away in his sleep at the Alexandra Hospital in Cheadle, Stockport, on 22 January. He had been the show's Godfather and had saved it from slipping off our screens. He turned *Coronation Street* into the number one soap and left the show in extremely good shape after thirteen years. He had an enormous warmth and likeability. He could get away with murder in conversation.

One famous story was how Arthur Lowe, who played Leonard Swindley in the Street, became the victim of one of Bill's cruel jokes. Arthur had a load of Rolls Royce shares and, in the early Seventies when the company was having trouble, he was very long faced. Bill came in one day and said: 'Arthur, have you heard the wonderful news, the Swiss are going to buy Rolls Royce.' Arthur immediately started to beam until Bill added: 'They're going to make Swiss Rolls.' He was blessed with a wonderful sense of humour and his passing hit me hard. Bill was the same age as me, sixty-two – and, just like me, he'd been a ferocious boozer in his time.

Nobody passed any nasty comments when I returned. They more or less ignored my enormous lips. Only Liz Dawn asked what was the matter with my mouth. I told her and a few other close pals in the cast what I'd had done. Someone asked me afterwards if it hurt and I replied: 'The only thing I felt was the twenty-four stabs in my back when I walked out of the green room.' I guessed they'd have been talking about me behind my back. That is how the atmosphere gets in there, and actors can be cruel.

Carolyn Reynolds came down for a quiet word and I told her they'd go down. I wish now I'd spent another week off work, because the TV cameras were very harsh on me. My first scenes were filmed and in the can when the day arrived for Bill's memorial service in Manchester. I'd thought about him a lot over the past few weeks. On the morning of the service I decided he wouldn't want me to go dressed all dull and drab. He was a larger than life character and would have wanted me to show a little panache. I put on a short black and white suit, high heels and a riding hat. The press photographers were knocked out and my arrival outside the church was greeted by a barrage of flash bulbs going off.

The service was very moving and I inevitably shed a few tears. But the event was a celebration of his life and scriptwriter John Stevenson provided a wonderful tribute to his pal Bill. He said Bill told some of his hospital visitors that he had been to the other side, but seeing there were no bars there he'd come back. Even on his death bed Bill had time for a gag. He really was a great man. My lips looked smashing in all the papers the next day and everyone commented on how well I looked. But a week later I made my first screen appearance since the break and my lips loomed large on the small screen. The same papers ran stories asking: 'What's happened to Poison Ivy?' But they'd all seen me the week before and my face was fine. They knew the filming had been carried out three weeks in advance and to be honest I wasn't prepared for all the fuss.

Some bitchy women columnists wrote nasty articles. All I can say to them is that they should use current photographs of themselves to accompany their columns, instead of pictures from ten years ago. I've always been one for immediate action. If I could have something lopped off or added on I'd rather suffer the surgeon's knife than the agony of letting my looks slip away naturally. I wasn't ashamed of that. Other members of the cast have had plastic surgery, but I won't name any names. Although it is common knowledge that Liz Dawn has had her eyes done. Once she walked on set with two shiners and I told her: 'Sorry, I don't work with pandas.' We had a relationship where it was easy for one to take the mickey out of the other.

I've a confession now that might shock fans of my holier-than-thou Street persona. I've always wanted a pair of boobs like Julie Goodyear's. I used to tell gags about it in my stage act. Big tits are something I've never had, but always wanted. I even once visited a cosmetic surgeon in Birmingham and discussed a boob job. It was funny. I'd taken a gay friend down with me and he sat there weighing these silicone bags. He was shuffling them between his hands saying: 'I think these are big enough for you.' I was all set to have the work done when the press got hold of the story. That stopped me going through with it.

Now I am glad I did not bother. You hear all these terrible stories of silicone implants going awfully wrong. Now I'm resigned to life with them the way they are. My main complaint is that, as I get older, they droop and the muscle tone goes. They are not as firm as they used to be. I'll do anything to stay young. I've got the Jane Fonda books and videos. I've seen Joan Collins video and her legs are lovely, but you should see her stomach.

I am a real sucker for special creams and potions that can enhance your complexion. I currently spend £325 on jars of Kinebo face cream. Derrick would go spare, if he ever found out. When I heard that Joan Collins only uses one cream, I thought pigs might fly. I'd seen her face with two tram lines on it, just like the ones I had after my first facelift twenty years ago.

Yes I had a facelift in 1974 and that was a lot more tricky than the lip implants, but I didn't get a fraction of the press attention back then. I had the op done on the NHS, because I was so depressed by the way the flesh had sagged under my chin that I was on the verge of suicide with it and the doctor feared I would have a nervous breakdown. I've always been open about everything, and I don't like pretending anything's natural when it is so obviously not. After that first facelift I was in Sheffield Infirmary for two weeks and the scars still show to this day. Cosmetic surgery is much more refined in the 1990s. When I had it done in the Seventies, they had to bandage me up like a mummy for two weeks afterwards. I looked shocking all bruised and bloodied.

But I can honestly say that I don't have any regrets about any of it. I feel better in myself for having fuller lips and that is all that matters to me. It is my business. My philosophy is that if I look good from the outside then I'll feel better on the inside. To be frank, I'd have myself completely resculptured if I could afford it. If I won the pools, or the *Sun* bingo, I'd spend the lot. Derrick once accused me of having knock knees, so I'd get them done. I'd have my bum done, my cheeks implanted, my eyes touched up and my boobs enhanced. If I'd stayed on *Coronation Street* after that lot they'd have had to start calling me Bionic Ivy Brennan – forget about Poison Ivy.

CHAPTER EIGHTEEN

Life After Ivy

Forgetting all about Ivy is something I could easily do. Since she was laid to rest Lynne Perrie has had hundreds of offers of work.

Within two days of leaving *Coronation Street* I had been offered a main part on the stage in *Wuthering Heights*, five pantomimes and the role of Rose in a musical about Gypsy Rose Lee, the infamous stripper, which was due to tour the leading venues in the British Isles.

I plumped to star alongside John 'I'm Free' Inman as Poison Ivy, the Wicked Witch, in *Mother Goose* at the Davenport Theatre in Stockport about ten miles from my Salford home. I have a feeling that show will be a real hoot. The only other time I did a panto was years ago in Stoke. I was starring as Widow Twanky, wearing a bright red wig and kettle on my head. Yet all the kids of three, four and five in the audience still recognized me as *Coronation Street*'s Ivy Tilsley. It was great fun.

To this day offers haven't stopped flooding in. A string of guest slots on TV chat shows await me. Newspapers, magazines and radio stations are perpetually chasing me for interviews. Until now, I have said nothing. A lot of people might leave the Street and find themselves with nothing to do. Not I. Before my twenty-three years in

Coronation Street I spent over twenty-five years doing cabaret, so I've got a very good grounding in show-business to fall back on.

My London-based agent Patsy Martin is delighted that I'm being innundated with offers of work and personal appearances. My overall plan is to keep on going for another couple of years, and then to embark on a semi-retirement. I'd never be happy doing nothing, so I'd have to keep my hand in with after-dinner speeches and the like.

I spent several weeks after leaving the show helping an old friend put the finishing touches on a musical he's written. He's a fantastic composer and has penned songs for me in the past. I've helped by sending a synopsis of the musical off to my old Street colleague Bill Kenwright. Bill, who played Gordon Clegg, the illegitimate son of Betty Turpin, is someone who has made a success of his life after *Coronation Street*. These days he's a West End impresario and must be a multi-millionaire.

So there's hope for me yet. My brother Duggie made his screen debut on *Brookside* on the very day I was finished on *Coronation Street*. On the strength of that we could team up as a double act under the heading 'Entrance and Exit'. But I am genuinely very excited about the future. And I suppose I could easily pop up as a guest character in rival soaps to *Coronation Street*. I'd love to do a spell in *Brookside* with Duggie, and I've been virtually offered a slot on *Emmerdale*. My ability to do a Scottish accent would make me easy to fit into something like *Take the High Road*.

But I really don't know what I'll be doing professionally in the next couple of years. The famous 'luncheon vouchers madam', Cynthia Payne, who I recently met at a party at my pal Kevin Horkin's remote Lancashire farmstead, gave me her card and told me I could still make a living with my body even though I'm in my sixties.

So if all else fails I might look her up some time.

Before I consider going on the game, I want to try going home to Derrick, to see if after all these years apart we can make our marriage work. He'll be shocked by some of the things I've disclosed in my life story. But I believe if you are going to tell your story you might as well do it warts and all. Let readers judge you for what you are. I don't try and make excuses for my life.

When my publisher told me my life story merited a hardback book, I was so relieved. My mean old man wouldn't splash out on one of those, he probably wouldn't even buy a paperback. Derrick will wait a few years until it's in the library at Maltby. Then he can get to see what I've said for free.

By then we'll either be living together as a loving couple, or we'll be happily divorced. I know myself which way I want it to go. But only time will tell. One thing I am sure of is that life without *Coronation Street* is going to be a great adventure. I'll keep you posted.